THE GRAND TOUR

PATRICK DELAFORCE

THE
GRAND
TOUR

PATRICK DELAFORCE

ROBERTSON McCARTA

First published in 1990 by

Robertson McCarta Limited
122 Kings Cross Road
London WC1X 9DS

© Patrick Delaforce

Managing Editor Folly Marland
Designed by Prue Bucknall
Maps by Rodney Paull
Production by Grahame Griffiths
Typeset by Columns of Reading
Printed and bound in Great Britain by
Butler & Tanner Limited, Frome

British Library Cataloguing in Publication Data
Delaforce, Patrick, 1923–
The grand tour: today's guide to twenty-five cities of
Europe in the footsteps of famous travellers of the past.
1. Europe. Cities. Description & travel
I. Title
914.04558

ISBN 1–85365–162–1

Every care has been taken to ensure that all the information
in this book is accurate. The publishers cannot accept any
responsibility for any errors that may appear or their
consequences.

CONTENTS

A NOTE FROM THE PUBLISHER

We have sought, in publishing The Grand Tour, and in these days of great European fervour, to bring today's reader closer to those eventful centuries through which great British and latterly American figures travelled.

Europe is the cradle of modern democracy, home of great art, literature and museums, and we invite you to discover something of the adventure and delight which still lies across the Channel.

By the same author

Family History Research – The French Connection
Pepys in Love: Elisabeth's Story
Burgundy on a Budget
The Country Wines of Burgundy and Beaujolais
French Riviera on a Budget
Gascony and Armagnac on a Budget
Burgundy and Beaujolais on a Budget
Provence on a Budget
The Dordogne on a Budget
Champagne on a Budget
Nelson's First Love: Fanny's Story
Wellington the Beau

INTRODUCTION

It was the fashion in Britain, from the sixteenth century, and for Americans, later in the nineteenth century, to travel on the 'Grand Tours of Europe'. It was considered essential to visit five cities: Paris, Florence, Venice, Rome and Naples. The 'paths to Rome' were varied, and *en route* the travellers visited the Low Countries, occasionally Germany, usually 'Swisserland', sometimes Austria, but invariably France and Italy. The 'Grand Tour' might take a few months, a year, or even several years. Finding a town that suited the traveller, a prolonged sojourn might be made, even in relatively unimportant places such as Reims, Dijon, Avignon or Geneva. From the middle of the sixteenth century to the end of the nineteenth century, from Sir Philip Sidney and John Evelyn to Mark Twain and Queen Victoria, the inquisitive and intrepid travellers made their way round this cultural circuit. The advent of the European network of railways and railway hotels late in the nineteenth century coincided with the package tour pioneers such as Thomas Cook, and brought the original concept of the Grand Tour to an end. Perhaps this book will help to recreate the pioneering spirit of those lost centuries.

Why did those curious travellers brave the hazards and discomforts so often encountered on the Grand Tour? Sometimes there were wars through which fearless (and lucky) voyagers rode or walked. Certainly there were '*banditti*' in every country (except 'Swisserland'). There were encounters with wild dogs, sometimes wolves, and usually vermin in the inns. Customs officials were a law unto themselves, with hands ever open for '*pour boire*'. Police officers, moneychangers, postmasters, tollkeepers and '*voiturins*' (the local travel packagers) exacted what they could get away with. The innkeepers vied with the postilions in insolence towards their temporary employers, as well as constantly overcharging them. Dirty inn rooms, indifferent food and wine, and the dangers of illness and pestilence, even plague, were inevitable hazards. Indeed some travellers died on the Grand Tour.

The accepted theory is that it was the young sprigs of nobility with their attendant tutors (known as governors or bearleaders) who went on the Grand Tours. They did indeed form the majority of tourists who travelled in the name of higher foreign education. Lord Chesterfield's comments on the young travellers in Paris were dated 10 April 1756. 'The life of Les Milords Anglais is regularly, or if you will, irregularly, this. As soon as they rise, which is very late, they breakfast together, to the utter loss of two good morning hours. Then they go by coachfuls to the Palais, the Invalides, and Notre Dame; from thence to the English coffee-house, where they make up their tavern party for dinner. From dinner where they drink quick they adjourn in clusters to the play where they crowd up stage, drest up in very fine clothes very ill made by a Scotch or Irish tailor. From the play to the tavern again where they get very drunk and where they either quarrel among themselves or sally forth, commit some riot in the streets, and are taken up by the watch. Those who do not speak French before they go are sure to learn none there. Their tender vows are addressed to their Irish laundress, unless by chance some itinerant English-woman eloped from her husband, or her creditors, defrauds her of them. Thus they return home, more petulant, but not more informed than when they left it: and show, as they think, their improvement, by affectedly both speaking and dressing in broken French.'

But there were a dozen quite different reasons for the Grand Tours. Sir Philip Sidney deliberately sought experience in order to become an ambassador at a foreign court. His tours were instigated and subsidized by his sovereign Queen Elizabeth. Arthur Young was an agricultural specialist and Sir James Edward Smith MD FRS was a botany expert. Young Edward Gibbon was initially despatched to Geneva to avoid Papist tendencies, Tobias Smollett, the Scots novelist, Sir Humphrey Morice, Lord Gardenstone and Queen Victoria went south for their health. William Kent, Robert Adam and John Ruskin went to study classical architecture, and John Milton and Joseph Addison to study foreign literature. John Evelyn travelled to gain military experience, and young Lord Lincoln went to Italy to perfect his military studies. James Boswell attempted to study law, but in practice wenched at bordellos in most towns on his route – and then boasted of his exploits in his journal. William Beckford and Lord Byron voyaged to leave disgrace behind them in England. John Wilkes left since he was *persona non grata* in London. J.M.W. Turner, Richard Wilson, B.R. Haydon and Bonington went as professional painters to gain inspiration.

Because Europe was so cheap, Thomas Howard, Earl of Arundel, and the Duke of Wellington's mother, amongst many others, lived there (temporarily) in genteel poverty. Keats, Shelley and Laurence Sterne travelled for sentimental and passionate reasons. The Barrett Brownings eloped for their Grand Tour. Matthew Todd, the 'gentleman's gentleman', travelled because it was his job but enjoyed immensely the wine, women,

9

songs and japes. Charles Dickens, Thackeray, William Hazlitt, Wordsworth and Edward Lear went to Italy to gather background material for their writing careers.

Other travellers went to seek solace for the loss of a spouse, such as Lord Stormont and Andrew Mitchell, or for the loss of a child, such as Thomas and Anne Barrett-Lennard, and Tobias Smollett and his wife. Some of the older wealthy men such as Joseph Leeson (first Earl of Milltown), Sir Matthew Fetherstonhaugh and James Alexander, went to Italy to purchase paintings, prints, statues, medallions and other 'old antiquities' for their collections. The older travellers were the best informed and wrote journals of taste and interest – for instance Lord Gardenstone, Messrs. Holroyd, Mitchell and Walker – although two young men, Lord William Bentinck and Thomas Pelham, wrote informed, sensitive and intelligent letters home.

A clutch of elegant ladies went on the Grand Tour and then wrote about their experiences. Mariana Starke, Lady Frances Shelley (Wellington's *petite amie*), Anna Jameson, Lady Elizabeth Craven, Mrs. Hester Piozzi/Thrale, Lady Knight, Lady Mary Wortley Montagu, Lady Anne Miller, Catherine Wilmot (and her Irish peer), Lady Pomfret, Anne Radcliffe and many others recorded their travels. Some wrote in the late eighteenth century, most in the period after Waterloo – and all are of great interest. Emily Birchall wrote a charming journal of her honeymoon Grand Tour in 1873. But the most notorious Lady of them all, and the most famous bearleader, was Emma Hamilton, who led her captive admiral and elderly husband on a Grand Tour from Naples through Switzerland, Austria and Germany back to London.

When it came to the point, many of the young milords misbehaved. They gambled and ran up debts. They chased young women and ran up debts. They disbursed large sums on clothes (as William Shakespeare noted in *The Merchant of Venice*) and ran up more debts. Many formed unfortunate relationships with '*filles de joie*' and courtesans. Many brawled in the streets, drunk as the proverbial Lord. *Plus ça change, plus c'est la même chose.*

As Lord Chesterfield wrote in 1748, 'The end which I propose by your education and which (if you please) I shall certainly attain is to unite in you all the knowledge of a scholar with the manners of a courtier: and to join what is seldom joined in any of my countrymen, books and the world.' But of the young travellers he observed, 'They are commonly twenty years old before they have spoken to anybody above their schoolmaster and the Fellows of their College. If they happen to have learning, it is only Greek and Latin, but not one word of modern history or modern languages. Thus prepared, they go abroad, as they call it, but in truth they stay at home all that while: for being very awkward, confoundedly ashamed and not speaking the languages they go into no foreign company, at least none good, but dine and sup with one another only, at the tavern.'

ADVICE TO THE TRAVELLER

Advice there was in plenty. Tourist guides, such as Thomas Nugent, advised on methods of transport; postchaise or one's own London coach, often sold in Paris at the end of the tour; and routes to Rome, usually via Paris and Lyon, thence by one of five routes into Italy, frequently down the pleasant river Rhône valley by boat. Advice was proffered on guides and provisions for the journey, such as medical supplies, an iron fastener to secure the bedroom door, broadbrimmed hat, plenty of handkerchiefs, waterproof buckskin breeches, a tea caddy, penknife, a dozen strong shirts, etc. Since food supplies might be inferior it was suggested that the traveller take with him – salt, mustard, pepper, plenty of tea, sugar, oatmeal (for the Scots), ginger and nutmeg.

The best advice of all to the novice traveller was to his father: 'Select the best possible tutor and bearleader, knowledgeable, sympathetic, kind, but firm!' And to the traveller, 'Never talk to strange ladies.' (There were plenty of negatives!) 'Never travel alone.' 'Never travel at night but seek refuge in the chosen inn before dusk.' 'Never fail to strike a bargain on terms and rates with innkeepers and other tradesmen *before* taking up the required services.' Moreover, 'Familiarity with fellow travellers beyond a certain degree is very imprudent.' The young milords were told to spurn their own nationals on tour, and to make acquaintanceships with the natives, thus perfecting their language studies. They were warned to be very wary of thieves and pickpockets everywhere! Letters of introduction to the English ambassador or consul were essential; to be solicited beforehand from Messrs. Hoare or others in London. The tourist was encouraged by the guide-books always to ask questions about local history, geography, climate, trade and crops, food and wines, flora and fauna, laws and politics, and even to take a look at the military fortifications.

By the end of the seventeenth century, the guide-books had detailed descriptions of the contents of the main churches, galleries and libraries, so that a great deal of homework could be done beforehand. The polish of foreign manners, the knowledge of foreign languages, the use of foreign clothes and mannerisms were the desirable requirements of the Grand Tour.

INTRODUCTION

Style was all important. The Italian style of Andrea Palladio (studied by Inigo Jones in Florence) influenced Sir John Vanbrugh, the American Charles Bulfinch, and other European travellers. Rich British and American tourists (including President Jefferson) were so taken with 'foreign' architecture that they ensured that it was faithfully reproduced on their return. (Burlington House and Mereworth Castle for instance.) As Tobias Smollett wrote, 'When an Englishman comes to Paris he cannot appear until he has undergone a total metamorphosis! At his first arrival it is necessary to send for the taylor, perruquier [wigmaker], hatter, shoemaker and every other tradesman concerned in the equipment of the human body. He must even change his buckler and the form of his ruffles.'

Dr. Peter Mark Roget, a bearleader, wrote in 1802 that 'the numerous coaches, chaises and cabriolets drive with amazing rapidity over an irregular pavement with a deafening noise, splashing through the gutters which run in the middle of the streets.' There were four thousand hackney carriages and cabriolets in Paris at the turn of the century, and accidents were frequent. On the roads between towns the traveller had a choice of a journey by 'carosse', a stagecoach with room for six passengers, a 'coche d'osier', a large wicker basket of a coach carrying sixteen passengers, twelve in the body and two on each side of it by the door. The 'diligence' was even larger, a public coach taking up to thirty passengers, whose horses were changed at each 'post' of six miles, though sometimes, if the going was good, a change was deferred to twelve miles. Despite its size, the large clumsy machine, badly sprung and overcrowded, was much faster as the horses were urged to a gallop. A carosse or coche travelled at three or four miles per hour and the diligence at six. The latter could cover nearly a hundred miles in a day, but the smaller carriages were more comfortable.

The various rates worked out at about two shillings per post of six miles, but the insolent postilions were another disadvantage, 'lazy lounging greedy and impertinent', as described by Tobias Smollett. The post route from Calais went through Boulogne, Montreuil, Bernay, Abbeville, Clermont, Chantilly and St Denis. The carosse route after Abbeville was via Poix, Beauvais and Beaumont.

Before Joseph Spence bear-led young Lord Lincoln, he wrote out a check-list of vital equipment needed on the tour: '3 pair of Pistols (Powder & Ball), A Blunderbuss, 3 saddles, 3 prs of Jackboots and Pumps (better purchased at Paris), 3 Hangers (swords), 2 pairs of sheets, Large Trunk, Portmanteau (from Lewis of Brumley St), An Escritoire, paper, etc. Maps of France, Italy, Germany and Low Countries. Travels of Misson, Addison & Burnet, Great Coats, Shoes & Stockings, Riding Britches, Livery suit, 2 waistcoats, 1 Frock (coat), 4 Hat & 3 Britches (from Ward of Castle Street) Knife & Fork, Tea & Sugar, Bill of Credit, Bankers-Allowance'.

Mariana Starke's advice in her travel guide was that persons of affluence, or travelling for reasons of health, should always travel in their own carriage (preferably English made), 'taking care that it be strong, and going post when the roads are good thru France, Swisserland, Germany etc. but travelling en voiturier over the Alps and Apennine into Italy owing to the peculiar excellence of the roads . . . always use best established Voiturins who will convey English carriages, 40–50 miles a day at four to five miles per hour.' She recommended 'the most frequented route by the shortest Post-Roads from Calais to Rome, via Beauvais, Paris, Lyon, over Mt Cenis, to Turin, Genoa, Lucca, Pisa, Poggisbensi and Siena. Beware of avalanches on Mount Cenis between the 3rd and 4th refuge posts. The best summer and autumn road [is] thru Dijon, over the Jura Alps, Simplon to Milan and thence to Rome.'

Although the first printed reference to 'The Grand Tour' was made in 1670 by Richard Lassells in his work *An Italian Journey*, 'the need and the pleasure to explore Europe' really started with the first Queen Elizabeth. She wished to establish a network of able young diplomats to represent their country at foreign courts. A knowledge not only of the appropriate language but also of the history, culture and ways of the 'foreigners' was considered vital. (The favoured courtiers were not, of course, allowed to go to cities where Jesuit influence was strong, such as Douai, St Omer and Reims; nor might they be allowed to Rome.)

Sir Philip Sidney was partly sponsored by the Queen on his Grand Tour, which cost a total of £1,700 – a huge sum in the sixteenth century. He left England in 1572 for Paris, travelling through France, Germany, the Low Countries and Italy, learning the languages and visiting the foreign courts. His tour took three years and he was accompanied by an Italian-speaking tutor, three servants and four horses. Sidney travelled in style, was painted in Venice by Tintoretto and Veronese, took riding lessons in Vienna, and on the way home visited Poland and Hungary. Doubtless he was helped by the first guide-book in Europe, published in 1549 (when the Queen was but sixteen) by William Thomas.

As usual, the perceptive William Shakespeare identified the fashion to travel in Europe. In 1596 he wrote in *The Merchant of Venice*, about Falconbridge, a young baron of England, suitor to Portia, [he] 'hath neither Latin, French nor Italian. He is a proper man's picture . . . I think he bought his doublet in Italy, his round hose in France, his bonnet in Germany and his behaviour everywhere.' Later the Bard wrote 'Farewell,

INTRODUCTION

Monsieur traveller, look you lisp and wear strange suits or I will not think thou hast swam in a gondola.'

By the end of the sixteenth century the Pope was complaining officially about the number of English heretics arriving in Venice. The Doge in Venice was informed in 1617 by King James I's ambassador that there were now more than seventy Englishmen in town. Thomas Coryat, an eccentric member of James I's court, and friend of Ben Jonson, was another intrepid traveller, and wrote in 1608 of his adventures as *Coryat's Crudities*. He thought that 'of all the pleasures in the world, travel was the sweetest and most delightful'. Of the *ghetto nuovo* in Venice he wrote 'the women there were as beautiful as I ever saw. So gorgeous in their apparel, jewels, chains of gold and rings adorned with precious stones, having marvellous long trains like princesses.' In the same year poor John Mole, a Protestant tutor to young Lord Roos, was imprisoned by the Inquisition in Rome for his faith, and spent the next thirty years in confinement, until his death.

Early guide-books included S.V. Pighius' *Hercules Prodicus*, the German Prince's tour in 1574–5; Varennes' *Le Voyage de France*; John Evelyn's *Kalendarium, My Journal 1620–1649*; Justus Zinzerling's *Itinerarium Galliae*; P. Totti's *Ritratto de Roma Antica* of 1627; François Schott's *Itinerarii Italiae Rerumque, Romanorum (Libre Tres)* of 1600; Pflaumern's *Mercurius Italicus* 1628; and John Raymond's *Itinerary contayning a voyage made through Italy in the years 1646–47*.

One of the earliest progenitors of the Grand Tour was Thomas Howard, Second Earl of Arundel (1585–1640). He was the most important patron of the arts in England during the early seventeenth century. Horace Walpole, writing 150 years later, described him as the 'Father of Vertu in England'. Howard travelled in state to Italy with Thomas Coke as his guide in 1612 and with Inigo Jones in the following year. For a long time Thomas Howard and his wife were established in Venice as ambassadors extraordinary, and later (in 1645–46) in Padua, where he died. Lord Arundel was the first great art collector among the English nobility and his collection is now dispersed throughout the British Isles. As a result of his encouragement of local artists, a remarkable industry was created. Pompeo Batoni (1708–1787) painted more than two hundred Englishmen on the Grand Tour, including the Duke of Richmond and his brother Lord George Lennox. Sir Henry Fetherstonhaugh commissioned a unique series of nine portraits of members of his family from Batoni. Painters as famous as Angelica Kauffman (1740–1807), Piranese (1720–1778), Vanvitelli, Luca Carlevaris, Zuccarelli, Giordano and the schools of Canaletto, Marieschi, and Van Lint were producing either portraits or commissioned views of 'antiquities' for the English aristocracy when they were on tour.

John Milton, that Protestant tourist, started his Grand Tour in April 1638 and was absent from England for fifteen months. Of Florence he wrote, 'I have always particularly esteemed [it] for the elegance of its dialect, its genius and its taste.' His friends Dati and Francini exchanged poems with him, talked of learning and religion 'for the manner is that everyone must give some proof of his wit and reading there'. He spent two months in Rome 'viewing the antiquities' and wrote with thanks to the Vatican librarian for his courtesy. In Naples the poet embarrassed the distinguished old Manso, Marquis of Villa. Milton 'had not been more reserved about religion' and Manso was sent a hexameter poem of thanks. On his way home Milton called in at Geneva to consult with the learned professor of Protestant theology Giovanni Diodati, and met by chance the debauched Franco–Scots professor Alexander More. Later Milton wrote smugly, 'I never once deviated from the paths of integrity and virtue and perpetually reflected that though my conduct escaped the notice of me, it could not elude the inspection of God.'

The seventeenth century produced a dozen or so books describing European Grand Tours – even though the Thirty Years War, which ended in 1648, was a hindrance to travellers. The quest for knowledge continued. After Richard Lassell's book, published in 1670, six years later came John Clenche's *A Tour in France and Italy*, Brereton's *Travels in Holland* (1634–1635), Peter Heylyn's *A full Relation of Two Journeys* (1656), Henry Logan's *Directions for such as shall Travel to Rome* (1654), John Walter Stoye's *English Travellers Abroad* (1604–1667) and Edmund Warcup's *Italy in its Original Glory, Ruins and Revival* (1660).

TUTORS AND BEARLEADERS

The eighteenth century saw a change of emphasis. Partly as a result of the low esteem in which the British universities were held, the aristocracy decided to send its sons on the Grand Tour accompanied by carefully selected older tutors. Some of these mentors were distinguished and able men; Dr John Moore, father of the General; Adam Smith, the Scottish economist; Thomas Hobbes, the philospher; Robert Wood; William Whitehead, subsequently Poet Laureate; John Horne Tooke, politician and philologist, and John Addison, poet, essayist and politician. Joseph Spence, the Oxford poet, bear-led three noble young charges in separate Grand Tours over a ten year period. Almost without fail these erudite tutors published accounts of their tours, with discreet descriptions of their stripling protégés. Their fee was a standard hundred guineas per tour with all expenses found.

Vicesimus Knox, an educational expert of the period, defined the bearleader's responsibilities. He should be 'a grave, respectable man of mature age', and should 'watch over the morals and religion of his pupil'. Thomas Wharton's tutor, Theophilus Gale, admitted to the young man's father, Lord Wharton, 'My Lord, as to Conversation Mr Wharton judgeth himself fit and capable to choose his company and thinks it too hard an imposition to be tyed up to such *as I shall judge meete* whereupon he has sometimes persons come to him whom I neither know *nor can approve of.*' Moreover, the young milord was a late riser, prayed insufficiently, and failed to observe the Lord's Day!

The tutors needed to be paragons. Chosen for their intellectual prowess, these travelling governors were rarely suited to face the hardships of travel, the dangers of bandits and wolves, and the insolence of postilions and innkeepers, or to cope with the numerous problems that beset all schoolmasters. Unruly, ill-disciplined, randy young men of a certain class looked down on their tutors socially. The bearleaders indeed were not to be envied. Lord Chesterfield wrote that scarcely one in a hundred of the youths who went abroad under tutors learned a language, or visited 'any person of quality, much less made an acquaintance with such from whose conversation he might learn what was good breeding in that country'.

PITFALLS AND PLEASURES

So, rich, intolerant, callow and insular, the young sprigs got into terrible scrapes during the eighteenth century. David Mallet boasted of 'having lain with a Sovereign Princess in Italy', and Horace Mann wrote, 'An English traveller frequently deranges the whole harmony of Cicisbeship' (the curious social system whereby young matrons were intimately chaperoned by a male friend).

Richard Pococke wrote in June 1734, 'Mr Wynn has been two or three years at Venice enchanted with a Mistress.' Venice was notorious for its prostitution and low morals, and three years later the Earl of Radnor's domination by a Venetian mistress attracted scandalous comment. James Stuart MacKenzie fell for the famous opera dancer Barberini, and promised to marry her in Venice. Fortunately the Duke of Argyll arranged for her to go to Berlin and for the young milord to be banned from Prussia. But

William Godolphin, the Marquess of Blandford, did marry an Italian woman, an Irish peer lived in Pisa with his wife and an Italian contessa, and George Viscount Parker's heavy involvement with an Italian woman nineteen years older than himself scandalized his friends and amused his enemies.

By contrast with those of Milton and Evelyn, the Grand Tour of James Boswell was the most hilarious and the most abandoned. In every town he visited he had explicit sexual adventures. ('A *fille charmante* cost fourteen paoli (7s).') He visited brothels on many occasions and caught venereal disease twice!

At the same time as Boswell was boasting of his brothel visits, Lord Lyttleton's son's engagement in England was broken off because 'he was detained by Circes & Syrens off the coast about Genoa'. One of the Earl of Chesterfield's brothers 'spent a great deal of money on a Venetian woman whom he thought in love with him'. And in 1785 a Mr Fox Lane, a young man of fashion and great fortune, 'in Turin from an infatuated complaisance to the lady he was in love with, changed his Religion [to] Roman Catholic . . . an act of Infatuation and childishness.'

Thomas Brand, bearleader for a decade, had good reason to consult the parents of his charges. In 1783 his pupil fell for the elder Miss Berry in Boulogne, and in 1793 young Lord Bruce fell for an older English tourist in Rome, and married her. Joseph Spence recalls how his handsome young charge (whom King George II declared was the handsomest man in England) fell desperately in love with the beautiful Lady Sophia Fermor and pursued her across Italy. Horace Walpole fell in love with Signora Grifone at Florence and profoundly worried her Cicisbeo. In the same town Lady Margaret Walpole, a married lady, eloped with young Samuel Sturgis.

Despite the plethora of good advice from a dozen well-written eighteenth-century guide-books, the love dramas continued. The *Gentleman's Pocket Companion for Travelling into Foreign Parts* was published in 1722, and Thomas Nugent's excellent four-volume guide *The Grand Tour* in 1743. His readers were warned that the French 'were fiery, impatient, inconstant, and of a restless disposition, [and] were addicted to gambling', while the young 'were debauched and irreligious'. Mr Bowman, tutor to Viscount George Harcourt, warned of 'the low vices of our countrymen in Italy'.

It was made plain by all the writers that Europe was no place for lady travellers, so it is a surprise to find a remarkably good travel guide published in 1791 (and subsequently) by Mariana Starke. This brave and intelligent lady was carried over the Alps in a sedan chair. She warned travellers against the climate in Genoa and the 'ill-educated nobles' there.

17

But she admired paintings in Bologna and recommended the Florentines as 'good humoured, open hearted and, though passionate, full of drollery.' Her guide-books were complete and comprehensive. For every city in Europe she had specific recommendations about the hotels, food, wine and cuisine. She was the Michelin Guide of the eighteenth century.

The scandals continued of course. Lord Euston, second son of the Duke of Grafton, eloped to Italy in 1744 with a wealthy Miss Neville of Lincolnshire. Lord Byron's father John Byron ran off with a married lady, Amelia D'Arcy, in 1778, and married her when Lord Carmarthen obtained a divorce. A few years later, in 1785, a Miss Murray wrote to Lord Keith, 'Mr M. is gone to France with Miss Johnson & left Lady Catherine to pray for his soul.'

Another problem, usually in Paris, was that of gambling. The young sprigs lost considerable sums of money at gaming and cards since, as Edward Mellish wrote, 'if one is expected to be well received by persons of the best fashions, one must be obliged to play deep and game sometimes . . .' Another Englishman, George James Cholmondeley, ran a public gaming table in Paris, and two MPs, Edward Wortley Montagu and Theobald Taaffe, were arrested in Paris in 1751 for cheating at cards.

CHANGING TIMES

The main European wars that temporarily reduced the flow of travellers to the Continent were the Anglo–Dutch wars in the seventeenth century, followed by the war of the Spanish succession, the Seven Years War (1756–63) and the French revolutionary wars at the end of the eighteenth century. The Peace of Amiens in 1802 saw a flood of travellers to France, which was sharply checked when Bonaparte became Emperor. Before Waterloo, the aristocracy, the gentry and their ladies flocked to Brussels and Paris where they seemed unconcerned during the One Hundred Days.

The arrival of steam-boats and the first railways shortly afterwards brought thousands of travellers to the south of France and Italy. As early as 1785, Edward Gibbon, then in Lausanne, had been told that there were forty thousand English on the Continent. From contemporary reports it appears that at any one time, except during the wars, about two thousand travellers were actually on the move. Boulogne had a resident English population of six thousand early in the nineteenth century. Paris, Calais, Rome and Florence, Geneva and Brussels could have had as many.

Progress and modernization of travel arrangements continued apace in the nineteenth century. The first steam-boat *Charlotte Dundas* was built by William Symington in 1789, and the first cross-channel steam passenger service was introduced in 1816 from Brighton to Le Havre. Four years later the *Rob Roy* was in service from Dover to Calais. In the 1820s and 1830s the steam-boat *Navrais* went from Le Havre down the Seine to Rouen.

The French railway system started up in 1843, when amidst great rejoicing the Paris–Rouen and Paris–Orléans lines were opened. Five years later there were ten trains a day from London to Folkestone, thence a steamer sailed with every tide across the Channel. The Boulogne–Abbeville railway was soon opened, and the coast to Paris train route of one hundred and seventy miles took only nine hours compared to the fastest *diligence* of fifteen hours. From the 1820s onwards it was estimated that one hundred and fifty thousand British travellers were going to Europe each year. The package tour operators moved in. Thomas Cook started in 1841, Joseph Crisp in 1844, and Henry Gaze in the same year introduced a tour to Paris and the battlefield of Waterloo.

THE ARRIVAL OF THE AMERICANS

After Waterloo, many Americans visited Europe on their Grand Tours. They started usually in London where George Bancroft, the ambassador there, kept an interesting journal. The year 1821 saw the first transatlantic crossing by steamer and soon there were sizeable American communities in Paris and Florence. Most of them recorded their Grand Tours for posterity, in books, novels or journals. George Ticknor of Boston was one of the first arrivals in 1815; others included James Fenimore Cooper in 1826 (*A Residence in France*), Bayard Taylor (*Views Afoot*), Nathaniel Hawthorne (*French & Italian Notebooks*), Oliver Wendell Holmes (*One Hundred Days in Europe*), J.L. Motley, Henry Brooks Adams (*Education of H.A.*), Robert Waldo Emerson, Thomas Jefferson, Harriet Beecher Stowe (*Sunny memories of Foreign lands*), Henry and William James (*A little Tour in France*), Washington Irving (*Tales of a Traveller*), H.W. Longfellow (*Outremer*) and a book written by his young female scribe Clara Crowninshield, Walter Savage Landor, and the inimitable Mark Twain (*A Tramp Abroad*).

The large artistic colony in Florence included painters, poets, writers and sculptors, who undoubtedly influenced the American cultural scene on their return. William Edward Mead, the American writer, wrote a book in 1914 on Americans on their Grand Tours, and Van Wyck Brooks wrote biographies of famous individual American travellers to Europe.

ART AND INSPIRATION

To view the ancient antiquities and seek inspiration in one form or another came many English artists. J.M.W. Turner made several journeys to Paris, the Loire, Switzerland and Italy, and the marvellous results can now be seen at the Tate Gallery in London. Bonington's paintings of the French coastal ports can be seen at the Wallace collection. Thomas Patch painted in Florence; Sir Godfrey Kneller studied in Rome and Venice; John 'Warwick' Smith and Francis Towne gained inspiration from Switzerland and Italy in the late eighteenth century. Richard Wilson lived for six years in Rome from 1749, and his oils and chalk drawings reflect the experience gained on his Grand Tour. John Robert Cozens (1752–1797) visited Italy twice in 1776 and 1782 and was an early inspiration to Thomas Girtin and Turner. During their stay in Naples, gouache watercolours of the Bay by local eighteenth-century artists were popular, and were brought back to the United Kingdom in large numbers.

Even now, neglected, forgotten Italian Renaissance paintings keep turning up in English country houses. In the attics of Holkham Hall in Norfolk, in 1988, four paintings were discovered which had been commissioned by Lord Leicester (1697–1759) during his Grand Tour. One was by Procaccini (1671–1734), another by Guiseppe Chiari (1654–1727), and two by Agostino Scilla (1629–1700). They have now been carefully restored and put on show in the room where Thomas Coke, First Earl of Leicester, also a veteran of the Grand Tour, originally intended they should go in 1750. A happy ending!

THE MODERN GRAND TOUR

A modern Grand Tour can be constructed quite easily. The only two problems are time and money! Any good travel agent will link Paris to Florence, Rome, Naples and Venice by air or train for a visit to the cities considered indispensable. Allow a minimum of three days in each city, stay at one of the hotels, and dine at one of the restaurants frequented by the original Grand Tourists.

Ideally, however, one should follow one of the major routes favoured by the early travellers. Assuming the starting point is in the United Kingdom, go by ship from Harwich to the Hook of Holland. No need to walk – take your car or catch a smooth, comfortable, Dutch train to Amsterdam, then go to Rotterdam via Utrecht, south to Breda, and across the frontier to

Antwerp and Brussels. Now you have three choices: either southwest via Paris and Orléans to Lyon, south via Charleroi to Reims, Troyes, Dijon and Lyon, or southeast via Namur, Metz, Nancy, Langres and Besançon to Geneva and Turin. Lyon was always the great crossroads, with three choices – east to Geneva, southeast to Chambéry, or south following the river Rhône to Avignon, Marseille and the Côte d'Azur to Genoa.

Once in Italy the traveller usually took the western coastal road through Pisa and Prato to Florence, then south via Siena to Rome and Naples. The return route would go towards the northeast again through Florence to Bologna and Venice. Most travellers returned via Padua and Vicenza to Milan, and then either to Turin/Lyon or Genoa/Nice. A few, braver than the rest, journeyed eastwards to Trieste, and inland to Graz and Vienna.

Two UK-based companies offer packaged city breaks, both of which can be recommended. **TIME OFF**, Chester Close, Chester Street, London SW1X 7BQ (012358070) offer four-city tours of the key cities in Holland, Belgium, France (i.e. Paris) and Switzerland. They also offer three-city tours in Italy.

PEGASUS HOLIDAYS (LONDON) LIMITED, 24a Earls Court Gardens, London SW5 0TA (013706851) offer multi-centre holidays in Italy, for which the traveller can choose his requirements from eleven cities, with a minimum of three days and nights in each – ideal for the modern Grand Tourer.

The modern painter can make the Grand Tour and spend six weeks on a Fine Art Course in Tuscany and Rome, with tours of the private palaces and gardens in Venice and Rome. Contact **FINE ART COURSES**, 15 Savile Row, London W1X 1AE (014378553).

A bus tour of Classical Italy of fourteen days duration is offered by **BADGERLINE LEISURE LIMITED** , Manvers Street, Bath, Avon BA1 1JJ (0225 445555).

THOMAS COOK also offer fifteen-day bus tours of Classical Italy: information from P.O. Box 36, Peterborough PE3 6SB.

Bon Voyage!

FRANCE

and the French

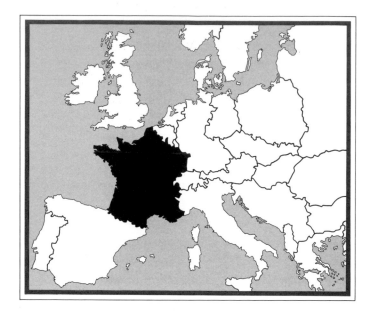

$\mathcal{O}$ver the centuries, many travellers have recorded their views of the French, their fashions, morals, honesty, customs, politics, streets, drains, music, theatre, food and wine. Occasionally one can also find French people's comments about the Grand Tour visitors to their country. Every traveller had to go to Paris *en route* to the Italian antiquities. Even if he or she started off in the Low Countries and the route from Brussels took them to Geneva, they would generally pass through Reims and Dijon, and return home through the coastal towns of Nice and Marseille, northwards via Aix en Provence and Avignon, and then up the Rhône valley to Lyon and Paris. The seven 'provincial' towns were visited with great regularity, and thus each has a chapter to itself.

The modern traveller will find there the best art, museums, and Roman antiquities in France; the gastronomic delights of Burgundy, Lyonnais and Provence; the '*événements*' of the wine harvest festivals; carnival battles of the flowers; opera seasons, theatres and modern jazz festivals.

The first stage was the crossing of the Channel from Brighton, more usually Dover, and occasionally Harwich.

ON BOARD SHIP

'My passage to Dieppe. We had not got out of the
Beachy Head lights, when it began to rain hard. I
was therefore driven into the cabin and compelled
to endure the spectacle and to hear the unutterable
groans and gasps of fifty sea-sick people. I went
out when the rain ceased but everything on deck
was soaked. It was impossible to sit so that I
walked up and down the vessel all night . . .'

LORD MACAULAY

LETTERS 1843

Then the customs officer at Dieppe charged Lord M. fourteen francs duty for some unworn cotton stockings!

He was fortunate in his crossing. Spark Molesworth had to rest at Calais 'after the great fatigue of ye sea'. In 1766 the Earl of Fife spent two terrible days at sea trying to cross the Channel.

The year before, young William Cole was injured changing boats in rough seas in the dark off Dover, and Lady Mary Coke was drenched in a little boat that landed four miles away from Calais!

Nowadays, of course, one crosses the Channel quickly, economically, and usually safely by air, ferry boat or hovercraft within a couple of hours.

ON ARRIVAL

'The first thing an Englishman does on going
abroad is to find fault with what is French because
it is not English. If he is determined to confine all
excellence to his own country, he had better stay
at home.'

WILLIAM HAZLITT

NOTES OF A JOURNEY THROUGH

FRANCE AND ITALY 1826

Still very true! Driving on the wrong side of the road. Distances in kilometres. Strange signs like *'Toutes Directions'* or *'Autres Directions'*. Prices in a different currency, and a different language. But Grand Tour travellers – then and now – take these minor problems in our stride, *n'est-ce pas?*

The French coastal ports of Calais and Boulogne have long been anglicized, and as the numbers of visitors grew, the inns rapidly improved their facilities. My Huguenot ancestor, Jean de la Force, kept the 'Mermaid Inn' at Calais in 1648. In 1673 my family owned the 'Golden Dragon' in Calais, and another relative of Jean's kept an inn at Dover. The most famous hotel during much of the eighteenth century, was Monsieur Dessein's 'Angleterre' in Calais where the traveller met with every courtesy and facility, including the supply of excellent coaches and reliable postilions. There were, however, many views about lodgings in France.

ON FRENCH INNS AND TRAVELLING

Travelling in northern France has not always been without its hazards. Thomas Coryat in 1608 wrote from Abbeville *en route* for Paris, 'false knaves in many places of the Forrest that lurke under trees and shrubbes, suddenly set upon travellers and cut their throtes.' In Burgundy he encountered 'roguish Egyptians, very Ruffians and swashbucklers'!

'A French gentleman travelling in company with
others, gets a cup of coffee at a little shop for three
halfpence and laughs at you for paying two francs
for a bad breakfast at the inn. They demand
payment for board and lodging beforehand which
shows either a grasping disposition or a want of
confidence.'
WILLIAM HAZLITT
ESSAYS 1824

'The waiters were tidy, noiseless, glided hither and
thither, hovered like butterflies, quick to compre-
hend orders, quick to fill them, thankful for a gratuity,
always polite. That is the strangest curiosity
yet – a really polite hotel waiter who isn't an idiot.'
MARK TWAIN 1867
of Marseille

Generally speaking in the seventeenth to nineteenth centuries the roads between the main towns in France were safe and adequate. Distances of 60–80 miles could be covered in a day. In the twentieth century they are superb, well maintained, well signed, and the travellers would be amazed at the French Autoroutes and Routes Nationales.

Passport holders now are usually nodded through at frontiers. No need for elaborate and complicated documents. John Milton's passport in May 1638 was issued by the Warden of the Cinque Ports. As recently as 1830, passports for France had to be issued by the French passport office in London. On arrival in France the British Foreign Office passport was liable to be taken away in exchange for a temporary 'passe provisoire', while the original was sent to Paris to be countersigned by the Ministry of the Interior. No need now for complicated letters of credit issued by London bankers to be negotiated with their correspondents in Paris and Lyon. Traveller's cheques, Eurocheques, plastic credit cards and the purchase of foreign currency before the start are now taken for granted.

Mark Twain, travelling in the mid-nineteenth century, never knew about the acute discomfort of the crowded smelly *diligence* ambling along at about five miles per hour over *pavé* through the French countryside. The new railway era in France he found most acceptable and praised the system highly. He would have liked the modern high-speed TGV that sweeps its passengers in great comfort from Paris to the Mediterranean in five hours.

ON FRENCH RESPONSIBILITY

'In France all is clockwork, all is order. They make no mistakes. Every third man wears a uniform and whether he be a Marshall of the Empire or a brakeman on a train, he is ready and perfectly willing to answer all your questions with tireless politeness, ready to tell you which car to take, yea and ready to go and put you into it to make sure that you shall not go astray. No, they have no railroad accidents to speak of in France. But why? Because when one occurs *somebody* has to hang for it! Not hang maybe, but be punished at least with such vigour of emphasis as to make negligence a thing to be shuddered at.'

MARK TWAIN 1867

25

On arrival in Paris, once lodgings had been organized satisfactorily, the immediate problems were dress, language, and servants.

ON DRESS

'My Lady Hertford has cut me to pieces and
thrown me into a caldron with tailors, periwig-
makers, snuff-box-wrights, milliners, etc. which
really took up but little time, and I am come out
quite new with everything but youth. The journey
recovered me with magic expedition.'

HORACE WALPOLE 1765

on arrival in Paris

ON LEARNING THE LANGUAGE

'It is certain that I have the greatest desire to learn
French but I fear that I am not learning it quickly.
Perhaps my keen desire makes me think myself
worse in acquiring the language than I am. I
certainly take a great deal of pains to improve. I
write two pages of a theme every morning. I read
for two hours in the works of Voltaire every
evening. When I do not understand words perfectly I look them up in the dictionary and I write
them down with their meanings.'

JAMES BOSWELL 1763

Nevertheless Boswell made terrible mistakes, and remarked ruefully, 'Such blunders make a man very ridiculous.'

ON GUIDES AND SERVANTS

'They lay all your tradesmen under contribution,
your taylor, barber, mantua maker, milliner,
perfumer, shoemaker, mercer, jeweller, hatter,
traiteur and wine merchant, even the bourgeois

who owns your coach pays him 20 sous per day.'
TOBIAS SMOLLETT 1763
on the 'valet de place'

'One (guide) looked so like a very pirate that we
let him go at once. The next one spoke with a
simpering precision of pronounciation that was
irritating. 'I speaky ze Angleesh pairfaitemaw. . .'
He would have done well to have stopped there
because he had that much by heart and said it
right off without making a mistake. But his self
complacency seduced him into attempting a flight
into regions of unexplored English and the reckless
experiment was his ruin. Within ten seconds he
was so tangled up in a maze of mutilated verbs
and torn and bleeding forms of speech
that no human ingenuity could ever have
gotten him out of it with credit.
The third man captured us.'
MARK TWAIN 1867
in Paris

'I might just as effectually argue with a horse as
with a French postilion.'
LADY ELIZABETH CRAVEN 1776

Many travellers had pithy comments – sometimes contradictory – about their Gallic neighbours' habits.

ON FRENCH MANNERS AND SOCIAL LIFE

'To complete this tissue of charges against French
manners, they are full of tracasserie, of trick and
low cunning; they are a thorough "nation of
shopkeepers". All their bonhommie and complaisance are at an end as soon as their interest is
concerned. They are rude or polite just as they
think they can make most of it . . . If you make a
bargain with them and someone else comes and

offers them a sou more they take it and smile at
your disappointment, or pretend not to have
understood you.'
WILLIAM HAZLITT
ESSAYS 1824

'I was taken for a Frenchman. I am insolent, I talk
a great deal. I am very loud and peremptory. I
sing and dance and go along and lastly I spend a
monstrous deal of money in powder.'
LORD CHESTERFIELD 1750

'The Parisian is industrious and inventive, polite
and gentle, curious, enthusiastic and inconstant,
endowed with wit and taste but satirical, frivolous,
a slave to fashion, fond of luxury, and eager for
pleasure. Naturally brave, his courage has been
seen to degenerate into cruelty. Living entirely for
the present, he soon forgets his afflictions, consoles
himself with songs and is too gay to think of the
future. The women have tolerably fair complexion,
[and] possess lively charms and graces which
many think superior to beauty. The tradesmen of
Paris and indeed all over France have an
impolitic custom of asking much more than they
will take. Even their own countrymen are obliged
to bargain and beat them down with the greatest
obstinacy.'
GALIGNANI'S GUIDE TO PARIS 1814

'All through this Faubourg St Antoine, misery,
poverty, vice and crime go hand in hand and the
evidence of it stare one in the face from every side.
Here the people live who begin the revolutions.
Whenever there is anything of that kind to be
done, they are always ready. They take as much
genuine pleasure in building a barricade as they
do in cutting a throat or shoving a friend into the
Seine. It is these savage looking ruffians who
storm the splendid halls of the Tuileries,

occasionally, and swarm into Versailles when a
King is to be called to account.'
MARK TWAIN 1867
in Paris

'The French are always open, familiar and talka-
tive . . . In France every one aims at a gaiety and
sprightliness of behaviour and thinks it an accom-
plishment to be brisk and lively . . .'
JOHN ADDISON 1703

ON ENTERTAINMENT

'All the surroundings were gay and enlivening.
Two hundred people sat at little tables on the
sidewalk, sipping wine and coffee: the streets were
thronged with light vehicles and with joyous
pleasure-seekers: there was music in the air, life
and action all about us and a conflagration of
gaslight everywhere. After dinner we sauntered
through the brilliant streets and looked at the
dainty trifles in variety stores
and jewellry shops.'
MARK TWAIN 1867
in Paris

'In the first place, the town is beautiful and the
people so genteel that it's a real amusement to
drive about the streets . . .the houses are dirty and
cold, but yet I own I like the stile of them
infinitely.'
LADY SARAH LENNOX 1765
in Paris

ON FRENCH FOOD

In the twentieth century one thinks of France as being a gastronomic
delight, and the food one of several excellent reasons for visiting that

country. Not so in the sixteenth to nineteenth centuries. Although the French cuisine was generally accepted to be superior to that of the Italians, Swiss or the residents of the Low Countries, it was not always greeted with acclaim.

'The French diet is not near so gross as ours. Their bread is exceeding good and so is their beef and mutton. They boil and roast their meat much longer than we do which exempts them from the gross humours to which the crudity of our meat subjects us. They are fond of soup ragoos and made dishes, which they dress the best of any people in Europe. Their vegetable food consists of kidney beans, white lentils, turnips, red onions, leeks, lettuce, white beets and asparagus. They have scarely any potatoes but great quantities of sorrel and mushroom, especially the latter of which they are very fond.'
THOMAS NUGENT 1750

'St Omer in a miserable inn, supper of stale mackerell, omelette of raddled eggs. Fridays stinking fish, rotten eggs.'
CHARLES BURNEY 1815
on staying at St Omer

Arthur Young travelled all over France in the pre-Revolutionary period, and stayed at many inns, dined at many tables d'hôte, and as a professional agronomist took a dispassionate view of the French cuisine.

He wrote in 1787, 'The English have half a dozen real English dishes that exceed anything in France (turbot and lobster sauce, ham and chicken, turtle, a haunch of venison, turkey and oysters). After those an end to an English table. It is an idle prejudice to class roast beef among them, for there is not better beef in the world than at Paris. The variety given by the French cooks to the same thing is astonishing. They dress a hundred dishes in a hundred different ways, and most of them excellent – and all sorts of vegetables have a savouriness and flavour from rich sauces that are absolutely wanted compared to our greens boiled in water. In France one would get 4 dishes to 1 amongst us, clean glasses in France, table linen cleaner in France, always clean knapkins at their inns.'

WHAT THE FRENCH THOUGHT
OF THE TRAVELLERS

The *Gentleman's Guide* for 1770 noted, 'Our young nobility and gentry collect mobs in the street by throwing money from the windows. People in trade find the English custom so vastly beneficial that they have their lookers-out on purpose to bring them to their shops and Taverns. All the guides receive commissions from the shopkeepers.' Even the bearleader/tutors, those 'unscrupulous needy bold men' were known to subcontract a boy's tuition to second-rate academics and pocket the difference in fees, or even take bribes from scheming foreigners to entrap the youngster into an unsuitable marriage. So what then did the French think of our travellers?

> 'How they hate us these foreigners, in Belgium as
> much as in France! What lies they tell of us: how
> gladly they would see us humiliated . . . They hate
> you because you are stupid, hard to please and
> intolerably insolent and air-giving . . .'
> W.M. THACKERAY 1840

> 'The French have no idea that there is any thing in
> England but roast beef and plum pudding and a
> number of round red faces, growing fat and stupid
> upon such fare . . .'
> WILLIAM HAZLITT 1824

MODERN FRANCE

The next seven chapters concentrate on cities which the travellers invariably visited on their way to or from Italy. It was essential for them to visit Paris where they would spend up to a year, whereas a month would be considered the maximum stay in the provincial towns. Dijon, Reims and Lyon are dignified wine cities with cuisine to match, and the modern traveller can reach them easily by autoroute, TGV or fast rail, or by the French Air Inter. Roman Provence, with its antiquities at Avignon, Aix, Marseille and Nice, should also be visited. The modern Provençal cuisine should please every visitor. Even the tetchy Scots novelist Tobias Smollett would approve of '*bouillabaisse*' and '*ratatouille*' washed down with a Côtes de Provence rosé sitting in the sun overlooking the Mediterranean.

A number of enterprising travel companies in the United Kingdom cater for wine lovers and gourmet travellers. Among them are **VINTAGE WINE TOURS**, 8 Belmont, Landsdown Road, Bath, Avon BA1 5D2, (0255 315834); **WORLD WINE TOURS**, 70 North Street, London SW4 0HE; **FRANCOPHILES**, 66 Great Brockeridge, Westbury-on-Trym, Bristol, Avon BS9 3UA, (0272 621975); and **BLACKHEATH WINE TRAILS**, 13 Blackheath Village, London SE3 9LD, (01 463 0012).

Several companies including **THOMAS COOK LIMITED**, **SAGA** and **SWAN HELLENIC** offer sophisticated package tours to France to see the 'Antiquities'.

PARIS

'This city of love and folly'

At one stage or another on the Grand Tour, the travellers *had* to visit Paris. One of the earliest visitors was the young Scotsman Fynes Moryson, who in 1595 wrote a concise account. He admired the stately unpolished stone houses with their outsides of plastered rough-cast, often four to six storeys high. Most of the streets were dirty but the 'fairest' were, in order, St Denis, St Honoré, St Antoine and St Martin. He noted that the river Seine often overflowed, and that the 'diet' was cheaper in Paris than in London. The 'Cittie of Paris' was divided into three parts – the Ville, the Island and the University. There were fourteen fountains, eight hospitals, and eleven market places.

Thirteen years later, in 1608, Thomas Coryat arrived in Paris and met Isaac Casaubon, the Huguenot 'divine'. The town 'was ten miles in circuit, very populous, goodly buildings of faire white free-stone, with durtiest streets'. He counted the fourteen Town Gates, admired the 'noble river Sequana, la rivière de Seine, their famous Sorbona, fruitful nursery of schoole-divines, but the Cathedral, nothing so faire as our Lady church of Amiens.'

John Milton in his *Works* published early in the seventeenth century, wrote cynically of the travellers, 'Nor shall we then need the monsieurs of Paris to take our hopeful youth into their slight and prodigal custodies, and send them back again transformed into mimics, apes and kickshows.' Young John Evelyn, accompanied by James Thicknesse of Balliol, visited Paris several times and in 1641 and 1643 stayed at the Hôtel Ville de Venize, the inn most frequented by the English. Thought to be the cultural capital of Europe, Evelyn described it as 'large in circuit, infinitely populous, but situat in a botome which renders some places very durty and makes it smell as if sulphure were mingled with the mudd – but one of the most gallant cittys in the World and best built.' On the Seine he marvelled at the 'prodigious number of Barges and boates of incredible length, full of hay, corne, wood, wine and other commodities which this vast citty consumes.'

Lady Mary Wortley Montagu thought the Paris of 1716 was half the size of London, 'the Tuileries finer than our Mall, the Cours with its high trees more agreeable than our Hyde Park.' She visited Versailles, Le Trianon, Marli and St Cloud. 'I was followed to Versailles by all the English at Paris.' She admired the neatly paved streets, the houses built of stone, the beautiful gardens and the regular lighting of the streets at night.

Thomas Gray, the poet, and Horace Walpole, the fop, stayed at the Hôtel de Luxembourg in the rue des Petits Augustins on their long visit to Paris in 1741. Other milords then in Paris included Holderness, Conway, Waldegrave, George Bentinck and Clinton. The former described the women as 'in general dressed as sacs, flat hoops of five yards wide, nosegays of artificial flowers on one shoulder and faces dyed in Scarlet up to the Eyes. The Men in bag-wigs, rolling-hose, Muffs and Solitaires (loose necktie of black silk, secured in front by a brooch).' They went to the Opéra ('orchestra of hum-strums, attentive house') and to the Comédie Française. 'Great part of our time is spent in seeing churches and palaces full of fine pictures, the quarter of which is not yet exhausted.' 'For my part', wrote the poet, 'I could entertain myself this month merely with the common streets and the people in them. The Pont Neuf is the charming'st Sight imaginable.' Walpole thought the Opéra music 'resembles a gooseberry tart'. He complained of 'the violent vanity of the French . . . it is very dishonourable for any gentleman *not* to be in the Army or in the King's service . . . [but] no dishonour to keep public gaming houses – one hundred and fifty people of the first quality in Paris who live by it . . .' He called Paris 'A dirty town with a dirtier ditch calling itself the Seine . . . dirty houses, ugly streets, worse shops and churches loaded with bad pictures . . .' Although bearleader Joseph Spence, who was in Paris at the beginning of the Wars in 1739–43, agreed about the Seine, he did *not* agree about the buildings and the pictures. 'No collection of pictures in France equals to that at the Palais Royal – 500 valuable pieces in it – 30 Titians, 15 Raphaels, 20 Paul Veroneses, 16 Giulio Romanos, 13 Guidos, 28 Carracis, 14 Correggios . . . the Luxembourg Palace reckoned one of the best in France.' The Place Vendôme, he noted, was uniform and handsome with the Louis XIV statue, 150 yards by 140 yards. Measurements of squares, spires and bridges were considered important by the curious travellers!

When James Boswell visited Paris on his Grand Tour he stayed at the Hôtel de Dauphin, rue de Tavanne. He met John Wilkes, patriot temporarily in exile, and Horace Walpole (on his third or fourth visit to Paris), 'a lean genteel man, talked about Corsica and the Pretender'.

Boswell visited the well-known brothel at Hôtel Montigny run by Mlle Dupuis, and recorded in his diary, 'sad work'. Another night he met Mlle Constance, an elegant *femme de joie* at Mme Charlotte Geneviève Hecquet's bordello. Boswell caught the pox again in Paris: on his way home to England he accompanied Rousseau's mistress, Mlle de Vasseur, twenty years his senior. Notwithstanding, he seduced her: the 'night was manly'.

Sentimental Laurence Sterne stayed in 1762 at the Hôtel de Modène. He described Paris as the clearing house of European intellect. In a single city he found Diderot, Voltaire, Rousseau, Crébillon, Marmontel, Madame du Deffand and many other literati.

The following year, Edward Gibbon stayed in Paris for three months at the Hôtel de Londres, rue du Colombiernon, near the Université. 'I devoted many hours of the morning to the circuit of Paris and the neighbourhood, to the visit of churches and palaces conspicuous by their architecture, to the royal manufactures, collections of books and pictures and all the various treasures of art, of learning and of luxury. An Englishman may hear without reluctance that in these curious and costly articles, Paris is superior to London since the opulence of the French capital arises from the defects of its Government and Religion . . .' David Garrick, the actor, was received rapturously both by the company of the Théâtre Français and by the literary world. George Primrose called Paris 'the city of venal hospitality . . . the people of Paris are much fonder of strangers that have money than of those who have wit!' Dr Oliver Goldsmith visited Paris in 1770 and stayed at the Hôtel Dannemark, rue Jacob, Faubourg St Germain, with Captain and Mrs Horneck. He took them to Versailles, and whilst showing off to the two beautiful Horneck daughters fell into the fountains. He described his voyage as 'remote, unfriended, melancholy, slow'.

His friend, Dr Samuel Johnson's, only visit to Paris was curious in that he was ashamed of his lack of knowledge of the language, so he spoke in Latin and rarely communicated! He was appalled at the Gallic habit of spitting, but his itinerary was amusing. 'The Tuileries to walk in the gardens redesigned in 1665 by Le Nôtre, not open to mean persons, upper classes dripping powder and paint. Then to Palais Royal, very grand, large and lofty. A very great collection of pictures – Three of Raphael – one small piece of M. Angelo – One Room of Rubens. Then to the Ecole Militaire, the Observatory, several private Hotels, many churches and courts of Justice.'

THE OLD HOTELS AND CAFÉS

Mariana Starke's guide-book of 1802, when the Peace of Amiens between Britain and France allowed freedom of travel, recommended the following hotels: The Meurice, Bristol, Hollande, Wagram, Lawsons, Pearcey's Prince Regent, des Princes, de France in rue Laffitte, the Angleterre in rue Filles St Thomas, and the Hungerford. The cafés suitable for English visitors were the Lemblin, the Valois, Orléans, La Rotonde, de Foy, Hardy, Tortoni, Richard's and Véry's.

When the allied armies defeated Napoleon in 1814, the painter B.R. Haydon took his family to Paris. 'Such is the intoxicating gaiety of French manners, such the fascination of French amusement, so easy is admission to all their public places, libraries and collections, that, though most men enter Paris with disgust, no man ever left it with disappointment.' In the same year Matthew Todd and Captain B. visited Paris twice. They stayed at the Hôtel de Suède run by M. Meunier, and at the Hôtel d'Angleterre. They dined at Brigier's Restorature, and drank expensive glasses of iced punch at the beautiful Coffee House des Milles Colonnes, kept by the once-famed beauty La Belle Limonadière. They visited gardens – the menagerie Jardin des Plantes, on foot, (avoiding the contents of a *pot de chambre* thrown from the upper storeys), the Jardin des Turcs, the Jardin des Princes, and the Catacombs 84 feet below the earth, with 24,000 thousand skulls piled up. Then to the Place de Grève to see a woman guillotined for child murder, and on to the Opéra House, Théâtre Français, the Tuileries, and to watch the dancing in the Champs Elysées. The scars of war were evident. At Montmartre they saw the battlefield fort to protect Paris, where 500 French soldiers were killed. They went by carriage to Versailles twelve miles away, the Palace and grounds 'superb, immense scale but in sad ruinous state undermined by curious rats called Bandecotes', and to St Cloud to see the Palace of Buonaparte.

The most comprehensive guide to Paris was first published by Galignani in 1814, and in subsequent years was updated. 'The Quartier Feydeau, Chaussée d'Antin, Bd. des Italiens are favourites of the bankers, capitalists and brokers. The Palais Royal environs peopled by rich tradesmen and shopkeepers speculating incessantly on the taste of the Parisien for novelty, luxury and pleasure. Here are the finest dresses, the newest fashions, the most precious trinkets. The hotels in this opulent and busy quarter are generally filled with strangers. Luxury diminishes in the rue St Denis, and warehouses of silk, stuffs and linen are near the Pont Neuf. The Quai de la Ferraille has hardware. The Quai des Orfèvres in the Isle de la Cité gold and silversmiths. The Quai des Lunettes are the opticians, mathmatical instruments. Les Halles, rue des Lombards are the wholesale groceries. Gauze, shawls and fancy stuffs in the rue Ste Apolline and Meslée. At the Gobelins on the river banks are the tanners, brewers, dyers, wool [and] cotton spinners.'

Three perceptive lady visitors in the middle of the nineteenth century expressed approval of the city. The poet's widow, Mrs Mary Shelley, in 1840 went on a Grand Tour and wrote, 'There is an air of cheerfulness in the aspect of Paris that at once enlivens the visitor – seems to take the burthen from your spirits which weighs so heavily on the other side of the Channel. Not perhaps in any city in the world is there a scene more magnifique – to use their own word in their own sense – than the view at high noon or sunset from the terrace of the Tuileries near the river overlooking the Seine and its bridges; the Place de la Concorde with its wide asphaltic pavements, sparkling fountains and fantastic lanterns looking on to the Barrière de l'Etoile one way or down upon the horse chestnut avenues of the gardens on the other. There is gaiety, animation, life – you cannot find the same in London.'

Elizabeth Barrett Browning wrote, in the summer of 1851, 'Well now we are in Paris and have to forget "belle chiese": we have beautiful shops instead, false teeth grinning at the corners of the streets, and disreputable prints, and fascinating hats and caps and brilliant restaurants and M. le Président in a cocked hat and with a train of cavalry, passing like a rocket along the boulevards to an occasional yell from the Red. Oh yes, and dont mistake me! for I like it all extremely, its a splendid city – a city in the country, as Venice is a city in the sea.'

The third lady was Queen Victoria, who visited Paris in 1855. 'I am delighted, enchanted, amused and interested and think I never saw anything more beautiful and gay than Paris – or more splendid than all the Palaces.'

John Murray's guides to France started in 1834. Thirty years later, steam-boats from the Pont Royal to St Cloud made a pretty and pleasant excursion, there were no fewer than 8 railway stations in Paris, 150 warm bathhouses and 26 bridges across the Seine. He recommended the Hôtel Bristol, the Hôtel du Rhin in the Place Vendôme and in the rue Castiglione, the Meurice, Windsor, and Brighton Hôtels. In the rue de la Paix, he recommended the Hôtels Mirabeau, de la Paix, Hollande, Westminster and de Douvres. The smart restaurants suitable for English travellers were the Vefour, Véry, Café Foy, Trois Frères Provençaux and the Palais Royal. By now there were three English churches, two American, two Wesleyan, and a Scots kirk. Murray was keen on cemeteries. In Montmartre many English tombs were to be found, but the Père-Lachaise in the northeast of the city was the oldest, largest, extramural cemetery. Guides cost two francs an hour, but a good walker could see all he required in two hours, including the tombs of many Napoleonic marshals, as well as those of Balzac, David, Le Brun, Talma and Bellini. M. Berlioz' *concerts philharmoniques* were commended, as were five other concert halls where one could listen to Haydn, Gluck, Handel, Mozart and Beethoven (in that order). The smart clubs were the Jockey, near the Grand Hôtel, the Ancien Cercle for whist players, and the Cercle de la Régence for chess players.

Places to visit included the Gardens of the Luxembourg (85 acres), the Palais des Thermes, the medieval Hôtel de Cluny, the Catacombs, the Bourse, the Bois de Boulogne, the Ave. d'Etoile, St Denis (6 kms north), and the Fête de St Cloud for three weeks in September.

The Americans loved Paris. Samuel Langhorne Clemens ('Mark Twain') stayed in June 1867 at the Grand Hôtel du Louvre et de la Paix, rue de Rivoli, and Henry James crossed the Alps in 1869 and was in Paris in 1876, where he met Alexandre Dumas, Zola, Daudet, Guy de Maupassant and Flaubert. Mark Twain wrote in *The Innocents Abroad*, 'It was a pleasure to eat where everything was so tidy, the food so well cooked, the waiters so polite, and the coming and departing company so moustached, so frisky, so affable, so fearfully and wonderfully Frenchy!'

VISITING PARIS TODAY

WHERE TO STAY

Since the official list of Parisian hotels has thirteen hundred entries in the twenty *arrondissements*, it is quite difficult to identify those used by the early travellers.

The **GRAND HÔTEL DE L'UNIVERS**, 6 rue Grégoire de Tours, *6ème* (Tel. 43 29 37 00), with 34 rooms, was originally a fifteenth-century inn. Although it has been skilfully modernized, the old beams and stone walls prove its antiquity. Situated on the left bank near the Bd. St Germain, it may not have attracted the milords, who preferred the area around the Palais Royal. In the same road the **HÔTEL DE FLEURIE** at No 32 (Tel. 43 29 59 81) dates from the seventeenth century and has been well restored. Still in the sixth *arrondissement* is the **HÔTEL D'ANGLETERRE**, 44 rue Jacob (Tel. 42 60 34 72), which was built in 1650 and once

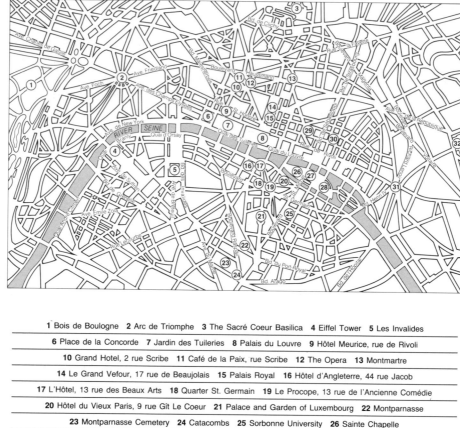

1 Bois de Boulogne 2 Arc de Triomphe 3 The Sacré Coeur Basilica 4 Eiffel Tower 5 Les Invalides

6 Place de la Concorde 7 Jardin des Tuileries 8 Palais du Louvre 9 Hôtel Meurice, rue de Rivoli

10 Grand Hotel, 2 rue Scribe 11 Café de la Paix, rue Scribe 12 The Opera 13 Montmartre

14 Le Grand Vefour, 17 rue de Beaujolais 15 Palais Royal 16 Hôtel d'Angleterre, 44 rue Jacob

17 L'Hôtel, 13 rue des Beaux Arts 18 Quarter St. Germain 19 Le Procope, 13 rue de l'Ancienne Comédie

20 Hôtel du Vieux Paris, 9 rue Gît Le Coeur 21 Palace and Garden of Luxembourg 22 Montparnasse

23 Montparnasse Cemetery 24 Catacombs 25 Sorbonne University 26 Sainte Chapelle

27 Ile de la Cité 28 Notre Dame Cathedral 29 Forum des Halles 30 Pompidou Centre 31 Place de la Bastille

32 Père Lachaise Cemetery

housed the British Embassy. In the same street is the **HÔTEL D'ISLY** at No. 29 (Tel. 43 26 32 39) with 37 rooms.

All four hotels have three stars, no restaurant, have been well modernized and have centuries of history behind them. The **L'HÔTEL** in nearby rue des Beaux Arts, No. 13, (Tel. 43 25 27 22) was called the Hôtel d'Alsace early in the nineteenth century. Now it is a highly modernized four-star hotel once frequented by Oscar Wilde – in fact he died there! Still in the *6ème*, the **HÔTEL DU PAS DE CALAIS**, 59 rue des Saints Pères (Tel. 45 48 78 74), has 40 rooms. It dates from 1815, as does the **HÔTEL DES SAINTS PÈRES** at No 65 (Tel. 45 44 50 00). Both are three-star hotels and have no restaurant. The **HÔTEL DU VIEUX PARIS**, 9 rue Gît-le-Coeur (Tel. 43 54 41 66) is off the rue St André des

Arts and the building dates from 1480. Indeed King Henri IV was once a guest! It is a two-star hotel with 16 rooms.

In the *9ème* near the Place de l'Opéra is the four-star **GRAND HÔTEL**, 2 rue Scribe (Tel. 42 60 33 50) with 600 rooms. It claims to be the largest old hotel in Paris and was designed by Charles Garnier, architect of the Paris Opera House. Next door is the famous Café de la Paix. The **HÔTEL CHOPIN**, 46 passage Jouffroy, is a two-star hotel from the early nineteenth century (Tel. 47 70 58 10).

The *1er* around the Place Vendôme has the **HÔTEL MEURICE**, 228 rue de Rivoli (Tel. 42 60 38 60), a four-star hotel with 214 rooms, which opened in 1816. Every crowned King of Europe has stayed at the Meurice at one time or another, as did Lady Shelley, who in 1833 found it a little noisy. The Ritz Hôtel opened in 1898, the Family Hôtel in 1899, the Hôtel (Inter) Continental in 1878, and the France et Choiseul in the 1870s, and so these do not qualify as 'Grand Tour' hotels. The **ST JAMES AND ALBANY**, 202 rue de Rivoli (Tel. 42 60 31 60) is in a Louis XIV building and was reopened successfully in 1981 with two excellent restaurants, including Le Noailles. Also in the same area is the **BRIGHTON**, 218 rue de Rivoli (Tel. 42 60 30 03), three stars, with 68 rooms, recommended by John Murray's *Guide* in the nineteenth century. Murray also commended the **WESTMINSTER**, 13 rue de la Paix (Tel. 42 61 57 46), a four-star hotel with 102 rooms in the *2ème arrondissement*. Matthew Todd and Captain B. stayed in the two-star **HÔTEL SUÈDE**, 106 Bd. Magenta (Tel. 46 07 43 13) in the *10ème arrondissement*.

In the *5ème arrondissement* on the left bank there are two very old hotels; **LE COLBERT**, 7 rue l'Hôtel-Colbert (Tel. 43 25 85 65), a three-star hotel with 40 rooms, and the **HÔTEL DU BRÉSIL**, 10 rue le Goff (Tel. 40 33 76 11), a modest one-star hotel with 30 rooms, where Sigmund Freud lived in 1885.

WHERE TO EAT

Most hotels do not have their own restaurant, and part of the charm of Paris is seeking out a 'new' eating place each evening or revisiting a favourite. The first genuine restaurants appeared in 1765, including Vérys and les Frères Provenceaux. Usually *traiteurs*, contractors who brought cooked meals to a hotel, or the proprietor's own 'table d'hôte', were the only sources of sustenance. In 1814 Galignani's *Guide to Paris* listed the dozen best restaurants – Grignon, Delaunay, Champeaux, Tellier, Ledoux etc. One or two have survived, but name changes are common among restaurateurs on a change of ownership. The eighteen now mentioned are a mixed bag ranging from the maximum of crossed forks to the minimum – but they share two things – their 'antiquity' and an excellent meal!

BEAUVILLIERS, 52 rue Lamarck, *18ème* (Tel. 42 54 19 50) is on the Montmartre hillside and was listed in 1814 as a 'good buy'. Try M. Edouard Carlier's *'terrine d'agneau à la fleur de thym'*, or *'tronçon de turbot en meurette'*. **LA PETITE CHAISE**, 36–38 rue de Grenelle, *7ème*, near Bd. Raspail claims to be the oldest restaurant in Paris. Métro rue du Bac. **LA COLOMBE**, 4 rue de la Colombe, *4ème* (Tel. 46 33 37 08) is on the Ile de la Cité. The house dates from 1275 and has been a tavern for centuries, now modernized. Their specialities are roast duckling with peaches, veal with almonds.

One of the grandest, most expensive restaurants in the city is **LA TOUR D'ARGENT**, 15 quai de la Tournelle, *5ème* (Tel. 40 33 23 31). The first restaurant on this site dates from 1582. Your *caneton* will have a numbered certificate to prove you have dined at La Tour d'Argent. **LE GRAND VEFOUR**, 17 rue de Beaujolais, *1er* (Tel. 42 96 56 27) was once known as the Café de Chartres, dating from 1760, and is one of the best restaurants in Paris. Napoleon and Danton were habitués. Speciality, *'Ragoût de brochet et d'écrivisses à l'anis'*, and a superb range of clarets. **LE PETIT RICHE**, rue le Peletier, *9ème*, descends from Galignani's Riche of 1814. Try their *'Pied de porc à la Sainte Menehoulde'* with Loire wines *en carafe*.

Opened in 1686 by a Sicilian as a café, **LE PROCOPE**, 13 rue de l'Ancienne Comédie, *6ème* (Tel. 43 26 99 20) was frequented by La Fontaine, Voltaire, Rousseau, Balzac and Benjamin Franklin. The speciality is *'côte de veau Gorgonzola'*. **CRÉMERIE-RESTAURANT POLIDOR**, 41 rue Monsieur le Prince, *6ème* (Tel. 43 26 95 34) is a characteristic bistro patronized by Verlaine, André Gide and James Joyce. Try their *'canard aux petits pois'*. **RELAIS LOUIS XIII**, 1 rue Pont de Lodi, *6ème* (Tel. 43 26 75 96) has a sixteenth-century *caveau* where one can eat their hot oysters or sole *soufflée*.

Once a sixteenth-century inn, the **AUBERGE DE FRANCE**, 1 rue Mont Thabor, *1er* (Tel. 40 73 60 26) was frequented by coachmen and insolent postilions. Try their snails in garlic sauce or *'filet Limousin'*. **HOSTELLERIE NICHOLAS FLAMEL**, 51 rue de Montmorency, *3ème* (Tel.

42 72 07 11) was an ancient tavern built in 1407. The speciality is '*rôti d'agneau*' with herbs.

The following were opened at the end or middle of the nineteenth century, and Mark Twain would have commended them. **LA CLOSERIE DES LILAS**, 171 Bd. Montparnasse, *14ème* (Tel. 43 26 70 50) frequented by Ingres, Lenin, Chateaubriand, Verlaine and Henry James. Specialities '*escargots*', ribs of beef in cider. **ESCARGOT-MONTORGUEIL**, 38 rue Montorgueil, *1er* (Tel. 42 36 83 51) was opened in the 1830s and the original Louis Philippe décor is well preserved. A favourite of Sarah Bernhardt. Try their turbot *soufflé* or the '*pieds de porc*'. **CHARTIER**, 7 rue du Faubourg Montmartre, *9ème* (Tel. 47 70 86 29) has kept its early nineteenth-century '*bouillon*' soup-kitchen atmosphere. Speciality '*croustade au jambon*'.

    Well known in the naughty nineties is **LUCAS-CARTON**, 9 Place de la Madeleine, *8ème* (Tel. 42 65 22 90) – red velvet bench seats and excellent Burgundian wines. **DROUANT**, Place Gaillon, *2ème* (Tel. 40 73 26 40) was founded in 1880. The Académie Goncourt meet here. Try the stuffed mussels, '*rognons d'agneau*' or '*loup de mer flambé*'. **PHARAMOND**, 24 rue de la Grande Truanderie, *1er* (Tel. 42 31 06 72), founded in 1832 in Les Halles area. Specialities '*tripes à la mode de Caen*', '*turbot au Champagne*'. **AU GRAND COMPTOIR**, 4 rue Pierre Lescot, *1er* (Tel. 42 33 56 30), founded in 1868. Specialities from the Limousin, haddock with fondue butter.

CAFÉS

In the year before the Battle of Waterloo, post-revolutionary France was to see a new phenomenon – cafés, where men, and ladies escorted by men, could meet in polite society outside their private town mansions or hotels. Galignani chronicles the most fashionable. La Belle Limonadière ran the elegant Café des Mille Colonnes, where Wellington's officers took their aperitifs in the Palais Royal. Chess players flocked to the Café de la Régence, while business men 'of the higher order' patronized the Café Hardi in the Boulevard des Italiens and the Café de la Paix. The fashionables congregated for good ices at Café Tortoni in the Boulevard des Italiens.

    Concerts, free music and rope dancing entertained '*le ton*' at the Café Turc, and the Café des Princes in the Boulevard du Temple.

Young women waiters served, and free concerts took place at the Café des Chinoises in the Palais Royal. In 1814 the world wanted to watch the rest of the world walk by. Cafés have been the heart and soul of Paris ever since. Poets, revolutionaries, and artistes of both sexes met each other, exchanged ideas and partners. Now, there are ten thousand of them selling 'tabac' products, stamps, state lottery tickets, sandwiches and croissants, and allowing phone calls and calls of nature.

The difference between a café and a bar is mainly in appearance. At the first one sees and can be seen, while in the second, dark secrecy is the order of the day or night. *Salons de thé*, *buvettes*, 'drugstores', 'pubs' and the familiar brasseries also serve hot meals throughout the day and evening. Some of the turn of the century cafés are to be seen on the left bank, and the more famous are **LE DÔME**, **LA COUPOLE**, and **CLOSERIE DES LILAS** in the Montparnasse area. **LE FLOR** and **LES DEUX MAGOTS** are in St Germain des Prés. On the right bank are the **CAFÉ DE LA PAIX** (12 Bd. des Capucines) now handsomely restored, the **ROYAL-OPÉRA**, the **FAUCHON**, and on the Champs Elysées, **FOUQUET'S** and **L'ALSACE**. In the Marais area look for **LA TARTINE** and **MA BOURGOGNE**.

Café-Théâtre is alive and well in Paris with sharp, cynical 'argot' quips at politicians and society individuals. Try the **AU BEC FIN**, 6 rue Thérèse, *1er*, and two in the *4ème*: **AU POINT VIRGULE**, 7 rue Sainte Croix de la Bretonnerie, and **LE CAFÉ D'EDGAR**, 58 Boulevard Edgar Quinet.

THE SIGHTS

The main **TOURIST OFFICE** is at 127 Champs Elysées, 75008 (Tel. 47 23 61 72) and is open every day from 9am to 8pm. Other information offices are in the Gare d'Austerlitz, Gare de l'Est, Gare de Lyon, Gard du Nord and the Invalides air terminal. Organized tours by double-decker bus can be made through **CITYRAMA**, 4 Place des Pyramides (Tel. 42 60 30 14). Leaving on the hour, the tours take three hours and during May-October there is an evening tour starting at 10pm. Another good way of seeing the city is by taking a boat tour on the river Seine on a *Bateau Mouche* from the Pont de l'Alma, the Pont d'Iéna or the Pont Neuf.

City communications are excellent. The Métro criss-crosses Paris from 5.30am to 12.30am. Books of ten tickets called 'carnets' are economical. Having found your target station on the Métro map (each '*ligne*' has a colour) look for the termination station on your selected route and follow it. The same tickets operate for the bus services, which start at 6.30am, but finish between 8.30 and 9.30pm. Four – or seven – day tourist tickets for unlimited travel are available at any Métro station. There are fifteen thousand taxis in Paris, equipped with meters. The postilion will expect a '*pour boire*' of at least ten per cent. Remember to '*composter*' your Métro and bus tickets (punch them in a machine) to validate them. Beware of pickpockets on Métro and buses. Car hire is easy but Paris is a city where walking to see the sights is usually a pleasure.

The traveller on the Grand Tour might allow several months' stay in Paris, certainly many weeks. That may not be feasible at the end of the twentieth century, but by concentrating on the twenty top sights, they can be fitted into three to seven days depending on one's interest. An ardent museum-goer could take two months to see the 56 museums in Paris. The Louvre itself could easily take a week. So one has to be *very* selective.

In the last decade or so, Paris has seen several very important changes to the overall landscape. The Pompidou Centre, or Beaubourg, *4ème*, as it is frequently called, is a colossal modern matchbox of steel girders, glass, pipes, concrete, and tubular external corridors in garish colours. It houses the Centre National d'Art et de Culture (closed Tuesday) with a magnificent collection of twentieth-century works. It acts as a forum for modern clowns and mountebanks, and in addition there is an excellent public library.

Ten minutes walk due west is the Forum des Halles, a 1979 development of the food and meat markets called Les Halles, founded in the seventeenth century. Now it is a glittering, ritzy, modern centre of two hundred shops, boutiques, cinemas and restaurants sunk four levels into a large courtyard often used, like the Beaubourg, by strolling players.

The third major development is the resuscitation of the old abandoned railway station, the Gare d'Orsay, on the south bank of the Seine opposite the Jardin des Tuileries. Opened in December 1986, the brilliant Impressionist collection of the Jeu de Paume, Picasso, Monet, Degas, Renoir, Cézanne *et al* has been transferred to the Musée d'Orsay, and can now be seen under the huge glass roof of the old station. These three new sites should have the highest priority for visits.

The classic splendours of Paris, which the travellers visited, still stand proudly. True that John Evelyn and Coryat could not envisage the Eiffel Tower, built to commemorate the centenary of the French Revolution in 1889, nor the Arc de Triomphe. Les Invalides, although designed by the Sun King in the 1670s, now houses Napoleon Bonaparte's tomb (and four museums). The old favourites are still there – the Palais du Louvre (select which of the six different departments you want beforehand – Paintings/Drawings, Egyptian Antiquities, Oriental Antiquities, Greek/Roman Antiquities, Sculpture or Objets d'Art), the Palais Royal and the elegant Jardin des Tuileries, Notre Dame, the Hôtel Dieu and Louis IX's beautiful Sainte Chapelle, all three on the Ile de la Cité, Louis XV's Panthéon church-mausoleum, and his Madeleine Corinthian church. The Palace and Gardens of the Luxembourg, built by Henri IV's widow, was visited by most travellers. Situated half an hour's walk due south of the Ile de la Cité, the Luxembourg certainly has enough attractions for a day's visit – two palaces, a museum, a library, an observatory and superb gardens with fountains.

The Basilique du Sacré-Coeur on Montmartre hill, the Butte, is a classic Parisian scene, conceived in 1873 and completed during World War I – well after the travellers' epoch. However, they all visited and admired the Basilique de St Denis, necropolis of the Kings of France, sited in the northern modern industrial suburbs of Paris.

The one individual who destroyed many of the travellers' memories of Paris was Baron Haussmann, Napoleon III's Prefect of the Seine, who replanned central Paris in 1853–70. His wide straight streets (difficult to barricade) around the Opéra, the Madeleine, and the rue de Rivoli, replaced the narrow dirty roads about which Horace Walpole complained.

The Champs Elysées became fashionable in the eighteenth century and its magnificent tree-lined avenue, fringed with parks running parallel to the Seine, is still one of the sights of Paris. The Arc de Triomphe at one end, the Louvre at the other, it is bisected by the Rond Point and the great Place de la Concorde.

Travellers on the Grand Tour always attended the serious and the comic opera in every town they visited in France (and Italy). Galignani listed ten theatres in 1814 including the Opéra in rue Le Pelletier, the Théâtre Français, 6 rue de Richelieu, and the Gaieté and Ambigu Comique, both in the Boulevard du Temple. Also the Théâtre des Variétés in Boulevard Montmartre, and the Vaudeville near the Palais Royale. At the end of the twentieth century there are now three operas – *The* OPÉRA in Place de l'Opéra, *9ème* (Tel. 47 42 57 50), the OPÉRA

COMIQUE, 5 rue Favart, *2ème* (Tel. 42 96 12 20), and the THÉÂTRE MUSICAL DE PARIS, Place du Châtelet (Tel. 42 33 44 44). The COMÉDIE FRANÇAISE, 2 rue de Richelieu, (Tel. 42 96 10 20) is one of the best classic theatres in France.

James Boswell would have approved of the Crazy Horse Saloon, the Folies Bergères, the Lido and the Moulin Rouge, but the eighteenth-century gambling saloons which so appalled and pleased the young sprigs have gone, probably forever. There are no public casinos in Paris, only a few private gaming clubs.

Some of the unusual 'attractions' of Paris are visits to the Père-Lachaise cemetery in the *20ème*, east of the Bastille, where Molière, Chopin, Rossini, Balzac and Oscar Wilde are buried – the Catacombs in the *14ème*, south of the Montparnasse Cemetery, open on most Saturday afternoons – the Egouts (sewers of Paris) open on Monday and Wednesday afternoons, entrance near the Pont de l'Alma, *7ème* – and, more salubrious, the Gobelins tapestry factories founded by Louis XIV and much visited by travellers. The Gobelins are one kilometre from the Gare d'Austerlitz, and are open Wednesday, Thursday and Friday afternoons.

Some interesting walking tours of Paris can be arranged through BONNE JOURNÉE, 6 Place Charles Dullin, 75018 (Tel. 46 06 24 17) or PARIS AVEC VOUS (Tel. 43 21 26 99).

Finally from a *Bateau Mouche*, Port de la Conférence, *8ème* (Tel. 42 25 22 55) one can see the heart of Paris and hear it beat – rather noisily!

The main excursions from Paris are to Fontainebleau (65 kilometres southeast), Versailles (24 kilometres southwest), Chantilly (50 kilometres north), Malmaison (15 kilometres west) and St Germain-en-Laye (21 kilometres west).

REIMS

the cross-road of Europe

It is appropriate that the large modern city of Reims (population 182,000) is twinned with Florence, Canterbury, Salzburg and Aix-la-Chapelle; all towns frequented by the early travellers on the Grand Tour.

Very badly damaged by German bombardments in World War I and

World War II, Reims has been rebuilt with fine boulevards, and the handsome centre round the Cathedral of St Nicaise still depicts some of its distinguished history. Reims was one of Julius Caesar's favourites under the '*Pax Romana*'. In AD498 Bishop Rémi baptized the powerful King Clovis, and three centuries later Charlemagne encouraged culture and the arts here. The first links with England came during the Hundred Years War when Joan of Arc crowned Charles VII and inspired him to turn the tide of battle. Since then the 'ville-sainte' has witnessed the spectacle of 25 coronations. The university was founded in 1547, and the English college became a focus of English recusants during the reign of Elizabeth I and James I.

Travellers on the Grand Tour coming south from Brussels passed through Reims on their way to Troyes, Dijon and the Alpine crossing. John Boteler visited Reims for the coronation of Louis XV in 1722 and drank excellent champagne; he wrote home that letters of introduction were essential for a traveller. Philip Thicknesse praised the prices in the inns he stayed in on the Reims-Dijon road, and found 'the meat tolerable'. King Henry VIII appointed an agent in the region to select Champagne table wines for his court, and many travellers visiting Reims appreciated the still wine. Later, Dom Pérignon shouted the immortal words, 'Brothers, brothers, come quickly; I am drinking stars'. The cellarer of the Abbey of Hautvillers had discovered towards the end of the seventeenth century the art of secondary fermentation inside the bottle. The sparkling wine brought prosperity to the Champagne wine trade. When Richard Pococke, who was travelling from Dijon to Calais via Reims in 1734, wrote of the red Champagne wine he drank, he referred to the rosé that is now so popular.

Thomas Nugent wrote in his travel guide that 'Reims attracted English tourists for weeks, even months at a time, comfortable living at low prices'. Of the cathedral he noted, 'the front of this stupendous church consists of a vast number of statues; saints in miniature, placed in little niches and in exact places so that the eye is pleased and shocked at the same time. Magnificence is mixed with littleness, grandeur with meanness, proportion with disproportion.' Bearleader Joseph Spence wrote that 'Reims makes a better appearance at a distance than when you come into it. Scarce anything handsome in it except churches and ecclesiastical houses. Both the Convents of the Benedictines have something grand in them. At their church of St Nicaise is the trembling pillar when the bell strikes or is only moved about. Saw the sacred ampoule in the church of St Remy. The good priest who showed it behaved as if it had really come from heaven. The monks of the convent seem to be great lovers of champagne. I counted 45 hogsheads flung by in one of their back courts by the church of St Remy!'

Arthur Young stayed at the chief inn, had a large well-served table d'hôte, excellent wine and a first class dinner. 'First view of the city from the hills at the distance of about four miles is magnificent. The Cathedral makes a great figure and the church of St Remy terminates the town proudly. The streets are almost all broad, straight and well built.' He noted that 'the vin mousseux of Champagne absolutely banishes the writhes of rheumatism'! Horace Walpole and his companion Thomas Gray, the poet, stayed for three months at M. Hibert's in the rue St Denis. Horace, the snob, recounted how they 'fell in with a party of men and women of the best fashion, one evening walking in the public gardens, one of the ladies suggested an '*al fresco*' supper'. Thomas Gray's diary mentioned the cathedral church, 'vast Gothic building of surprising beauty and lightness covered with little statues', and that within the Kings of France were traditionally crowned by the Archbishop of Reims. He thought 'the streets had a melancholy aspect, houses all old, the public walks run along the side of a great moat under the ramparts'. He liked the croaking of the frogs, and the fact that the 'country round about is one great plain covered with vines . . . nothing to drink but the best champagne in the world'. That was in 1740!

At the turn of the century Mariana Starke wrote in her guide of Clovis, the Cathedral and the coronation of Kings, but also noted that in this town of 30,000 population the Roman sarcophagus called the Tomb of Jovinus, the Roman Porte de Mars, and the large fossil discovery at Méri and Courtagnon merited visits. She commended the Hôtel de l'Europe. John Murray's guide of a few years later, when the population had increased to 36,000, recommended the Hôtel Lion d'Or, 'a good house, rather dear, in excellent situation facing the Cathedral.' Shortly after Waterloo, Lady Frances Shelley wrote of her visit, 'Suddenly the city of Rheims burst upon our view. It stands in the midst of an extensive plain with its noble cathedral so far above the other buildings that even the remains of a Roman triumphal arch seemed dwarfed and insignificant. . . . At last turning the corner of the street I beheld the beautiful portal of that sacred edifice. The sublimity of that work so far surpassed my expectations, affected me so deeply, that I shed tears.'

Lady Shelley was very young, very beautiful, in love with the Duke of Wellington and wrote perhaps a little emotionally of her three Grand Tours, of which this was the first. She would have wept unrestrainedly if she had seen in 1919 the awful devastation caused by nearly five years of bombardment. Nearly twelve thousand houses were destroyed including most of the 'inns' mentioned in the late nineteenth-century guide-books – the Grand Hôtel, the Lion d'Or and the Maison Rouge. A pity, because

Monsieur J. Radle, proprietor of the Lion d'Or not only offered choice wines but also had perfect sanitary arrangements – the highest accolade of all!

VISITING REIMS TODAY
WHERE TO STAY AND EAT

In the late twentieth century the two most appropriate hotels for today's Grand Tourists are the two-star **BRISTOL**, 76 Place Drouet-d'Erlon (Tel. 26 40 52 25), with 40 rooms, and the two-star **VICTORIA**, 35 Place Drouet-d'Erlon (Tel. 26 47 21 79), with 28 rooms. Neither has a restaurant, but are central, comfortable, and near the main sights.

Fortunately there are many fine restaurants in Reims. Undoubtedly the finest is **LE CHÂTEAU DES CRAYÈRES**, 64 Boulevard Henry Vasnier (Tel. 26 82 80 80), quite close to the famous Basilica and Museum of Saint Rémi, and equally close to the five leading champagne shippers. This restaurant is run by M. Gerard Boyer and his wife Eliane and they have many superb specialities. The '*salade Père Maurice*' contains *haricots verts*, *céleris*, *fonds d'artichauts*, *champignons de Paris*, *foie gras*, *truffes*, and *homard* – the whole seasoned with chopped herbs, olive oil and *vinaigre de champagne*. Another dish is '*le feuilleté d'escargots à la Champenoise*'. In their cellar they have over one hundred and fifty *different* champagnes to offer you!

The **RESTAURANT LE FLORENCE**, 43 Boulevard Foch, (Tel. 26 47 12 70) is to the west of town near the station and public gardens. M. Jean-Pierre Maillott and his charming wife have three specialities: '*Salade de queues de langoustines au vinaigre de champagne*', followed by '*le blanc de turbot braisé avec une sauce legère au Champagne*' (of course) and ending with '*le filet de boeuf au vin rouge de Vertus*'.

Finally **LE VIGNERON**, Place Paul Jarnot (Tel. 26 47 00 71), is situated 300 metres east of the cathedral. In summer, meals are served outside in the terrace-garden. M. Hervé Liegent is the patron. His cheese-board is famous and includes '*le carré de Reims*', '*le chèvre d'Asfeld*' from the Ardennes, '*le cendre de Champagne*', '*le Chaource*', '*le Rondeau*' and '*la Vignote*', a triple cream cheese prepared in the Aube département. The classic menu starts with '*salade au lard*', '*les truffes d'Argonne au vin de Champagne*', and '*le brochet poché dans une sauce au Champagne*'. Local desserts include '*le médaillon de Reims*' and '*gâteau aux poires de Rousselet*'.

This dish – a pear tart – was offered to King Charles X on his coronation in 1825 by Ruinart de Brimont, Mayor of Reims, who said *'Sire, nous vous offrons ce que nous avons de meilleur, nos vins et nos poires.'*

1 Hôtel Victoria, 35 Place Drouet d'Erlon **2** Hôtel Bristol, 76 Place Drouet d'Erlon **3** Porte de Mars

4 Cathedral of Notre Dame **5** Palais du Tau **6** Basilica of Saint Remy

7 Le Château des Crayères, 64 Boulevard Henry Vasnier

CHAMPAGNE

There are many excellent Champagne Houses, or négociants, in Reims. There is no question, however, of which one should be visited. **CHAMPAGNE RUINART** were founded in 1729, *before* Messrs Young, Walpole, Gray *et al.* visited the region. (To be fair Gosset of nearby Ay were making wine in 1584.) Dom Thierry Ruinart, a Benedictine monk and friend of Dom Pérignon, was the uncle of Nicolas Ruinart who was the first to sell champagne. Ruinart are sited at 4, rue des Crayères and produce 100,000 cases each year. The wine is described by Jane MacQuitty as having a light, flowery-citrussy style. She recommends their 1976 Dom Ruinart Blanc de Blancs. Visits can be made by prior appointment by telephoning 26 85 40 29, but not at weekends. Of the western group of shippers are **LANSON**, 12 Boulevard Lundy (but make an appointment; 26 40 36 26), **HEIDSIECK MONOPOLE**, 83 rue Coquebert (26 07 39 34), or **MUMM**, 34 rue du Champ de Mars (open throughout the year).

Other famous champagne shippers are open to the public without notice, including **POMMÉRY**, 5 Place du Général Gouraud; **TAITTINGER**, 9 Place St Nicaise; **PIPER-HEIDSIECK**, 51 Boulevard Henry Vasnier and **VEUVE CLICQUOT-PONSARDIN**, 1 Place des Droits de l'Homme. The latter screen a fine film about the famous widow, Veuve Madame Clicquot.

WHAT TO SEE AND DO

The **TOURIST OFFICE** is at 1 rue Jadart, 51100 (Tel. 26 88 37 89). It is tucked away in a side street, three minutes' walk southwest of the cathedral. The modern visitor on the Grand Tour should allocate a full two days to a stay in Reims, and three to include a day's tour of the vineyards around Epernay and Ay.

On the first day start with the Cathédrale de Notre Dame, standing proudly in its cobbled square. Although badly damaged in World War I it has been skilfully restored. Begun in 1211, it is, as all the visitors in the eighteenth century noted, a magnificent Gothic monument. The façade rises and rises with a succession of deep-set portals, the great rose window, the Gallery of the Kings and two immense proud towers. The thirteenth-century medieval statuary around the doorways was also much admired. The inside is simple and elegant, enlivened by the brilliant stained glass windows and rich fifteenth-century tapestries. Next door is the Palais du Tau, once the Archbishop's palace and now a museum, containing the Cathedral treasure, Charlemagne's talisman, and relics of various royal coronations. Between the two buildings is the magnificent thirteenth-century Chapel of the Archbishops. Near the tourist office is the Abbey of St Denis, now an art gallery/museum, at 8 rue Chanzy (closed Tuesday). Here there are 28 landscapes by Corot, portrait drawings by Cranach, paintings by Sisley, Poussin, Gauguin and fifteenth-, seventeenth- and nineteenth-century French school paintings.

In the nearby Place de la République is the Porte de Mars dating from the third century, one of four triumphal arches that decorated the city in Gallo-Roman times in Caesar Augustus' honour. The three-arched monument is huge, and bas-reliefs depicting Romulus and Remus, Jupiter and Leda, can still be seen.

During the afternoon the possibilities include a trip in a Montgolfière hot-air balloon. Contact **AIR SHOW**, 15 bis Place St Nicaise (Tel. 26 82 59 60). Or make a visit to two champagne shops: **LES SPÉCIALITÉS RÉMOISES**, Parvis de la Cathédrale (Tel. 26 47 64 32), or **LE MARCHÉ AUX VINS**, 3 Place Léon Bourgeois (Tel. 26 40 12 12), a museum and exhibition where 500 of France's finest wines from 62 châteaux are on display and sale.

The second day might take in a visit to the vineyards (if you are staying three days in Reims). The Tourist Office can arrange three different tours – 'La Montagne de Reims', 'La Vallée de la Marne' and 'La Côte des Blancs'. On a more serious note a tour can be arranged to World War I battlefields and cemeteries. At the **FORT DE LA POMPELLE** is a World War I museum; it is located five kilometres east on the Chalons road, the N44. Besides collections of uniforms, weapons, documents, photographs and paintings, there are the original trenches and redoubts to be seen. If you are a military survivor of World War, entry is free. The museum is open all year. Still on a martial note you can visit the 'Surrender Room' of 7 May 1945, where the Allies and the German Command signed the surrender documents ending World War II. Called *la Salle de la Reddition*, it is near the railway station on the west side of Reims, within easy walk of the Porte de Mars.

On your final day, the main sight to see is the mighty **BASILICA OF SAINT RÉMI**, consecrated by Pope Léon IX in AD1049. It is situated one kilometre southeast of the cathedral in a large, quiet square. Once a Benedictine monastery and a pilgrim hospice, it was commented on favourably by the Grand Tour visitors. Inside is the tomb of St Rémi, who converted the Frankish King Clovis. The beautiful modern stained glass windows are by Charles Marq. Next door is the **ABBEY OF ST RÉMI** which is an archeology museum of repute (closed Tuesday).

If you are an antique car fan you will appreciate the '**CENTRE DE L'AUTOMOBILE FRANÇAISE**' at 84 Avenue Georges Clemenceau (Tel. 26 82 83 84). It is five minutes' walk from Champagne Pommery, and houses 150 vintage cars dating from 1769, and more than 2,000 different toy cars!

The Tourist Office has a '*billet commun*' providing entrance to six museums at a very reduced price. Other museums include the seventeenth-century Ancien Collège des Jésuites, 1 Place Museux; Chapelle Notre Dame de la Paix, 33 rue du Champ de Mars; Musée Hôtel Le Vergeur, 36 Place du Forum; and Cryptoportique gallo-romain, also in the Place du Forum.

During the summer there are '*Son et Lumière*' displays outside the cathedral, and many festivals, exhibitions and 'spectacles' arranged by the Comité Central des Fêtes. In the evening there is a choice of four theatres. The **GRAND THÉÂTRE**, 9 rue Chanzy, has a programme of opera, ballet and classical music concerts; the Centre Dramatique National performs contemporary drama. The Centre National Art et Technologie de Reims, 1 rue Eugène Wiet, produces a wide range of artistic activities. The Centre Saint Exupéry, Parc Leo-Lagrange, has a wider, more democratic style of cultural programmes. Reims is a university town and has high standards of entertainment. Try the **THÉÂTRE DE LA COMÉDIE**, also at 1 rue Eugène Wiet, or the **MAISON DE LA CULTURE**, 3–5 Chaussée Bocquaine, for films, plays and dances. Jazz can be heard at **LE SUNSHINE**, or **CLUB 51** or **CLUB ST PIERRE**. **LE PALAIS**, 14 Place Myron-Herrick is a smart evening '*café de luxe*'.

DIJON

city of mustard and gingerbread

Burgundy is famous throughout the world for its cuisine and for its wines. The French, however, regard Dijon, the capital (population 160,000), as the '*Carrefour d'Art et de culture*'. It is on a major crossroads. The roads from Paris to Geneva and Turin passed then (and now by modern autoroutes) through or close to the city. The lateral west-east route lay between such places as

Bourges, Nevers, and Autun to Besançon.

Charlemagne's grandson Charles the Bald, followed by John the Fearless, Philip the Good and Charles the Fearless – a dynasty of fourteenth- and fifteenth-century Valois Dukes – established the richest, the most cultured, and almost the most powerful country in Europe. They occupied Flanders and the rich Fleming wool trade brought prosperity to Burgundy. The Valois Dukes encouraged the finest artists in Europe, who flocked to Dijon during the Renaissance. The sculptor Claus Sluter, the painters Jan Van Eyck and Roger Van der Weyden and a score of brilliant Flemish artists and writers made Dijon, for a century, the greatest cultural centre in Europe. During the Hundred Years War the Burgundians allied themselves to the British, and ever since the 'entente cordiale' has been strong. Burgundian cuisine and wines are now famous worldwide, but the early visitors on the Grand Tour were more interested in seeing the famous sights – legacies of the Valois Dukes and their inspired artists.

The young Scotsman Colin MacLaurin was very sceptical of the sacred relics he encountered in Dijon in 1722. But he was amazed by the height of all foreign beds, grumbled at the food and lack of wine in 'Picardie', and disliked Sens for its narrow twisting streets, associated (by him) with dirt, disease and poverty. Eight years later young Lord Middlesex, bear-led by his tutor Joseph Spence, the Oxford doctor of poetry, encountered five other milords in Dijon. Spence noted that Dijon was a handsome city, the streets broad and well-paved, that the river Suzon passed through the town concealed under the arches. In the intervals between learning how to dance, 'I believe verily [I] shall come home very much a gentleman', Spence almost made a cuckold out of his landlord – with his wife, Madame Cotheret, *proche la place Royale*! 'The French women are not so beautiful as the English', he wrote, 'but then they make it up in a sprightliness and freedom of behaviour that is universal among them. Their headdress here for the people of fashion is called "*Tête des Muttons*" *(moutons)*, tis a very small head just on the top, without flaps or anything coming down on the sides . . . They wear a sort of sultanas (rich gowns trimmed with buttons and loops) or at least a vest of silk that comes up almost quite to the neck and falls loose every way down to the feet. The breast is invisible [in England in 1730 the ladies' bosoms were uncovered] and there is no pretence to a waist in this dress – but yet I must say very graceful!'

Spence and the young Lord Middlesex liked Dijon so much they spent several months in residence. They visited the vignerons, 'they are busy, March 27, in their vineyards setting up the sticks and tying the vines to them . . . a whole vineyard when the poles are set like a large plantation of raspberries.' They commented on the fine Burgundian cuisine, 'Eating is a delight in fowl, a pullet or capon on the table, pigeons, two plates of sparagrass – one dressed with oil and vinegar for the good people of the country and the other with honest butter for the poor Englishmen. Dinner begins with 'soupe', ends with dessert, a bottle of Burgundy at each end of the table. The dessert of curds and cream and [table] cloth stay as long as you do . . . Best burgundy at the taverns costs eight pence, from the best cellars of the merchants sixteen pence. Lowest price is halfpenny per bottle.'

The milords were introduced to *fricassée* of frogs for the very first time, 'a sort of chickeny taste'. This classic Burgundian dish was also commented on by Robert Wharton in 1775, 'who found upwards of thirty English in Dijon'. 'I was helped to an excellent Fricassée but was much puzzled to find out what it was, there being an uncommon quantity of bones and especially of small merry-thoughts.' It turned out to be frogs' legs, but Wharton took the recipe home with him – 'a curiosity like white veal'. Boiled artichokes, cold, with pepper and salt, was another new dish.

Thomas Gray, the poet, and the supercilious man about town, Horace Walpole, found Dijon in 1741 one of 'the gayest and most agreeable little cities of France for beauty and cleanliness.' They admired the rich convents and churches, the Palace of the States, the famous Abbey of the Carthusians and the Cistercian Abbey. They spent four days at the Hôtel Croix d'Or and found the town 'full of People of quality, very agreeable Society'. Lady Mary Wortley Montagu agreed: 'There is not any town in France where there are not English, Scotch or Irish families. Here in Dijon are no less than sixteen English families of fashion.' *The Gentleman's Guide* published in 1770 said of Dijon, 'There the French language is spoke with greater propriety than at Paris or any other town in the Kingdom tho' Blois had formerly that reputation. I do not know of any town in France preferable to this for the residence of any gentleman.' 'Dijon, on the whole', he wrote, 'is a handsome town, the streets though old are wide and very well paved, with the addition, uncommon in France, of trottoirs (pavements).' He visited the 'Clos de Veaugeau' (Vougeot), walled and belonging to a convent of Bernardine monks, 'vineyards so famous in France'.

The 'gentleman's gentleman', Matthew Todd, was in Dijon in 1814 with his amiable country squire Captain Barlow. They dined each day at the Count d'Artois inn 'everything was uncommonly well dressed and the wine very good tho' high charges. Vin de Hermitage five francs, ten sols per bottle; vin de Bourgoine one franc ten per bottle which was not so cheap considering this town the capital of Burgogne. However the place had so many My Lord Angles passing through it was not so very astonishing. Our dinners including wine came to eleven francs ten sols. Went to the top of the great church and had a very extensive view of the country for miles.' Matthew noted that the townsfolk were still Bonapartistes and not yet for Louis XVIII. He 'had a good lark with the young ladies of the house who were kept under the fear of God and a broomstick by their father.' He found the diamond-shaped, fortified town very 'airy and pleasant' and enjoyed walks around the ramparts. Later in the century Mark Twain visited Dijon by rail, 'called it Demijohn, poured out rich Burgundian wines and munched calmly through a long table d'hôte bill of fare [of] snail patties, delicious fruits and cheeses then paid the trifle it cost.'

VISITING DIJON TODAY

WHERE TO STAY AND EAT

Two centuries ago, Mariana Starke, the intrepid and distinguished lady traveller and guide-writer, visited Dijon and recommended two hotels, the du Parc and the de la Cloche. A century later John Murray, in his famous French guide, recommended the Grand Hôtel de la Cloche, then run by Monsieur E. Goisset, and the Hôtel de Jura.

These three hotels have survived the years remarkably well. The four-star **HÔTEL DE LA CLOCHE** is at 14 Place Darcy (Tel. 80 30 12 32). It has 76 rooms and four apartments, an interior garden and private parking. Security should be good as the main *gendarmerie* is 150 metres away in the rue Devosge. **LES CAVES DE LA CLOCHE**, 1 rue Devosge, with the same telephone number, is presided over by the famous M. Jean-Pierre Billoux, Meilleur Ouvrier de France. This is one of the most renowned restaurants in Burgundy, where our travellers Messrs Wharton, Spence, Gray, Walpole and Mark Twain would have felt quite at home in the famous vaulted cellars. The candle-lit dinner includes '*terrine moelleuse de pigeon aux mousserons, filets de turbots à la nage de homard, granité au marc de bourgogne, foie gras poêlé en crépinette de choux rouges, noisette de lapin au ragoût d'artichaut, plateau de fromages, mille-feuilles à la nougatine au miel, pamplemousse* and *mignardises*'. Recent specialities are '*salade de ris de veau aux poireaux frits*', '*paillasson de langoustines*' and '*suprême de pintade au foie de canard et aux cèpes*'.

Dijon, Beaune and Mâcon are the three chief wine towns of Burgundy, and you should try an aperitif '*un Crémant de Bourgogne*' – a delicious sparkling white wine made with the champagne chardonnay

1 Chartreuse de Champmol   2 Hôtel du Jura, 14 Avenue Maréchal Foch   3 Hôtel de la Cloche, 14 Place Darcy

4 Cathédrale Saint Bénigne   5 Notre Dame Church and Clock Tower, Rue de la Chouette

6 Palais des Ducs et des Etats de Bourgogne   7 Musée des Beaux Arts, Salle des Gardes

8 Hôtel du Parc, 49 Cours du Parc

grapes, by the *'méthode champenoise'*, in the same limestone soil as its northwest neighbour Reims. With your fish course a white 1985 Chablis, perhaps from Paul Droin, Alain Geoffrey or William Fèvre, or perhaps a delicate Meursault from Remoissenet. Monsieur Billoux will commend his St Romain or Monthélie. With your main meat course the choice is overwhelming. The red wines of Burgundy depend solely on one factor – the depth of your pocket. There are modest country wines – look on the label for *Côte* (hillside) or *Hautes Côtes*. There are medium-priced red wines of Nuits St Georges and Pommard. Or the exotic, gorgeous Vosne-Romanée perhaps from Jaffelin, or Gevrey-Chambertin from the Trapet family. But if you are still undeterred by the bottle prices think very seriously about the greatest – Le Chambertin, La Romanée Conti or Le Musigny – the Grands Crus. With your '*mignardises de Dijon*' try the marc de Bourgogne of Gabriel Boudier (who are also well-known for their blackcurrant Cassis de Dijon).

The four-star **HÔTEL DU JURA** is at 14 Avenue Maréchal Foch (Tel. 80 41 61 12), five minutes walk west of the Place Darcy and close to the SNCF Gare de Dijon-Ville. The Jura has 75 rooms and its bar 'Le Refuge' is welcoming, but it has no restaurant. Closed 20 December–15 January.

The smaller **HÔTEL-RESTAURANT DU PARC**, 49 Cours du Parc (Tel. 80 65 18 41) is more modest, and is one kilometre from the Place Darcy due south on the D 996 signed for Seurre, near the Parc de la Colombière. There are only seven rooms, inexpensively priced, and a reasonable menu of two fork status. Closed during the second two weeks in August and February.

Two other excellent restaurants are the **CHAPEAU ROUGE** 5 rue Michelet (Tel. 80 30 28 10), opposite the Church of St Philibert, and **PRÉ AUX CLERCS ET TROIS FAISANS** 13 Place de la Libération (Tel. 80 67 11 33), near the Ducal Palace.

WHAT TO EAT

Dijon is famous for its mustard. Try the blue and white china pots at Moutarde 'Grey Poupon', 32 rue de la Liberté. Since 1777 their special formula blend has been sold to Grand Tourers. Gingerbread '*pain d'épices*', made with honey, is a local speciality. '*Escargots*' (snails) *de Bourgogne*', '*jambon persillé*' (ham pâté with parsley), '*terrine bourguignonne*', '*boeuf*' and '*coq au vin bourguignon*' are famous throughout France. '*Tourte bourguignonne*' is a pie made with meat and mushrooms in a creamy sauce. The local fish soups are delicious, as is the freshwater fish stew called '*pochouse*' simmered in white wine. The local cheeses are called *Citeaux*, *Cabrion* and *Epoisses*. Kir or blanc-cassis is an aperitif made with blackcurrant juice blended with dry white wine. Serve lightly chilled in summer. Although most of the famous wine négociants are in Beaune and Mâcon, there are a few in Dijon. Lejay-Lagout, L'Héritier-

Guyot and Grands Chais de Dijon will show you their cellars. It is no wonder that Dijon plays host to an International Food Fair in November each year.

A TOUR OF THE CITY

The ideal stay in Dijon is of three days, with the second day reserved for a vineyard tour to Beaune on the Route des Grands Crus via Fixin, Gevrey-Chambertin, Clos de Vougeot and Nuits St Georges. In Beaune the main sight, unique in France, is the Hôtel-Dieu and Museum founded by the wealthy (and rather guilty) Burgundian Nicolas Rolin – a hospital for the poor – in an exquisite building.

On the first day head for the Quartier Ancien based around the Place de la Libération where the Palais des Ducs et des Etats de Bourgogne is much mentioned by the Grand Tourers. Climb the Tour Philippe-Le-Bon (free on Sunday) to see the city, and then explore the enormous kitchens. The main building is the Hôtel de Ville (town hall). Around the corner is the Musée des Beaux-Arts (closed on Tuesday, free on Sunday) in the modern East Wing of the Palace. The Claus Sluter tombs of Philippe le Hardi and Jean sans Peur, a carved altar-piece with wings by Jacques de Baerze, and a 'Nativity' by Robert Campin are the stars amongst the Flemish primitives. Ask for the Salle des Gardes. The museum's collection houses works by Veronese, Caracci and Titian as well as a wide range of French painters from Mignard to Manet. This is the second museum and gallery in France after the Louvre. Dijon is so rich in museums – there are seven more – that after the rich feast of the Beaux-Arts, leave the others to the third day.

Take a stroll after lunch through the pedestrian zone. From the Place Darcy (near the SNCF station) where you will find the helpful **TOURIST OFFICE** (Tel. 80 43 42 12), walk eastwards along the rue de la Liberté to the Place St Michel. On the north side is the market, the Hôtel Chambellan courtyard, the rue de la Chouette and rue de la Verrerie with grooved centre pavements, i.e. Arthur Young's 'trottoirs', leading to the seventeenth-century Eglise de Notre Dame. Note the gargoyles and the splendid Horloge à Jacquemart, the pride of Dijon. Philippe le Hardi commissioned the clock and bell in 1382 after defeating the Flemish. Next you see the fifteenth-century church of St Michel, a mixture of Gothic and Renaissance styles. Call in at the Grey

Poupon shop or ask the tourist office to arrange a visit to a Burgundian wine négociant/shipper.

On the third day in Dijon explore the thirteenth-century Cathedral of Saint Bénigne in the rue Dr Maret and then the Musée Archéologique next door. Both are five minutes' walk south of the Place Darcy. The church of St Jean is two hundred metres east, *en route* for the Palais de Justice and near the Musée Magnin (a collection of French painters displayed among elegant seventeenth-century furnishings).

After lunch, walk or take the bus (No. 12) west for one kilometre to the Chartreuse de Champmol, once visited by all the Grand Tourists, now a psychiatric hospital, where two of Claus Sluter's famous works are to be seen. The 'Well of Moses' and the 'Portal' are notable, and there is no entrance charge. Other museums of interest are the François Rude in the rue Vaillant, and the Natural History museum near the Arquebuse gardens, considered to be the second greatest botanical gardens in Europe. In the rue Sainte Anne are the Sacred Art Museum (No. 15) and the Burgundian 'La Vie Bourguignonne' (No. 17) in the cloister of the Bernardines.

AFTER DINNER

In the evening Dijon has much to offer. During June there are concerts every night. From mid-June to mid-August the Estivade presents dance, music and theatre in the streets. The **THÉÂTRE DE DIJON**, Place du Théâtre, produces autumn, winter and spring opera, operettas and classical music concerts. The Grenier de Bourgogne organizes free jazz and entertainment during the summer in the Place Darcy. The antiques fair (mid-May), Jazz dans la Rue (mid-July), Festival de Folklore and Fête de la Vigne (September), and the Festival of the Nuits de Bourgogne (alternate Decembers) produce almost non-stop cultural opportunities for the modern Grand Tourer.

After dinner, if your French is adequate, try the Nouveau Théâtre de Bourgogne at the **THÉÂTRE DU PARVIS ST JEAN**, Place Bossuet, or '**LE MESSIRE**', '**LE CARILLON**' or '**LA CATHÉDRALE**' night clubs.

So that is Dijon. A smaller version of Paris, a delightful city of knights and ladies, of wine and *coq au vin*, of music and theatre, of mustard and gingerbread. A marvellous legacy of the cultured great Valois Dukes, the 'Grands Ducs de l'Occident'.

LYON

———————— the city of 'Grand Guignol' ————————

It was very difficult for travellers on the Grand Tour to avoid Lyon. Either on the southern route from Paris, or the northern route from what we now know as the French Riviera, Lyon, the second city of France, on the juncture of the mighty rivers Saône and Rhône, simply had to be visited.

As a result, every traveller who committed pen to paper on his *escritoire* had a few words to say about 'Lions'. Now it is a vast sprawling urban area of nearly one and a quarter million inhabitants, with the original old town of St Jean facing Bellecour across the river Saône.

Roman legacies abound. 'Lugdunum' was from the first a local capital town, with the theatre of Augustus, Hadrian's Odeon, the Agrippan Way and the amphitheatre of Drusus. Early Christian saints were martyred here, and Sainte Blandine was one of the earliest victims. The old quarters of the city are still called St Paul, St Georges and St Jean, and the Cathedral of Gothic bourguignon style is called St Jean. There are important Roman remains on the Fourvière hill above St Jean and there is a major Gallo-Roman museum. The St Nizier church is built in flamboyant Gothic style, and St Martin d'Ainay is built in Romanesque style. The prosperity of Lyon and its cultural heritage is derived from its strategic position at the confluence of two major rivers, the Rhône and the Saône, with the Massif Central in the west and the Alps in the east. By the sixteenth century Lyon had surpassed Paris in both population and wealth, and Kings Louis XII and François I took up residence. In the seventeenth century it became a centre of the silk industry. The present fabric museum has a collection of 300,000 pieces from every period and country.

Travellers on the Grand Tour usually arrived by flat-bottomed boat on the Rhône from Chalon. They then had a choice of continuing by boat south through Vienne, Valence, Montélimar, Orange, Avignon and Arles to Marseille, or striking east by road to Grenoble and Briançon to Turin.

Tom Coryat rode through the town in 1608 and commented on the many buildings, six or seven storeys high, windows made of white paper, and walls of white freestone. There were no fewer than 39 churches in Lyon, possibly because Pontius Pilate reputedly slew himself in the town! There was a good grammar school, and the brave young man stayed at the Inn of the Three Kings, 'fayrest Inne in the whole citie'. He needed 'billes of health' before he could leave Lyon to visit Italian cities.

John Evelyn chose the Hôtel Golden Lion (Lion d'Or) and 'met divers of his acquaintance who coming from Paris were designed for Italy'. He boated down the Rhône from Lyon to Avignon. The current was so strong that boats arriving from Geneva were sold in Lyon, that course being preferable to the cost of a team of horses hauling them back upstream. On his return from Italy again through Lyon to Paris via Roanne he reported that they 'lay that night in Damask beds, were treated like Emperours.'

The first detailed look at Lyon came from Richard Lassells in 1686; 'One of the greater and richest towns in France, intercepts all the Merchandise of Burgundy, Germany and Italy, it licks its fingers notably and thrives by it. It expresseth this in its looks for here you have handsome people, noble houses, great jollity, frequent balls and much bravery – all the marks of a good town.'

Many visitors in the eighteenth century commented favourably on the city. Dr John Moore counted Lyon as the most magnificent town in France after Paris for commerce, wealth and population. The inns (Three Kings, Dauphin, Auberge du Parc) were famous for their lavish display of plate, and the merchants lived on a grand scale. Later in the century Mrs Piozzi wrote, 'Such was the hospitality of the Lyonnais at table [that] I counted 36 dishes where we dined, and 24 more where we supped. Everything was served up in silver in both places.' Robert Adam noted that the shops had a varied stock of 'prettiest things for ladies'.

Lady Mary Wortley Montagu in 1716 visited the Roman aqueduct outside the gate of St Justinius, the monastery of St Mary, and the ruins of the Imperial Palace where the Roman Emperor Claudius was born. She admired the clock on the great Gothic Cathedral of St Jean, and the French statues in the well-planted Belle Cour with their gilded full-bottomed wigs.

Four years later Edward Wright noted the Jesuit and Dominican churches richly adorned with marble, the Franciscans' well stored with pictures, and that the canons of the church of St John were all Counts! 'The famous clock figures move at twelve o'clock, the Angel opens a little door, discover the Blessed Virgin and figure of God the Father descends to her and a brazen cock crows a-top.' The fashionable town houses did not have glass, but oiled paper windows. Wright drank Côte-Rôtie wine ('on the roasted side of the hill') visited the Château de Pilate, drank Hermitage wine grown near Tein on a famous hill, went to the King's cellars and ate fricassée of frogs at his inn.

Sir J.E. Smith stayed at the Hôtel du Parc and visited the Hôtel Dieu hospital where the beds had large, thick, woollen curtains with two, or even three patients to a bed. The public library was excellent, with 60,000 volumes. Thomas Nugent's *Guide* was a bit depressing, reporting that 'The women would be very handsome if it were not for losing their hair and teeth so soon, which some attribute to the frequent fogs that cover the town'! But despite the 'villainous ragged paper windows', he found a 'great many remains of antiquity'.

James Boswell also stayed at the Auberge du Parc, went to the '*baigneur*', and M. Le Blanc, the bath-keeper, allowed him to stay with him for three livres a day for room and wax candles, including shaving and dressing.

By the end of the eighteenth century the population had grown to 160,000 and Mariana Starke wrote in her guide how Lyon was encircled by rich and beautiful country, had four theatres, and good inns (Ambassadeurs, Provence, L'Europe, du Nord and du Parc). There was a daily *diligence* to Marseille, and three '*coches d'eau*' by river to Avignon each week. She thought the quays on the Saône and Rhône were magnificent, and the Hôtel Dieu one of the best hospitals in Europe with one hundred and fifty nuns watching over the sick. Of the antiquities she commended visitors to see the Taurobolic altar, with its mosaic pavement, sacrificial vases, ancient lamps, lares and armour.

Lord St Vincent thought Lyon the 'pleasantest city in France' but the harbour porters were 'sharpers and imposters'. The long boat journey was very convenient, producing no fatigue. Robert Wharton claimed the 'Peaches of Lyon are the best fruit I have yet met with'. He noted the women bathing in the Saône and wrote home suggesting that British women adopt the habit of summer bathing. Charles Thompson wrote 'wine plenty and tolerably good', but he was delighted with the food. The Lyon bankers, including M. Auriol, were helpful and lent money to Edward Mellish, Richard Hoare, Robert Wharton and a hundred Louis d'Ors to a Mr Godfrey. Sir John Swinburne paid 216 livres for a waistcoat of rich Lyons stuff, 84 livres for six pairs of worked ruffles.

Joseph Spence criticized the prison of Pierre Lize, admired the Jesuit College library and said the variety of vineyards, church convents and water-houses made Lyon 'delightful'. At the good playhouse and opera he met the Duke of Kingston travelling with his tutor, Dr. Nathan Hickman, Sir Edward Bellew and Sir William Stuart. He purchased a coat, a light camlet (made of silk and camels' hair) with silver buttons, a green silk waistcoat with silver lace, and stockings with silver clocks [patterns].

At the beginning of the nineteenth century, Catherine Wilmot and her Irish peer stayed at the Hôtel d'Europe, rue Bonaparte, Place de Belcour, and there met the Acklam and Foster families. She went to 'Messe' in the old Gothic Cathedral, noted that Lyon-made chocolate was good, visited silk factories and admired the 2,000-year-old Roman baths. Lady Frances Shelley stayed at the Hôtel de l'Univers, visited the silk mercers, and the silk and velvet manufacturers in the rue Constantin, listened to the band on the Place Belcour, and drove to the new Faubourg Napoléon and the Citadel. Matthew Todd, the valet, and his master put up at the Hôtel du Nord, thought Lyon 'much more beautiful than Paris, and the theatre better too'.

Still in the year before Waterloo John Mayne, a young Irishman of 23, travelled to Avignon with his brother Charles and his wife. At the Hôtel de l'Europe he was amazed that men worked as maids, '*filles de chambre*'. He wrote, 'The river quays and bridges are extremely handsome, and the river boats are rowed by women! The people are less French and the women infinitely handsome . . . the Alps look like clouds on the horizon. The town filled with tapestry and decorations of all kinds, triumphal arches, orchestras and preparations to greet Monsieur with painted Bourbon friendship.' The Maynes were visited after an excellent dinner by a police officer who demanded to know who they were, their names, ages, place of birth, nationality, last place of residence, and object in travelling. They saw a grand display of fireworks on the bridges, went to St John's Church for Mass, and to two theatres (the music was good at the opéra comique). They encountered their first religious procession in France, with fifty women and girls in white carrying lighted wax tapers, marching in two rows, holding shrines, relics, crucifixions, transparent lanterns, and silver vessels, led by priests magnificently dressed. The Maynes visited a silk manufacturer, saw many looms at work, and rich materials in production. They commented that 'Lyons was the most cheerful handsomest city yet seen in France, in an opulent state, much commerce.' Moreover, the hotelier was very honest and gave them a free bottle of wine.

John Murray's guide of 1840 was less enthusiastic. 'No really good inn here, the dirt and insects horrible, appearance of grandour limited to the quais, bridges and noble rivers, and the two Places of de Bellecour and des Terreaux: it is deficient in fine streets and long open thoroughfares. The interior is one stack of lofty houses, penetrated by lanes so excessively narrow and nasty as not to be traversed without disgust. Here seethed the silkweavers, amongst them many English who are in the lowest state of degradation . . .'

At Lyon 'Boz' and the Dickens family in 1844 were fascinated by the Cathedral clock. Thinking that evil was being overcome by the little clockwork puppets, Charles Dickens exclaimed 'Ah! ha! Le Diable!' but the priest corrected him, 'Pardon, M'sieu, c'est l'ange Gabriel!' He was worried,

63

like John Murray, about the miseries attending a manufacturing town without adequate drains!

VISITING LYON TODAY

WHERE TO STAY

Of the many inns mentioned by the travellers to 'Lions', many survive in one form or another. The two-star **HÔTEL UNIVERS**, 33 rue Ney (Tel. 78 52 09 18) with 48 rooms, and the **HÔTEL LE BRITANIA**, 17 rue Professeur Weill (Tel. 78 52 86 52), two-star with 22 rooms, are both in the Brotteaux area of Lyon, which is on the east side of the river Rhône. In the Bellecour area, where most travellers stayed, is the two-star **HÔTEL DU DAUPHIN**, 9 rue Victor Hugo (Tel. 78 37 18 34) with 14

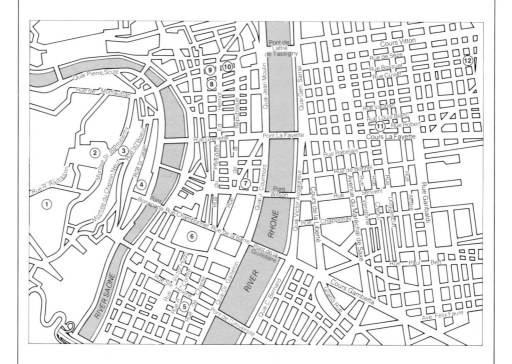

1 Théâtres Romains   2 Basilique de Fourvière   3 Vieux Lyon   4 Cathédrale Saint Jean   5 Fabric Museum

6 Place Bellecour   7 Grand Hôtel des Etrangers, 5 rue Stella   8 Musée des Beaux Arts   9 Place des Terraux

10 Hôtel de Ville   11 Brotteaux Area   12 Hôtel Le Britania, 17 rue Professeur Weill

rooms, and the three-star **GRAND HÔTEL DES ETRANGERS**, 5 rue Stella (Tel. 78 42 01 55) with 52 rooms. In the Perrache area, near the railway station between the rivers, and just south of Bellecour, are the two-star **HÔTEL DAUPHINE**, 3 rue Duhamel (Tel. 78 37 24 19) with 31 rooms, the three-star **HÔTEL BRISTOL**, 28 cours de Verdun (Tel. 78 37 56 55) with 131 rooms, and the **HÔTEL VICTORIA**, 3 rue Delandine (Tel. 78 37 57 61) with 53 rooms. It is rare to find a hotel in Lyon with a restaurant – none of these mentioned has one.

WHERE TO EAT AND DRINK

The traditional Lyon restaurant is called a *'bouchon'* (wine cork) and many of them are found in the Terreaux area, north of Bellecour, and in Vieux Lyon of St Jean, west of the Saône. The famous Paul Bocuse restaurant, one of the top three in France, is to be found twelve kilometres north near the Pont de Collonges. His influence over the gastronomy of Lyon has been immense and he has set very high standards for others to follow. M. Chavent runs the **TOUR ROSE**, 16 rue Boeuf in Vieux Lyon, and serves Côte-Rôtie and St Véran wines with his salmon or duck or *'rouget barbet poêlé aux pois gourmands'*. **VETTARD**, 7 Place Bellecour, serves Pouilly Fuissé and Beaujolais-Villages with *'loup à l'huile de basilic'*, *'paupiette de saumon'* or *'blanc de poularde'*. **ORSI**, 3 Place Kléber; **HENRY**, 27 rue Martinière, and **NANDRON**, 26 quai J. Moulin, are all high class, quite expensive restaurants. Less expensive *'bouchon'* restaurants serving cuisine Lyonnaise are the **CAFÉ DE JURA**, 25 rue Tupin; **GARIOUD**, 14 rue du Palais-Grillet; **L'OUVRE-BOÎTE**, 5 Place du Change, and **LE 21**, 21 quai Romain Rolland. Look also in the rue Mercière near Place Bellecour.

Local specialities to ask for are *'tripes à la Lyonnaise'*, *'andouillette grillée'*, *'quenelles sauce Nantua'*, and *'cochonailles chaudes'* or *'froides'*. Lyon has been famous for its *charcuterie* for centuries with names like *'Jésus de Lyon'*, *'Rose de Lyon'*, *'saucisses de Lyon'*, *'caillettes'* etc. Frogs' legs, snails and chicken as well as river fish feature frequently on menus.

There are several good wine-bars in Lyon. **LE MITONNE**, 26 rue Trouchet; **CHEZ SILVAIN**, 4 rue Tupin; **CAFÉ DES FEDÉRATIONS**, 8 rue Major Martin, and **DASSAUD**, 12 rue Pizay, all serve a wide range of Beaujolais and Côtes du Rhône wines. The restaurant **LÉON DE LYON**, 1 rue Pleney, also has an excellent selection of local wines. Wine classes are held by Lucien Chapat in the **HÔTEL SOFITEL**, 20 rue Gailleton

(Tel. 78 42 52 50) at very reasonable fees for one class or a course of six classes.

Three large open food markets are held every day except Monday at Quai St Antoine, Boulevard de la Croix Rousse and on the Quai Victor Augagneur.

EXPLORING THE CITY

Lyon, like most French cities, is divided into *arrondissements*. Bellecour and Perrache are in the second and Vieux Lyon is in the fifth. The Métro links Perrache, Bellecour, the Cordeliers and Hôtel de Ville, and *carnets* of tickets are available. *Funiculaires* go from St Jean up the hill of Fourvière to the Théâtre Romain and the Basilica. Travel tickets for Métro, bus and *funiculaire* can be purchased for 48 or 72 hours, with unlimited use in each period.

The **TOURIST OFFICE** is in the Place Bellecour near the flower market, 69002 Lyon (Tel. 78 42 25 75).

Sightseeing tours are interesting, varied and sophisticated. Among those to be recommended are:

1 The Gallo-Roman tour, which takes in the amphitheatre, Odéon, Cybèle Temple, Roman theatres and the Museum of Gallo-Roman civilization. Every Sunday, 3.30pm, at the Museum, 17 rue Cléberg.
2 A Renaissance walk around 'Vieux Lyon', the three villages of St Paul, St Jean and St Georges, on Friday evenings and Saturday at 2.30pm.
3 A tour of the silk-weaving area of La Croix Rousse. In the seventeenth century there were 10,000 weaving looms in Lyon. There are guided tours of the Canute Museum and the *'Traboules'* narrow medieval alleyways on Saturday afternoons.
4 *Bateaux Mouches* boat cruises on the rivers Saône and Rhône.
5 Minibus tours to the Beaujolais vineyards, daily at 9.30am.

Apart from the Gallo-Roman antiquities, the dark, cobble-stoned streets, and the Renaissance houses in Vieux Lyon on the west bank of the Saône, the main architectural sights are the bourguignon-style Cathédrale St Jean with its fourteenth-century clock in the north transept and flamboyant Gothic rose window; the nineteenth-century

Basilique de Fourvière on the hill overlooking the cathedral and the Renaissance Hôtel de Ville, and the churches of St Martin d'Ainay, St Bonaventure, St Nizier and St Paul. There are nine parks, of which the largest, the botanical Parc Tête d'Or, northeast of the city, is on the banks of the Rhône.

Of the fourteen museums, besides the two already mentioned (Civilization Gallo-Romaine and the silkweavers Maison de Canute), the Musée des Beaux-Arts, Place des Terreaux, open all week, free, is a huge museum with a complete range of French and Lyonese paintings. A Rubens, Jordaens, Zurbarán, El Greco, and some sixteenth-century Venetian paintings should also be seen. It houses so many paintings that the two Impressionist rooms, and the early twentieth-century paintings (Picasso, Matisse, Dufy) should perhaps be seen first.

In the month of June, Lyon hosts the Biennale du Théâtre, a grand festival of theatre from all over the world. Details can be obtained from **HÔTEL DE VILLE**, 69680 Lyon (Tel. 78 27 71 31). The Opéra, just east of the Hôtel de Ville, has a good reputation. All the travellers visited it on their tours of Lyon.

WINE TOURS

Lyon makes a perfect base from which to visit the regional vineyards mentioned by the travellers. Northwest is the Beaujolais area, reached easily by the A6 towards Villefranche-sur-Saône. Although the best areas are between Villefranche and Mâcon (Juliénas, Chénas, Fleurie, Morgon etc.) there are twenty friendly wine cooperatives close to Villefranche on the western side. Practically every village has one.

To the south of Lyon on the A7 past Vienne is the Côte-Rôtie, which is both rare and delicious. A perfumed, fragrant red grown by producers such as Champet, Guigal and Jasmin.

The Hermitage wines lie between Vienne and Valence on both sides of the river Rhône. Look for Auguste Clape, Verset, Juge for Cornas black fruity red wines; Crozes-Hermitage from Jaboulet; St Joseph wines from Florentin, Gripa and Coursodon. The whole area is only fifty kilometres north to south, and five to ten kilometres wide. As Catherine Wilmot observed nearly two centuries ago, 'Good local wine from St Foit near Vienne and Côte-Rôtie. The Wine Press is full everywhere. At supper we eat Carp, Eels and Pike for which the Rhône is famous and drink

Hermitage wine.' The Maynes visited the vineyard and noted the 'vines were 5–6 feet high, looked like great raspberry beds'.

And Guignol?

This unique character was created in 1808 by an unemployed silk weaver in Lyon. He is a red-faced Lyonnais puppet who makes jokes at the bureaucracy, at the bourgeoisie, at everyone in fact. 'Grand Guignol' was cynical, bloody-minded and often disturbing: in many ways out of character with modern Lyon! The Festival International de la Marionette is held in Lyon on the first week-end in September, and throughout the winter **LE NOUVEAU GUIGNOL DE LYON** performs adult puppet shows (Tel. 78 37 31 79). The Musée des Marionettes in the Hôtel Gadagne houses an international collection of puppets as well as the original famous Lyonnais Guignol 'family'.

Allow three days to see Lyon, including half a day on a *Bateau Mouche* and a day in the vineyards.

AVIGNON
————————————*city of the old popes*————————————

The words of the old song, '*Sur le pont d'Avignon l'on y danse, l'on y danse*' are no longer quite correct, since if you include the rail bridge there are now three '*ponts*' over the river Rhône. The St Bénézet bridge with the St Nicolas chapel is the one referred to in the famous nursery rhyme. Avignon is the Préfecture city of Vaucluse, with a population of nearly 100,000, and all the Grand Tour travellers taking the boat route south from Lyon had to pass through it, and for the most part welcomed the chance. As Charles Dickens wrote 150 years ago, 'There lay before us, that same afternoon, the broken bridge of Avignon and all the city baking in the sun: yet with an underdone-pie-crust, battlemented wall, that never will be brown, tho' it bake for centuries'.

When Pope Clement V in 1309 moved the papacy from Rome to his own country he chose Avignon as the perfect compromise between 'obeying' his sovereign King Philippe Le Bel and avoiding the notorious corruption of Rome. Seven popes – French popes of course – succeeded, until in 1377 Pope Gregory XI transferred the seat back to Rome. Avignon was by then rich and corrupt. The Palace of the Popes was a huge white stone Gothic fortress – the church embattled – with towers and ramparts. These buildings attracted all the Grand Tour milords, although medieval pilgrims were brutally tricked and swindled here.

Richard Lassells in 1686 listed the ten key points about Avignon, which still hold good. They were, 'No 1 the Cathedral church and tombs of the Popes, No 2 Church of St Didier with tomb of Petrus Damianus, full of learned works and sanctity, No 3 Church of Celestins with tomb, chapel of Cardinal Peter of Luxemburg, No 4 Carthusian Monastery in Bourg of Villeneuve (which has a good pantry), No 5 The Dominicans' fair Convent has a picture of St Vizentius Ferrerius, No 6 The Cordeliers church with [the tomb of] Madame Laura de Sade rendered so famous by Petrarch's verses, No 7 church of the Father of the Christian Doctrine, No 8 Fine free stone walls of the Town, No 9 the admirable Bridge, many handsome palaces, curious gardens, No 10 Town trading in silk stuffs, perfumed gloves, Ribbands and fine paper'. Lassells, a Roman Catholic priest, and skilled governor, wrote with first-hand knowledge and with admirable precision.

During the eighteenth century many travellers visited Avignon. Bearleader Joseph Spence remarked 'Avignon is an old fashioned town in a very pretty country: the Rhône washes its walls on one side (for it seems to be a sort of square) with a fine long island in it that, as it were, divides it into two rivers on that side, and there are the remains of a bridge which went over both of them and the island quite from Avignon to the Castle of Philip the Fair.' Visitors were startled on stepping ashore to see the crowds of bronzed sailors on the river banks, carrying talismans around their necks to guard them from shipwreck, and wearing distinctive fringed sashes.

James Boswell bounced merrily into Avignon in 1765 and found it 'a good warm town, put up at St Omers, table d'hôte excellent, warm wine and bread'. He visited the church of St Laurent and noted the nuns were adorned with hangings of elegant lace. 'Avignon is a very agreeable place to live at. The air is excellent and there are many nobles.' He met a French Marquise who took snuff, pulled up her gown and warmed her legs. Boswell was mildly shocked. 'The French women may be virtuous but they look like strumpets. The Italian women may be licentious but they look modest.'

Still in the eighteenth century, William Bennett thought the cathedral not as good as an English principal market town equivalent, but praised the active Jewish community. Robert Wharton was unhappy with the food, but Charles Thompson 'found all sorts of fish, flesh, fruit and wines in the greatest plenty – at the most reasonable rates'. Lady Elizabeth Craven was there in July 1785 having arrived by *bateau de poste*, a flat-bottomed, very rude construction, the materials always being sold for plank and firewood on arrival in Avignon. Her cabriolet on board served her as a cabin, although bilge water needed frequent bailing.

Arthur Young disliked the '*vent de Bize*' (the modern *mistral*) which blew strongly for several days with a clear sky tempering the heat of August. He approached the town 'with [an] interest, attention and expectancy that few towns have kindled'. He was sad to see Madame Laura's tomb was but a stone in the pavement in the church of the Cordeliers. A monument to brave Crillon was in the same church. He noted that 'from the rock of the Legates Palace there is one of the finest views of the windings of the Rhône, [which] forms here considerable islands richly watered, cultivated, covered with mulberries, olives and fruit trees'.

Mariana Starke commented in her turn of the century guide that the population was 23,000, 'the Cathedral most striking, the church of the Cordeliers, the museum, the tombs of Laura and gallant Crillon are near a large cypress and should all be seen. The best hotel is the L'Europe although the Petrarque et Laura between Avignon and Vaucluse is celebrated for its trout and fish dinners.' So much did Lady Mary Wortley Montagu like the place that she lived there from 1742 to 1746.

Catherine Wilmot, travelling a few months before Waterloo, liked Avignon, noting 'its incircling ramparts, Popes Palace top of a rock, the Pagan temple to the Goddess Diana with its arched entrance, vestibule, Corinthian pillars, les Cordeliers and the church of St Nizier. An annual fête and pilgrimage with much incense took place there by the women of Avignon who had passed the dangers of childbirth.' She, too, admired the countryside covered with olive trees, full of fruit, mulberries, figs and vines.

In the same year bustling young Matthew Todd stayed at the Palais Royal Hôtel, and visited the great prison, Pope Pius palace and convent, where 3,000 Spanish prisoners were incarcerated. He visited the valuable collection of paintings and marble statues, saw the Hôtel des Invalides and a convent. Todd was given breakfast '*à la François*, half seas over, not accustomed to wine in the morning . . . Supper was stewed eels, anchovies, fritters of pears, custard pudding, sweetmeats, most excellent wines, afterwards coffee, eau de vie de cognac . . .'

Dickens and his family attended mass in the cathedral with a few old crones, a babe in arms and an excited dog! He also visited the offices of the Inquisition. On a frescoed wall was the story of the good Samaritan. Puzzled Boz bought a local history guide to Avignon!

Later in the century, in 1858, John Stuart Mill retired to Avignon and spent the next fifteen years there until he died.

VISITING AVIGNON TODAY

WHERE TO STAY AND EAT

John Murray's guide of 1843 recommended the Hôtel L'Europe, where the attentive landlord was one of the best in France, and the Hôtel du Palais Royal, where Matthew Todd and his master stayed. **THE HÔTEL L'EUROPE** is still the best in Avignon, situated at 12 Place Crillon (Tel. 90 82 66 92), near the Pont Edouard Daladier. It has 53 rooms and was built originally in 1580 as a palace for the Marquis of Gravezon, but has been a hotel since 1799. Inside is a courtyard, a remarkable collection of Aubusson tapestries, Empire consoles and Directoire pieces. It has a good restaurant. The **HÔTEL D'ANGLETERRE**, 29 Boulevard Raspail, near the Pont de l'Europe (Tel. 90 86 34 31), has 40 rooms but is more modest with two stars.

The best restaurant is the **HIÉLY-LUCULLUS**, 5 rue de la République (Tel. 90 86 17 07), just a few minutes' walk from the Préfecture. Their *pièce de résistance* is '*l'agneau des Alpilles grillé sur feu de bois*' with a Tavel rosé wine or Châteauneuf-du-Pape. **LE VERNET**, 58 rue Joseph Vernet (Tel. 90 86 64 53), and the **BRUNEL**, 46 rue Balance (Tel. 90 85 24 83), which has hot curried oysters with a Côtes du Rhône, are both good alternatives. The best wine bar is **LE BISTRO D'AVIGNON**, Place de l'Horloge (Tel. 90 86 06 45).

WHAT'S ON IN AVIGNON

The **TOURIST OFFICE** is at 41 Cours Jean Jaurès (Tel. 90 82 65 11). Avignon is a rectangle; 1.2 kilometres on each side, with ramparts all round the perimeter. The Tourist Office is in the south-centre of the rectangle, off the main rue de la République between the police station and the Musée Lapidaire.

A stay of two days is recommended to do justice to Avignon; three if you are there in July and August when the Festival, established by Jean Vilar, is in progress. There are concerts, plays, films, '*événements*' and much excitement – *but book early*!

The massive and luxurious Palace of the Popes, the Palais Vieux, was built on the hill by Pope Benoît XII, and the neighbouring Palais Neuf by Pope Clement VI. In the huge Place du Palais is the Chapelle St Martial and the Cathedral of Notre Dame des Doms, a heavy

Romanesque church with a richly decorated interior, where Pope John XXII is buried. Note the unusual nave and impressive dome. At the end of the Place is the Petit Palais, a cardinal's palace which now

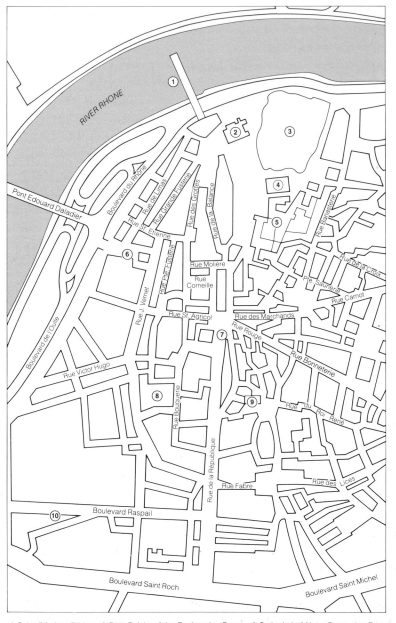

1 Saint Bénézet Bridge **2** Petit Palais **3** Le Rocher des Doms **4** Cathedral of Notre Dame des Doms

5 Palace of the Popes **6** Hôtel l'Europe, 12 Place Crillon **7** Hiély Lucullus, 5 rue de la République

8 Musée Calvet **9** Church of Saint Didier **10** Hôtel d'Angleterre, 29 Boulevard Raspail

houses a fine collection of Italian paintings of the thirteenth to sixteenth centuries, and local paintings and sculptures of the twelfth to sixteenth centuries. From 1440 the town became the centre of French painting, founded by Enguerrand Charonton. Traces of Flemish tradition were blended with characteristics of Italian art. The best way to see the art treasures in the Palais des Papes is to take a guided tour of about fifty minutes which starts every half hour from 8am, excluding two and a half hours for lunch – siesta time.

The Musée Calvet, 65 rue Joseph Vernet (closed Tuesday) is five minutes' walk southwest from the Palais des Papes. Here there is an excellent collection of seventeenth- and eighteenth-century French and Flemish paintings by Breughel, and the school of Bosch, Dufy, Utrillo, Manet and Soutine. Other sections include prehistory, Egyptology and local wrought-ironwork collections.

In the seventeenth-century Jesuit College nearby at 18 rue de la République, is a fine lapidary and sculpture museum (closed Tuesday).

The ramparts around Avignon were built in the fourteenth century, with battlements, turrets and old gates. One visitor called them 'squat and very thick, like huge children's blocks placed there according to a playful up-and-down design'. Viollet-le-Duc restored them in the nineteenth century, after Notre Dame in Paris and the fortified walls at Carcassonne.

In the old quarter there are many fascinating buildings, and bordering the Sorgue are the unusual waterwheels used by the dyers of the Middle Ages. Between the Petit Palais and the Rhône are the remains of the St Bénézet bridge with the St Nicolas chapel of nursery rhyme fame. Now only four of the original twenty-two arches are intact. A souvenir shop will sell you a ticket to *danser sur le pont d'Avignon*.

The best view of all is from the top of Le Rocher des Doms, a lovely park at the north end of the Palais des Papes complex. There are ponds full of fish and ducks, a view of the Rhône, of Mount Ventoux, the St Bénézet bridge and the fortified town of Villeneuve-lès-Avignon on the west side of the Rhône. A little train runs from the palace to Villeneuve, through the Alpilles, the Lubéron and Châteauneuf-du-Pape, 18 kilometres away. This makes an admirable excursion to see the Pope's Château and taste the excellent wine from that small town. For real '*amateurs de vin*' the Comité Interprofessionnel des vins des Côtes du Rhône is located at the same address as the Tourist Office (Tel. 90 86 47 09). The wine festival '*Baptême des Côtes du Rhône*' is held in Avignon on 14 November each year.

AIX-EN-PROVENCE

———————————— *capital of Provence* ————————————

John Evelyn passed through Aix on 'a most delicious journey to Marseilles through a Country sweetly declining to the South and Mediterranean coast, full of vineyards and Olive-yards, Myrtils, Pomegranads and the like sweete Plantations'. Forty years later, in 1686, Richard Lassels commented favourably on the parliament town (of Provence) and called it 'one of the neatest towns in France'. It is now, most appropriately, twinned with the elegant spa town of Bath, in England.

It was jolly King René of Naples and Anjou, cultured artist and genial poet, who introduced the muscatel grape to the region and made Aix his headquarters from 1471 to 1480. The town became part of France two years later. In 1536 it was captured by the Emperor Charles V who was crowned 'King of Arles' in Aix Cathedral. There have been Catalan, Angevin and Neapolitan influences in this small, elegant, cultured town of 125,000 population. It has no river, no port, and little commercial power. Indeed Sir Nathaniel Wraxall commented two centuries ago that it had an 'air of silence and gloom, so commonly characteristic of places destitute of commerce and industry'. Because of its sunny climate and warm spa water (the thermal baths are west of the cathedral on the Cours Sextius), Aix was a popular small health resort on the way to Lyon or Marseille. The *Gentleman's Guide* of 1770 remarked, 'Aix is much admired, much visited for its squares and fountains, being considered more beautiful than any other in France save Paris . . . this town will perhaps please you better than any you have yet seen in France . . . in winter it is extremely pleasant'. But Robert Wharton, travelling in a mule-drawn coach and averaging only three miles an hour, grumbled 'Never in my life did I pass such bad roads [as those] to Aix'. Sir John Swinburne paid an Aix tailor's bill of 45 livres, and 'bills for cloth, lace etc. for making into clothes, of 591 livres'. Arthur Young travelled there for 'scholarship' and noted the lack of glass windows. James Boswell spent a Christmas there, had his shoes cleaned in a café, and 'mounted with my great jackboots to courir à franc étrier à bidet' (roughly, to ride at full speed on a pony express). He enjoyed the bread, figs, and almonds baked with honey into a Christmas gâteau. Today the Aix '*calissons*', an almond-paste confection, are a well-liked speciality. Rather surprisingly Boswell behaved himself here, possibly because Aix had no bordellos!

The seventeenth and eighteenth centuries were relatively peaceful for the town. The Cours and the Spa were developed and many distinguished English visitors came, and some, like William Wilson, stayed. For charitable works over a fourteen-year period he was made an honorary citizen in 1790.

Philip Thicknesse described Aix as a 'well built city', and Joseph Spence commented in his diary on 'The pretty Cours . . . between the two double rows of trees and with three fountains'. He was alluding to the Cours Mirabeau, one of the most beautiful boulevards in France, with tall leafy plane trees screening the cafés from the hot Provençal sun on one side, and old sandstone 'Hôtels' from the seventeenth and eighteenth centuries on the other side. Spence wrote in his working bearleader's notes, 'See the baths and two Roman tours by Fennhouse and if possible the library that belongs to Mr Peyrete. Lodge at the Mulet Blanc without the town. The cours at Aix is perhaps what makes it be called so pretty a town. 'Tis 1,500 f. long and 125 f. broad (20 f. street, 20 f. sidewalks, 45 middle; 20 side and 20 street). Four streets fall into it on each side at right angles, opposite each other, most of them tirés à corde.'

Tobias Smollett, the slightly tetchy Scots novelist, took the waters and had to admit that 'as many of its inhabitants are persons of fashion, they are well bred gay and sociable'. But many English visitors without the prefix 'Milord' were snubbed by the Governor of Aix, the Duc de Villars, although Laurence Sterne spent a month or two in Aix in 1762 relatively happily!

Thomas Jefferson visited the town in 1787. Gabriel Mirabeau, the French Revolutionary leader (1749–1791) lived in Aix and was elected deputy in 1789. His writings greatly influenced the start of the French Revolution. At the turn of the century Mariana Starke in her guide wrote that Aix, with a population of 23,700, was 'a cheap town for permanent residence, handsomely built in the Italian style. The mineral waters and Hot Baths are celebrated. View the Cathedral, La Rotonde adorned with columns, the Temple of Vesta and the College Chapel'. She recommended the best inns; Hôtel du Cours, L'Hôtel des Princes and La Mule Blanche.

The year before Waterloo, Matthew Todd and Captain B. were staying in Aix at the Hôtel des Princes, near a coffee house on the road entrance from Marseille. He found the countryside 'pretty but hilly, not much wood, except olive trees, soil on the rocks by no means good, not much cultivation . . . Olive, figs, almonds, grapes grow in wild state, also lavender, mignonette, sweet marjoram.' Matthew went to the mineral baths and reported, 'the water is strong, about new milk warm, the baths rather too small tho' not dear at only 22 sols/sous per bath. But the Lady of the Wash Tub made a heavy charge.' He priced the local wines as usual. Lunette rouge, Tavel rouge and Chably blanc all at one franc ten sous per bottle:

Petit Champagne blanc one franc fifteen, Muscat de Frontignac two francs – ten shillings – 'all too new new for an English stomach'!

VISITING AIX TODAY
WHERE TO STAY AND EAT

The **STATION THERMALE** (mineral water spa) is at 55 cours Sextius (Tel. 42 26 01 18) and many 'curistes' stay at **L'HÔTEL DES THERMES**, 2 Boulevard Jean Jaurès (Tel. 42 26 01 18). Probably the oldest Hôtel-Restaurant is the two-star **HÔTEL DE FRANCE**, with a restaurant named **LA VIEILLE AUBERGE**, 63 rue Espariat (Tel. 42 27 90 15). It has 27 rooms, and is situated 300 metres east of the Place de Général de Gaulle, a huge roundabout in the southwest corner of Aix. Alternatively, there is the three-star **LE MANOIR**, 8 rue d'Entrecasteaux (Tel. 42 26 27 20).

The two best restaurants in Aix are the **CAVES HENRI IV** very near the Hôtel de France and the **ABBAYE DES CORDELIERS**, 21 rue Lieutaud, near the Hôtel de Ville. Try the excellent local Palette wine made at Château Simone; the reds are best from grapes called Mourvèdre, Grenache and Cinsault.

CULTURE

During the nineteenth century Paul Cézanne (1839–1906), Impressionist painter, and Louise Colet (1808–1876), authoress and friend of Flaubert and Musset, helped reinforce Aix's vital cultural life. Eight of Cézanne's paintings now hang in the Musée Granet, and his *atelier* was restored by American patrons and is at No. 9 Avenue Paul Cézanne, open for visits except on Tuesdays. The literature and language courses offered in July are very popular with English and American literati. They are held by the **UNIVERSITÉ DE PROVENCE**, 29 Avenue Robert Schumann in Aix (Tel. 42 59 22 71).

During the summer the town is host to a grand music festival, more refined and formal than the one held in Avignon. Opera, concerts, conferences and a major painting exhibition are held at the Fondation Vasarely. Enquiries should be addressed to 'Festival d'Aix, Palais de l'Ancien Archevêché, 13100 Aix-en-Provence (Tel.

1 Station Thermale 2 Cathedral of Saint Sauveur 3 Musée des Tapisseries 4 Le Vieil Aix

5 La Vieille Auberge, 63 rue Espariat 6 Municipal Casino 7 Musée Granet

42 23 37 81). Each year the 'Artistes du Pays d'Aix' have a three-week exhibition, lectures and a conference at the Salon de Puyloubier, based on the works of Paul Cézanne and his school, including Louis Leydet, Joseph Ravaison and others. The Ecole d'Aix is well known and their annual event is usually held in September.

WHAT TO SEE

The helpful **TOURIST OFFICE**, 2 Place Général de Gaulle (Tel. 42 26 02 93), and the main police station are near the main bus station and the casino. The splendid 1651 Cours Mirabeau runs for half a kilometre east from the Place Général de Gaulle. The seventeenth-century town mansions known as 'Hôtels' worth looking at are No. 2, de Villars, No. 10, d'Entrecasteaux, No. 14, de Rousset Boulbon, No. 19, Arbaud Jouques, and No. 20, Hôtel de Forbin (1656). Altogether there are 80 town mansions of the seventeenth–eighteenth century in Aix. Within walking distance to the north are Le Vieil Aix, the Place des Tanneurs, and the Hôtel de Ville, with its handsome seventeenth-century balcony and sixteenth-century clock tower. The main post office is in the historic Corn Market. Two notable cloisters are the St Sauveur and the St Louis, at 60 boulevard Carnot. The Quartier Mazarin in the old town is the most intriguing sector.

Prince René's court painter was Nicholas Froment, who helped introduce Flemish painters to Aix. In the Cathedral of St Sauveur can be seen his beautiful 'Triptych of the Burning Bush' with portraits of Prince René and his wife. Have a look too at the collection of Flemish tapestries. In the church of Ste Marie-Madeleine is the 1442 'Annunciation' by Jean Chapus.

Aix has ten permanent museums, and the best is the Granet in the Palais de Malte, Place St Jean de Malte (closed Tuesday). François Marius Granet and his friend Jean Auguste Ingres have several delightful paintings here including the latter's 'Jupiter and Thetis'. See too the Cézanne gallery.

The Museum of Old Aix is in the Hôtel d'Estienne de St Jean, designed by Puget. The seventeenth-century Hôtel is at 17 rue Gaston de Saporta and is closed on Monday. The collection is an interesting ragbag of local history and popular customs. See the gallery 'jeux de Fête-Dieu'.

The Musée des Tapisseries has a collection of seventeenth-century Beauvais tapestries, the Fondation St Jean Perse has the MSS of this modern poet, and the Fondation Vasarely, 1 Avenue Marcel Pagnol, Jas de Bouffan (to the west of Aix) is an extraordinary modern building housing the modern artist's pop-art murals. (Closed Tuesday.) Cézanne's *atelier* is in the north of the town at 9 Avenue Paul Cézanne, in its own small park. Well worth a visit (closed Tuesday). The '*route de Cézanne*' is a tour outside Aix, eastwards on the D17 towards the Montagne de Ste Victoire via the village of Le Tholonet. Incidentally Picasso is buried at Vauvenargues, only 17 kilometres east of Aix.

In the evening Aix has various entertainments. The **OPÉRA** is at the eastern end of the Cours Mirabeau. The **THÉÂTRE DE VERDURE** is the open air summer theatre at Paysage du Jas de Bouffan (to the west of the town). The **THÉÂTRE DE L'ARCHEVÊCHÉ** hosts theatre and concerts. The municipal **CASINO**, at 2 bis avenue Napoléon Bonaparte, is open from 3.00pm and in addition to its gaming facilities also has Sunday tea-dances.

Besides its International Music Festival Aix holds its International Dance Festival in July, with performances ranging from classical ballet to modern dance and jazz. Contact the Comité Officiel des Fêtes, 2 bis avenue Victor Hugo (Tel. 42 26 23 38). The Tourist Office arranges daily town tours and half a dozen mini-bus tours to Cassis, Avignon, the Camargue, Roussillon etc. So allow one or two days for a stay in Aix, the cultural city of Provence.

MARSEILLE

gateway to the Orient

This ancient city, founded by the Greeks as 'Massilia' in the sixth century BC, has always been a busy mercantile port, and usually prosperous. Travellers on the Grand Tour came here frequently, but rarely to see the 'antiquities' or excellent museums. The city was seen mainly as a staging point on their journeys to and from Genoa by sea, usually via Nice. John Evelyn visited the town and found it 'well wall'd with an excellent port for ships and galleys'. He admired the large fast King's galley, but pitied the thousands of slaves manacled together as crews. Richard Lassells, also in the seventeenth century, noted 'Marseille stands upon the Mediterranean Sea . . . and hath a most neat Haven and Harbour for ships and Gallies'.

Joseph Addison admired the orchards and gardens of Marseille, 'green olive trees, laid out in beautiful Gardens in depths of winter. I plucked about five different sorts that grew within a yard of each other – also Wild-Time, Lavender, Rosemary, Balme and Myrtle.' Edward Wright was there in 1720–22 and found it 'very pleasant, strait streets, houses well built, the Corso Course, the rendezvous of company in summer evenings with fountains, double row of trees. The Hôtel de Ville a fine building, good sculpture by Monsieur Puget. The Harbour has 20 Galleys, 270 slaves in each. The church of St Victor said to be the first Christian church in France. The Cathedral church said to have been a temple of Diana.'

Many eighteenth-century travellers visited Marseille; Dr Josiah Hort, Bishop of Ferns, in 1720 for his health; Sachaverell Stevens in 1739 took a *felucca* [a small coastal vessel] from Marseille to Genoa, with a good stock of provisions for the voyage, cold tongue, ham, bread and water; Philip Thicknesse wrote that 'the city was crowded with men of all nations walking in the streets in the proper habits of their country'; John Wilkes, the emigré patriot, spent a dissipated month's holiday in Marseille during 1765; Laurence Sterne also spent a month there seven years later, but became ill and suffered from the cold Mediterranean wind, and from a '*bouillon infraîchissant*'. Thomas Glyn in 1784 spent a lengthy 'quarantine' in Marseille, probably because he did not bribe the customs and passport controllers sufficiently!

Most of the travellers referred to the town's export trade in almonds, cloth, salted eels, figs, anchovies, cotton waistcoats and stockings to Italy; and taffetas, box-combs, dimities [cotton fabrics], paper, gum arabic, hardware and drugs to Spain. The population then was 90,000 compared to nearly 900,000 at the end of the twentieth century.

One of the most famous Marseille landmarks is the Château d'If, the castle made legendary by Alexandre Dumas' *Count of Monte Cristo*. Thomas Brand, bearleader, described the château in 1793 as 'a sort of Bastille wherein are held a few state prisoners and young men whose excesses have procured them lodgement, recommended by their fathers!' Sir James Smith commended the Hôtel des Deux Pommes in which he stayed, pronouncing it, 'very good, like Amsterdam'.

When Joseph Spence visited the town with his young charge, his working notes said 'see Mr Olivier who eats at the 13 Cantons table d'hôte and desire him to make the walk of the old town which he did with me and explain to you our reasoning about Caesar's seige of the town'. He approved of 'the new town, several noble streets, country about a long run full of bastides. Port has a fort close to the sea with a Louis XIV fortress (by Vauban).' He counted 17 galleys in the harbour and was told that 8,000 slaves were at work in the port. During a recent plague (1720) 70,000 people had died out of the population of 90,000.

By the end of the eighteenth century, Mariana Starke reported 'Marseilles founded BC 539, a capacious safe harbour for merchant vessels, depth only 4 fathoms, magnificent promenade in the Cours. Puget's Hôtel de Ville has splendid paintings by Seurre, David, Puget. The Lazaretto the best in Europe. One good theatre.' The population had risen to 110,000 and she recommended the Hôtel des Ambassadeurs and the Hôtel des Empereurs. She thought the quay and environs were beautiful but warned against mosquitoes, 'beware scorpions, even in bed'. John Murray in 1840 was more dismissive; 'Marseilles has few fine places, buildings or sights for strangers'.

Four years later 'Boz' and the Dickens family arrived – he in a 'perfectly torpid state' after a long road journey. His 'berline' carriage was hoisted aboard the steamer *Marie Antoinette* bound for Genoa via Nice. On his second visit to Marseille Dickens arrived by '*mailleposte*' and took the steam packet *Charlemagne* for Italy. Lady Shelley walked round the port in 1854, noting that it was 'completely mercantile, reminds me of Liverpool'.

Mark Twain stayed at the Grand Hôtel du Louvre et de la Paix and was displeased with his host, who 'wrote down who we were, where we were born, what our occupations were, the place we came from last, whether we were married or single, how we liked it, how old we were, where we were bound for and when we expected to get there and a great deal of information of similar importance – all for the benefit of the landlord and the secret police'. Even now unwary travellers in France may be asked to complete a *fiche* for the bureaucrats to pore over in our modern EEC!

VISITING MARSEILLE TODAY

WHERE TO STAY

John Murray's hotel recommendations of 1843 included the Orient ('first rate, dear, table d'hôte four frs'), the Richelieu ('good, quiet and moderate, kept by three old ladies, table d'hôte excellent at three frs'), the Hôtel Beauvau ('like all the inns suffers from the evil of horrid smells'), and the Hôtels des Empereurs and du Paradis.

Later in the nineteenth century, the Grand Hôtel du Louvre et de la Paix in the rue de Noailles (where Mark Twain stayed), was deemed to be excellent, as was the Grand Hôtel de Marseille.

Now, the three-star **GRAND HÔTEL DE NOAILLES**, 68 La Canebière (Tel. 91 54 91 48), has 71 rooms, but no restaurant. The more modest one-star **LE RICHELIEU**, 52 Corniche Président J.F. Kennedy (Tel. 91 31 01 92) has 21 rooms and has a restaurant on the ground floor. The **PORTE DE L'ORIENT**, 6 rue de la Bonneterie (Tel. 91 90 68 64), two stars, has 51 rooms.

WHAT TO EAT AND DRINK

Marseille fish cuisine is known the world over. Try '*bouillabaisse*', a fish stew with saffron; mussels, eels and lobster may be included, but it is

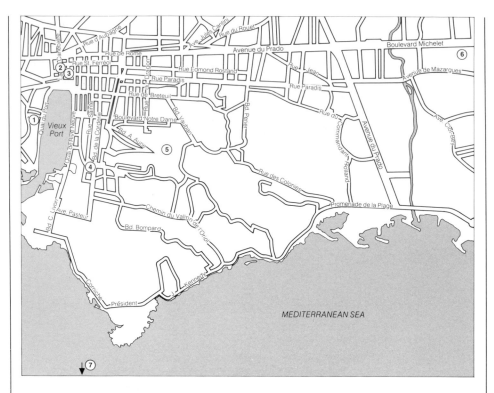

1 Musée du Vieux Marseille   **2** Grand Hôtel de Noailles, 68 La Canebière   **3** Hôtel Beauvau, 4 rue Beauvau

4 Basilica Saint Victor   **5** Basilica of Notre Dame de la Garde   **6** Corbusier Cité Radieuse   **7** Chateau d'If

essential that they are fresh – think of poor Laurence Sterne! In the Vieux Port there are many fish restaurants on the Quai de Rive Neuve (the Rascasse-Dauphine, and the Aux Deux Soeurs), and the Quai du Port (the Miramar and the Caruso) which serve excellent *bouillabaisse*. (Note that for this speciality most restaurants prefer to have your order in advance.) At the Quai des Belges the fishermen sell their catch direct from their boats each morning. Try the New York restaurant's '*bouillabaisse de baudroie*', '*bourride Provençale*', and '*poissons du goffe*'. Perhaps the best sea-food of all is at **MICHEL** (Brasserie des Catalans), 6 rue des Catalans, sited at the southeast end of the Vieux Port and run by the Visciano family. The best area for regional specialities is around the Cours Julien. Try **LE TIRE-BOUCHON** at No. 11, **LE CAUCASE** at No. 62, the **FACÉTIES** at No. 38, **LA GARBURE** at No. 9, and **CHEZ BENOÎT** at No. 26. If you like North African *couscous* then the area round the rue Longue des Capucins is the place – *in daytime*.

The regional wines are the vins de Cassis (served at the Michel and Calypso restaurants). The small port of Cassis is between Marseille and Bandol to the east. The white wine is delicious, made from a blend of Marsanne, Ugni Blanc, Clairette, Grenache Blanc and Sauvignon grapes. Only three-quarters of a million bottles are produced each year from 150 hectares. Look for Clos Boudard and Château Fontblanche. The Fête du Vin in Cassis is held on the first Sunday in September.

The vineyards of Bandol are between Toulon and Marseille, producing mainly red and rosé from 1,000 hectares of limestone soil. The famous reds need eighteen months in wooden casks, are strong, spicy, almost peppery, and have a long life. Look for Le Moulin de la Rogue from the Co-op, Domaine de Pibarnon and Domaine de l'Hermitage. The Fête des Vins de Bandol is held on the first and second Sundays in December.

WHAT TO SEE

Alexandre Dumas called Marseille 'the meeting place of the entire world' and many travellers commented on the diversity of races to be seen there. There are North Africans, gypsies, Indians and sailors from all around the world. It is a tough town, an exciting town; make the best of it, but at the same time be careful – particularly at night.

Marseille is famous for a wide variety of reasons. It is France's greatest port, and 40 per cent of her exports start here. During the French Revolution five hundred volunteers sang a rousing song known as the 'Marseillaise', which subsequently became the National Anthem. The principal and best-known street is La Canebière, which winds down from the squares of Verdun and Stalingrad (close to the zoo) to the Vieux Port. Take a stroll down this exhilarating boulevard, more famous now than the long, right-angled Prado which attracted the travellers. Dumas' island of Château d'If is a fifteen-minute boat trip from the Quai des Belges. One can book boats to the Ile de Frioul, a large green island, and in the summer along the coast to Cassis.

Marseille is also known for Le Corbusier's seventeen-storey Cité Radieuse, built in the early 1950s. It houses 2,000 people, (east of the Prado) with apparently modern, moderately priced housing. It is doubtful whether the travellers would have approved – *chacun à son goût*! The Vieux Port is most picturesque, although no large boats use it now. It is flanked on west and east sides by restaurants, and ships' chandlers catering for the hundreds of yachts. The Port Moderne was rebuilt after World War II.

The ecclesiastical buildings are not amongst France's greats! The fortified Basilica of St Victor, southeast of the Vieux Port, with a fifth-century crypt, is worth a visit. So too is the Basilica of Notre Dame de la Garde, on a limestone rock one kilometre east of the Vieux Port, which has a superb view, best seen at sunset. The Cathedral of Sainte Marie-Majeure was built in Romano-Byzantine style in the nineteenth century (as was La Garde).

The **TOURIST OFFICE** is well sited at the top end of the Vieux Port at No. 4 La Canebière (Tel. 91 54 91 11), close to the Hôtel de Ville. They recommend two town tours, either by coach or on foot. The former calls at Porte d'Aix (Triumphal Arch), the Cathedral, St Laurent's Church, Hôtel de Ville, Notre Dame de la Garde, Corniche Président J.F Kennedy, Parc Borely, Le Corbusier estate and La Canebière. The tour on foot covers the old town to the west of the Vieux Port with sixteen 'ports of call' and takes a complete morning. Ask for the leaflet '*17 panneaux autour du vieux port*'. The 24 markets are open in the mornings, including fish, flower, general food, *aux puces* and *aux timbres*.

The travellers on the Grand Tour would be amazed at Marseille's modern Métro system. The main stations are Vieux Port, Colbert, St Charles, Noailles, Castellane and Estrangin. Fast, clean and quiet, it makes sightseeing easy. There are two lines, and a map is available at the Vieux Port station.

Many people do not realize that Marseille, the most important city in the south of France, has a wealth of museums. To be precise there are twelve, of which the Musée des Beaux-Arts in the Palais Longchamp is the best-known. The French School of the seventeenth to nineteenth centuries includes drawings and sculptures by Pierre Puget and Daumier, and paintings by Perugino, Rubens and David. Sited in the Place Berner, the spectacular fountain, colonnade and the bird collection in the *jardin zoologique* (look for Mark Twain's stork) make the Beaux-Arts an essential visit. The Corot, Ingres and Dufy works are noteworthy too.

Nearby is the Musée Grobet-Labadié, 149 Boulevard Longchamp – a superbly furnished mansion which houses a diverse collection of Provençal armour, musical instruments, Italian and Flemish primitives, faiences, and Gobelins tapestries. The Musée Cantini, 19 rue

Grignan, a seventeenth-century town mansion, has a good collection of Provençal ceramics and modern art, as well as frequent temporary exhibitions. The Musée du Vieux-Marseille, in the 1570 Maison Diamentée is at No. 2 rue de la Prison. Appropriate too, because part of the permanent exhibition concerns the arsenal of the notorious galleys and their thousands of wretched slaves, seen by John Evelyn and James Boswell. The salle des Santons, little biblical statuettes of coloured clay, is certainly worth seeing. Marseille runs a Santons fair in December. The santons are made traditionally by twenty families living on the coast between Nice and Marseille. The Musée des Docks Romains du Lacydon, Place Vivaux, is in the old quarter of the town, and is devoted to the excavations of the Roman docks dating two thousand years back in time. The archeological museum is housed in the Château and Park of Borely.

MUSIC IN MARSEILLES

Marseille has a selection of music festivals throughout the long summer, held mainly in the Palais and Jardin du Pharo, on the southeast side of the Vieux Port. Classical music concerts are given at the Eglise du Sacré Coeur, and Cathédrale de la Major. The London Symphony Orchestra plays at the Centre de la Vieille-Charité, there is international folk music at the Château Gombert, opera at the Château Borely. Circus, jazz, Glenn Miller Revival Orchestra, Carmen and Joan Baez at the Théâtre aux Etoiles. The Golden Jazz Club is at 40 rue Plan Fourmiguier, and the Opéra is at 1 place Reyer. In addition there are a dozen theatres offering a wide variety of choices. There are four Café-Théâtres. The 'Gateway to the Orient' has a very wide range of '*événements*', so plan to spend a couple of days here.

NICE

_____ *capital of the Riviera* _____

Originally 'Nicaea' was founded by Phoenicians from Marseille in the fourth century BC. The Romans, however, built the small town of Cemenelum (modern Cimiez) just west of the river Paillon. The glorious Bay of the Angels must have been beautiful to every beholder. For the next thousand years, ownership of Nice-Cimiez changed hands repeatedly, belonging to the counts of Provence, of Savoy, of Monaco, of Tende and of Sardinia. Although it was French-owned in 1792, it was handed over in 1814 to Sardinia, and as recently as 1860 it voted for union with France at the Treaty of Turin. Its population in 1815 was 23,500, in 1860 it was 40,000 and today it stands at 340,000.

Lord and Lady Cavendish lived in Nice in the 1730s and introduced English society to the town. Their son, Henry Cavendish, the chemist, was born there in 1731. Edward Young, author of *Night Thoughts,* spent the winter of 1736–37 in Nice, as did William Dowdeswell MP in 1744.

In the middle of the eighteenth century Nice was a large village *en route* from Marseille or Toulon to Genoa. As most travellers made that journey by sea, and there were no remarkable 'antiquities' in Nice, it was quite undiscovered, although James Paterson, a general in the King of Sardinia's army, was Commandant of Nice from 1752 to 1765. The Duke of York went there in 1764, as did James Boswell aged 25, in the following year. He saw a religious procession, met M. Julien the French Consul, Lord Breadalbane, Lord and Lady Glenorchy and Dr Ramsay of Edinburgh.

In January 1764 the irascible Scottish novelist, Tobias George Smollett, went to Nice for his health and rented a flat there for fifteen months. He never liked the place. 'A stranger must conduct himself with the utmost circumspection to be able to live among these people without being the dupe of imposition.' He bathed, and his health improved, but he remained tetchy. The shopkeepers were 'greedy and over-reaching', the artisans 'lounge about the ramparts, bask themselves in the sun, or play at bowls in the streets from morning till night'. 'There are no tolerable pictures, busts, statues or edifices . . . There is not even a bookseller in Nice . . . they are unacquainted with music.' Nevertheless, he was involved with the building of the port of Lympia. The first esplanade was laid out in 1770 when the Duke of Gloucester visited Nice, and the first casino appeared in 1777.

By 1784 three hundred English tourists were regularly spending the winter in Nice *en route* for Italy. They bathed each day for their asthma, bronchitis, and neurasthenia, since the climate is as near perfect as can be. They lived mainly in the Quartier de Villanuova in the west of Nice, then moved to the Quartier Croix de Marbre. They called it Newborough. The Duke of Bedford, Lady Fitzgerald, Duchess of Cumberland, and Lady Penelope Rivers (wife of George Pitt) gave Nice much 'ton'. The French Revolution had a considerable effect on the English colony. Arthur Young passed through in 1787 and wrote that in the previous winter 57 English and 9 French 'families' had wintered there, but on his visit the reverse was true.

During his lengthy stay, Arthur Young put up at the Hôtel de Quatre Nations for five shillings a day all in. He visited the remains of the Roman amphitheatre and aqueduct and thought Nice a flourishing town with new prosperous buildings and many gardens full of oranges. The streets were straight and broad, very well built, and the sea views fine. He went on walks and gathered some plants that were in blossom. But Nice was the resort of foreigners, principally English, who passed the winter there.

Mariana Starke's guide recommended the Hôtel des Etrangers as very good, and the Hôtel de York as adequate. 'The situation of Nice is cheerful, the walks and rides are pretty, the lodging houses numerous and tolerably convenient, the eatables good and plentiful, the wine and oil excellent. The Citadel of Mont Albano overhangs the town and the Paglion torrent separates it from the English quarter.' 'Beware,' she wrote, 'the Vent de Bise, a searching wind.'

The orange crops failed in 1822 and the Reverend Lewis Way, a wealthy clergyman, started a fund 'for the repair of the English Walk by the Unemployed Poor,' and thus the magnificent Promenade des Anglais was built from 1820–24. When it was finished, Talleyrand and Metternich, powerful, influential statesmen both, visited Nice and its popularity was thereby assured. Henry Lord Brougham, a friend of King Louis-Philippe visited Nice in 1834, then aged 56, with his sickly daughter. Cholera had broken out in Provence and no entry visas were available, so they put up at the Hôtel Pinchinat on the Fréjus road. He fell in love with Nice, purchased the Villa Eléonore for his daughter, and they wintered there ever after.

A few years later Lady Blessington made 'a dangerous undertaking on the mule track route' to see Lord Byron at Genoa. In 1815 there had been 100 English families in Nice, by 1827 147 families and in 1857/8 it had risen to no less than 800 families. In 1839 there were 21 auberges and inns for a population of 34,000; this had risen by 1858 to 20 hotels and 60 auberges. Nice was much cheaper for the English than Aix-en-Provence, and the English doctor J.B. Davis ministered to them. In the Faubourg la Croix de Marbre, the transient English had 'leurs habitudes, leur temple, leur cimitière'. In 1847 the English church was charged with 'prosélytisme au profit de l'anglicanisme' and the vicar had to flee to neighbouring Cannes!

John Ruskin was on his architectural Grand Tour in 1845. He travelled via Dijon, Digne and Draguignan towards the Italian frontier and breakfasted on fried trout, sweetbread and asparagus on the way to Nice. 'The Corniche above Nice and Monaco is far finer than I thought. It is very superb and the entrance here among the Indian figs and heavy laden lemon trees with crowds of peasantry coming home with their orange baskets full of yellow fruit and glittering leaves upon their heads and the intense purple sea are more to me than I could have conceived.'

Queen Victoria and her family set the royal seal of approval. Calling herself the Comtesse de Balmoral (hence the rash of hotels of that name) she travelled in the Royal Train from London to the Riviera. Her party spent five winters in Cimiez/Nice, one in Hyères/Toulon, and one in Grasse as well as Aix-les-Bains and Florence. The Queen strolled and sketched, visited *all* the cemeteries, and watched the Battle of Flowers in Nice. Initially she stayed at the Grand Hôtel or the Hôtel Excelsior Regina in Cimiez, and in 1897 she opened the Regina Palace. Her son, the Prince of Wales, played the games of chance (and with the ladies of the stage) at Cannes – but not when Mother was in residence in Nice!

VISITING NICE TODAY

WHERE TO STAY

In 1893 John Murray made recommendations to travellers about hotels in Nice. The Hôtel-Pension Suisse near the Grand Opéra and casino had a Sanitary Certificate signed by Hugh Smith, Engineer Surveyor of the English Sanitary Company of Nice. The Grand Hôtel d'Angleterre, the Métropole, and the Paradis (M. Crepaux) were good. The Hôtel de Nice was excellent, with the best situation for asthma and sufferers of nervous afflictions. The Hôtel de France was one of the best.

The world-famous white Hôtel Négresco with its pink-tiled roof was built as recently as 1913 and so does not qualify as a Grand Tour Hôtel. The **HÔTEL SUISSE**, 15 quai Rauba-Capeu (Tel. 93 62 33 00), with two stars, has 40 rooms, superb views and a very good value restaurant. The **HÔTEL DE FRANCE**, 24 Boulevard Raimbaldi (Tel. 93 85 18 04), with one star, has 45 rooms. The **HÔTEL NICE-PALACE**, 2 rue Eugène Emmanuel (Tel. 93 87 96 14), two stars, has 48 rooms. Others with Victorian links are the Westminster, the West End and the Windsor, but the Victoria is modern.

WHERE TO EAT

There are several hundred restaurants, brasseries and pizzerias in Nice. As in Marseille, '*bouillabaisse*' is a seafood stew speciality. Some of

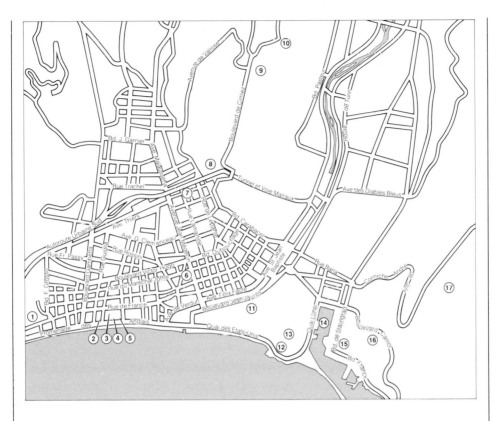

1 Musée Chéret 2 Hôtel Négresco, 37 Promenade des Anglais 3 Musée Massena

4 West End Hôtel, 31 Promenade des Anglais 5 Westminster Hôtel, 27 Promenade des Anglais 6 Russian Orthodox Cathedral

7 Hôtel de France, 24 Boulevard Raimbaldi 8 Musée Chagall 9 Cimiez 10 Roman ruins

11 The Cathedral of Saint Réparate 12 Hôtel Suisse, 15 Quai Rauba-Capeu 13 The Château Sainte Hélène

14 Vieux Port 15 Lazaret 16 Lympia 17 The Citadel of Mont Albano

the best restaurants in which to try this dish are on the Quai des Etats-Unis, the eastern continuation of the Boulevard des Anglais. Try **GIRELLE ROYAL** at No. 41 or **PRINCES** at No. 57. At the harbour called Bassin Lympia is the excellent **LA CASSINE** at 26 Quai Lunel. Try their '*soupe de poissons à la rouille*', or the '*friture de la Baie des Anges*' with '*ratatouille*' (the famous Niçois dish of tomato, onions, egg-plant, garlic, peppers and olive oil).

At the **BARALE** restaurant, 39 rue de Beaumont (Tel. 93 89 17 94), the eccentric family of that name have been in business for a century. **LA MERENDA**, 4 rue de la Terrasse, is the best place for specialities Niçoises (no phone), but the **CHANTECLER**, 37 Promenade des Anglais (main restaurant of the Négresco) has the most stars. Try their '*gratinée* *de lapereau aux champignons'* with a local vin de Cassis, or *'le Cannet des Maures'*. **L'ÂNE ROUGE** and **LA POULARDE CHEZ LUCULLUS** are also highly starred, and both serve Bellet wines (see below), as does the **BOCCACCIO** in the rue Masséna with excellent sea-food and wines. One of the best wine bars on the Riviera is the **BISTRO DE LA PROMENADE**, 7 Promenade des Anglais (Tel. 93 81 63 48).

WHAT TO EAT AND DRINK

Nice cuisine is a happy blend of Provençal and Italian. A typical dish is *'pissaladière'*, an open tart with onions, olives, anchovies and tomatoes. *'Salade Niçoise'* is composed of tomatoes, beans, anchovies, olives, peppers and boiled eggs. *'Pistou'* is a sauce of cheese, garlic and basil, pounded in olive oil. Fish dishes are prepared from red mullet (*rouget*), tunny (*thon*), monkfish (*lotte*), sea bass (*loup*), scorpion fish (*racasse*) and of course sardines and anchovies.

Now for a secret. Nice has its very own Appellation Contrôlée wine called Bellet, grown on 40 hectares (100 acres) of vineyards a few kilometres from the northern suburbs. There is red, rosé or white, but the latter is best, grown from the grape varietals called Rolle, Roussanne, Clairette, Bourboulenc and the more familiar Chardonnay. Look for the Château de Bellet wine from St Roman de Bellet. Not inexpensive however! Also the Château de Crémat has a classic red, Folle Noire. Incidentally for wine lovers interested in the wines of Provence there are courses at Les Sommeliers de Provence, Lycée Hôtelier de Nice, 144 rue de France, 06000 Nice (Tel. 93 86 92 11).

WHAT TO SEE AND DO

The eighteenth and nineteenth century travellers would approve of modern Nice. Now one of France's five largest cities, it has the best communications outside Paris. To the west of the Promenade des Anglais is Nice Airport (Tel. 93 72 30 30), with runways pushing out into the Mediterranean; it handles more traffic than any other provincial airport. To the north of the town is the Autoroute A8, running 58 kilometres to San Remo in Italy to the east and 188 kilometres to Marseille to the west. The smooth comfortable railway line hugs the coast, parallel to the A8, with frequent express and local services. Ferry-boats leave Nice port regularly for Corsica. Bookings from SNCM, 3 Avenue Gustave V. The bus station (*Gare routier*), Promenade de Paillon, has services to Monaco, Menton, Antibes, Juan-les-Pins and Cannes.

The main **TOURIST OFFICE** in Avenue Thiers (Tel. 93 87 07 07) is adjacent to the railway station. There, the staff cater manfully for the eight million tourists who visit Nice each summer. Amazingly the city absorbs these tourists without too much fuss. There are nearly three hundred Council gardeners who start work at 5.00am to keep the 750 acres of parks and squares pristine.

The most interesting section of the town, apart from the three-mile-long palm-tree-lined Boulevard des Anglais, is the Vieille Ville, a triangle between the Château-dominated hill, the Quai des Etats Unis and the parks of the Boulevard Jean Jaurès. The old town is still called Nizza and maintains its medieval Italian atmosphere.

The travellers of old would have complained of the winding, narrow, inevitably dirty streets, with the old ochre, pink and terracotta houses six or seven storeys high, leaning towards each other. Geraniums and petunias and songbirds mingle with the washing strung across streets often only twelve to fifteen feet across. Down below in the Cours Saleya are bread shops with *real* pizza, '*fougasses*' and '*tapenade*', and the flower, fish and vegetable markets are in the lee of the château. Fascinating, but watch out for pickpockets (probably tenth generation pickpockets!).

The next sector of interest is Cimiez, three kilometres inland, with streets named Prince de Galles, Avenue George V, Boulevard Edouard VII, Avenue Colonel Evans, and Avenue Reine Victoria clustered around the Roman antiquities and the Musée Matisse (closed Monday). The Chagall Museum, closed Tuesday, is half-way between Cimiez and the Hôtel Négresco.

There were once nine '*palais-hôtels*' housing the royal families of Britain, Russia, Belgium, Portugal, Sweden and Denmark. Tobias' Smollett, the Scots writer, has a street named after him too, inland, and parallel to, the rue Bonaparte. He would have liked that! Our Captain Scott, Edith Cavell and Shakespeare have also been remembered by the Niçois.

The new town, well laid out and prosperous, starts on the front with the Hôtel Négresco, the excellent Musée Masséna, closed Monday (Napoleon's Field Marshal and Garibaldi were two of Nice's leading sons), the Casino, the Jardin Albert I and, inland a little, the marvellous Russian Orthodox Cathedral, Boulevard du Tzarewitch, first consecrated in 1912. To the west near the sea front is the old-fashioned hotel harbouring the Musée Jules Chéret (closed Monday) which contains lovely works by Raoul Dufy, and the Impressionists, Monet, Boudin and Sisley.

There are many more museums – Art Naïf in the Château Ste Hélène; the Palais Lascaris; the Terra Amata; the Prieuré du Vieux Logis; the Musée Naval; but the jewels in the crown are the Matisse, Jules Chéret, Marc Chagall and the Masséna. It is doubtful whether any town outside Paris can match Nice for the high quality and diverse range of these 'antiquities'.

The three churches of interest, besides the Russian Cathedral, are the Eglise St Jacques, the Cathedral of Ste Réparate and the church of St Martin–St Augustin, the first two being in the old town, the latter near the main post office.

One clue to the cultural background of Nice can be gathered from the names of these streets and squares: rue Berlioz, Félix Faure, rue Gounod, place Mozart, rue Paganini, rue Rossini and rue Verdi. Not surprisingly, Nice is host to operas, concert orchestras and a world famous jazz festival in July.

The grand highlight of Nice, indeed of the whole Riviera, is the Carnival usually held 11–24 February each year. Processions, confetti throwing, floats, beauty queens, papier-mâché comic heads – the Carnival dates from 1830 when the aristocracy threw bouquets from their carriages to the crowds watching the King (their King) of Sardinia go by. The effigy of King Carnival is burned on Mardi Gras (Shrove Tuesday).

Each summer there are two one-day Battles of the Flowers about 23 July and 6 August. Fireworks, balls, the Casino, folklore festival, many night-clubs, opera, horse racing, three miles of beaches and two hundred restaurants – Nizza la Bella!

ITALY

and the Italians

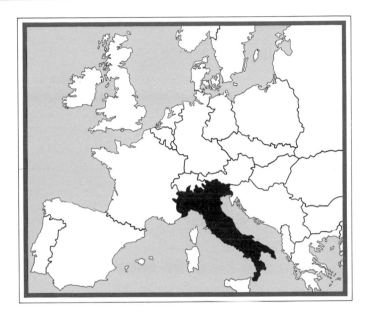

The main object of the Grand Tour was to visit the 'antiquities' of Italy. Florence and Rome were considered essential, Naples and Venice most desirable, and the cities in between – Genoa, Milan, Turin, Pisa, Bologna, Vicenza and Padua – were of varying degrees of importance. Italy was famous as a country of great 'Musicke'. Of the fifteen finest opera houses in Europe no less than eleven were to be found in Italy. The four best were Bologna, Reggio, Milan and Naples, and in the second rank Vicenza, Genoa, Rome, Siena, Florence, Padua and Turin.

The travellers' itineraries varied in that the border in the northwest was crossed either laboriously by '*voiturin*' through the Alps to Turin and Milan, or along the coast road from Marseille to Genoa, or by ship from Toulon or Nice to Leghorn. Coming from Flanders or Germany, one route came via Trento and Treviso to Venice. Rome and Naples were visited on the outward-bound route and vice versa on the return, thence to Venice via Perugia, Bologna and Padua. From Venice the usual routes were a return westwards via Vicenza, Verona, Brescia and Milan or north through the

Dolomites to Bolzano, into Austria and on towards Vienna.

During the nineteenth century large numbers of artists, writers and sculptors – English and American – were to be found in Florence and Rome. Some of our greatest men and women of letters, verse and oils looked for and found inspiration in Italy. They included Byron, Shelley, Keats, Dickens, Turner, Bonington and many others. Royalty too came to the south. Jacobite Kings, Henry IX and Charles III are buried in Rome, and Queen Victoria came to Florence to sketch.

Travellers had widely varying views of France and the French, but for the most part, for the three centuries recorded in this chapter, opinions on Italy and of the Italians were generally unanimous. Their music was praised, their inns were condemned out of hand, the squalor of their towns was noted, their light-hearted dishonesty was accepted, and their antiquities were usually admired, but unlike the French, the Italians were, usually, loved!

'Italy is the garden of the world, so is Lombardy
the garden of Italy, and Venice the garden of
Lombardy, wholly plaine and beautified with such
abundance of goodly rivers, pleasant meadowes,
fruitful vineyards, fat pastures, delectable gardens,
orchards, woods – the butter thereof is oyle, the
dew honey and the milk nectar.'
THOMAS CORYAT 1609

'There are a good many things about this Italy
which I do not understand – and more especially I
cannot understand how a bankrupt government
can have such palatial railroad depots and such
marvels of turnpikes. Why, these latter are as hard
as adamant, as straight as a line, as smooth as a
floor and as white as snow.'
MARK TWAIN 1856

'I have the Pisan mountains, the noble peaks of
Carrara and the Apennines towards Parma, all
burning in the sunset, or purple and dark against
it, and the olive woods towards Massa, and the
wide rich, viny plain towards Florence – the

ITALY

Apennines still loaded with snow and purple in the
green sky, and the clearness of the sky here is
something miraculous. No romance can be too
high flown for it – it passes fable.'

JOHN RUSKIN 1845

at Lucca

'The gardens are adorned with statues, laber-
inthes, fountaines, vines, myrtle, palme, cetron,
lemon, orange and cedar trees with lawrels,
mulberries, roses, rosemary and all kinds of fruits
and flowers so as they seem
an earthly Paradice.'

FYNES MORYSON 1595

from Naples

'I love the Italians. It is impossible to live among
them and not love them. Their faults are many –
the faults of the oppressed – love of pleasure,
disregard of truth, indolence and violence of
temper. But their falsehood is on the surface
– it is not deceit. . . . They are affectionate, simple
and earnestly desirous to please. There is life,
energy and talent in every look and word, grace
and refinement in every act and gesture. They are
a noble race of men – a beautiful race of women
. . . the country of Dante and Michael Angelo and
Raphael still exists.'

MARY SHELLEY 1840

'Two thirds of these [the population] are women, I
think, and at least two thirds of the women are
beautiful. They are dressy and as tasteful and as
graceful as they could possibly be without being
angels. They are very fair and many of them have
blue eyes, but black and dreamy dark brown eyes
are met with oftenest.'

MARK TWAIN 1856

in Genoa

'The Italians are generally reckoned men of spirit
and of a character rather more serious than light;
but when the season requires foolery there are no
people in the world that give in to it so much. Why
are the Italians that are a solid and grave people
the most fond of drolleries on their stage and
greater dealers in burlesque than any other nation?
But their drolleries are very low and violent.'
. . . 'Most of the churches in Italy are refuges for
rogues: in Florence there were eight or ten
idle fellows lying on the grass; robbers,
but the greater part murderers,
playing at cards.'

JOSEPH SPENCE 1740

ON ITALIAN CARNIVAL

'There are but three days more but the last two
are to have balls all the morning at the fine
unfinished palace of the Strozzi and the Tuesday
night a masquerade after supper: they sup first to
eat *gras* and not encroach upon Ash-Wednesday.
What makes masquerading more agreeable here
than in England, is the great deference that is
showed to the disguised.'

HORACE WALPOLE 1740

in Florence

ON ITALIAN STYLE

'The more I see of Italy the more I am persuaded
that the Italians have a style in everything which
distinguishes them almost essentially from all
other Europeans. Where they have got it, whether
from natural genius or ancient imitation and
inheritance I shall not examine, but
the fact is certain.'

LADY MARY WORTLEY MONTAGU 1716

96

ON 'CICESBOES'

'Every lady when she marries fixes on a gentleman, sometimes a relation, not always. He visits
her at the toilette, determines where to pass the
evening, leaves her till the afternoon.
They go together on public walks,
to the 'conversazione' or to the opera.
He hands her about, presents her
coffee, sorts her cards and attends her with as
much assiduity as if he were her lover.'

JUVENILE TRAVELLERS

describing the strange 'Cicesbo' Social System

ON ROMANCE

'Floated through the streets in my gondola and
received charming salutes from barred windows:
from one notably where a very pretty damsel lost
in langour hung with her loose-robed bosom
against the iron and pressed amorously to see me
pass, till she could no further . . . return, and lo as
I came slowly into view she as slowly arranged her
sweet shape to be seen decently, and so she stood,
but half a pace in the recess with one dear hand on
one shoulder, her head slightly lying on her neck,
her drooped eyelids mournfully seeming to say
"No, no never! tho' I am dying to be wedded to
that wish of yours" . . .'

GEORGE MEREDITH 1861

from Milan, of Venice

ON 'LADIES OF THE NIGHT'

'Here [at the Ridotti] you meet ladies of pleasure
and married women who under the protection of a
mask enjoy all the diversions of the carnival, but

97

are usually attended by the husband or his spies.
Here the gentlemen are at liberty to rally and
address the ladies but must take care to keep
within the bounds of decency, lest they meet with
bravoes or assassins. Those who could not afford
to keep a mistress for their own particular use join
in with two or three friends and have one in
common amongst them.
When the nobility have done with
their concubines, they become courtesans.
Of these there are streets full, who receive all
comers . . . these dress in the gayest colours with
their breasts open and their faces bedaubed with
paint, standing by dozens at the doors and
windows to invite their customers.'
THOMAS NUGENT'S *GUIDE* 1750

ON ITALIAN CUISINE AND INNS

'Italians use little forks when they eat their meats
so no need to use your fingers, made of yron or
steele, or silver by Gentlemen. [The] Italian
cannot by any means indure to have his dish
touched with fingers seeing all men's fingers are
not alike cleane.'
THOMAS CORYAT 1609

(Subsequently Coryat adopted this strange habit on his travels in Italy, Germany and back home.)

'The Italians frequently eat kites, hawks, magpies,
jackdaws, and other lesser birds [and] even
buffaloes and crows. They are fond of boiled snails
served up with pepper and oil, fried frogs dressed
the same. Antipasto, a dish of giblets boiled with
salt and pepper, mixed white of eggs, next two or
three different ragout, then minestra
di grasso, or di magro.'
THE TRAVELLERS' GUIDE 1770

'Give what scope you please to your fancy, you
will never imagine half the disagreeableness that
Italian beds, Italian cooks, Italian post-houses,
Italian postillions, and Italian nastiness offer to an
Englishman in an Italian journey; much more to
an English woman. At Turin, Milan, Venice,
Rome, and, perhaps, two or three other towns, you
meet with good accommodation; but no words can
express the wretchedness of the other inns. No
other bed but one of straw, and next to that a dirty
sheet, sprinkled with water, and, consequently,
damp; for a covering you have another sheet, as
coarse as the first, and as coarse as one of your
kitchen jack-towels, with a dirty coverlet. The
bedsted consists of four wooden forms, or benches;
an English Peer and Peeress must lye in this
manner, unless they carry an upholsterer's shop
with them, which is very troublesome. There are,
by the bye, no such things as curtains, and hardly,
from Venice to Rome, that cleanly and most useful
invention, a privy; so that what should be collected
and buried in oblivion, is forever under
your nose and eyes.'

ARTHUR YOUNG 1786

ON THE ENGLISH IN ITALY

'The winter I passed at Rome, there was an
unusual concourse of English, many of them with
great Estates and their own masters. As they had
no admittance to the Roman ladies, nor understood the language, they had no way of passing
their Evenings, but in my Apartment where I had
allwaies a full drawing room. Their Governors
encourag'd their assiduities as much as they could,
finding I gave them lessons of Oeconomy and good
conduct and my Authority was so great it was a
common Threat amongst them – "I'll tell Lady
Mary what you say" – I was judge of all their

disputes and my Decisions allwaies submitted to.
While I staid, there was neither gameing, drinking, quarrelling or keeping.'
LADY MARY WORTLEY MONTAGU 1741
in Rome

'The English indeed are true Romans . . . they are
lawmakers and bridge builders, they carry England with them wherever they go – even to clothes:
his shooting jacket, checked trousers and brown
gaiters proclaim his nationality before he begins to
speak: he rarely yields to the seduction of a
moustache: he is inflexibly loyal to tea: and will
make a hard fight before consenting to dine at an
earlier hour than five' . . . 'The most ignorant men
I saw on the Continent were Englishmen. No
American would be found upon the soil of Europe
so profoundly ignorant. Though he might have left
home with as little knowledge, he would have
bolted the contents of half a dozen guide-books on
the voyage.'
GEORGE STILLMAN HILLARD
(*from Boston*) 1847, *writing from Florence*

But let dear 'Boz' have the last word. Charles Dickens and his ladies
enjoyed their Grand Tour, and Pictures from Italy recounts their adventure.
'Let us not remember Italy the less regardfully, because in every fragment of
her fallen Temples and every stone of her deserted palaces and prisons she
helps to inculcate the lesson that the wheel of time is rolling for an end . . .'

MODERN ITALY

There are so many marvellous towns and cities that should be seen that it is
difficult to give impartial advice. Certainly any modern tour *must* take in
Venice, Florence, Rome and Naples. No question that these cities of the
antiquities were the main *raison d'être* of the Grand Tour. But what of the
university towns of Bologna, Padua and Verona? Perhaps if time is limited

the northwestern cities of Turin, Genoa and Milan *can* be dispensed with. The travellers coming by carriage had to visit these cities and indeed found them more enchanting perhaps than would the traveller of today.

Communications now are absurdly easy. International airports abound in Italy, served by Air Italia, British Airways, and Air France from Paris or Nice. The modern *autostradas* bring far-flung Naples within easy distance, as do the remarkably cheap Italian railways (despite their cumbersome system of surcharges).

Parking in the big cities is difficult, and Italian driving anywhere is aggressive, so there is a lot to be said for the admirable package tours by bus, or fly and train holidays offered by many companies such as Pegasus, Thomas Cook, The Magic of Italy, Saga, Swan Hellenic and Time Off.

ROME

the 'Eternal City'

William Shakespeare was the greatest publicist for the Grand Tours. Who could not long to visit Venice, Florence, Verona, and above all Rome after seeing *Julius Caesar* at the Mermaid? Under Pope Urban VIII, Bernini's baroque talent had made Rome the undisputed artistic capital of Europe.

Three early travellers to Rome were Sir Philip Sidney, Sir Henry Wotton and Fynes Moryson. Fear of the Inquisition caused the Protestant visitors to adopt various disguises. Wotton in 1587 came wearing a 'mighty blue feather' in his black hat, disguised as a German Catholic. Moryson appeared as a poor, humble pilgrim with a letter of introduction to the English Cardinal Allan and one Master Warmington, who guided him in Rome. His recollections of 1595 are still valid four centuries later. Rome was, he wrote, 'a terrestriall Paradise by reason of the fountains, statues, caves, groves, fishponds, cages of birds, Nightingales flying loose in the groves, and the most pleasant prospect'. He climbed the Seven Hills of Rome – the Palatine, Aventine, Capitoline, Esquiline, Viminal, Caelian and Quirinal. The River Tiber overflowed during his visit, but he drank the celebrated wines of Fondi and Cecubo instead. He inspected St Peter's, the Pope's Palace and famous Library ('147 walking paces long, had three rowes of cubbards filled with books'), the House of Pontius Pilate, the Caracalla Baths, the Pillar of Emperor Trajan and numerous other famous antiquities.

John Milton spent two months in Rome 22 years after Shakespeare's death, viewing the antiquities and the Vatican library. The three most precious relics were considered to be the spear which had pierced Christ on the Cross, St Veronica's handkerchief, and a piece of the True Cross. Other relics to be seen were the bodies of St Peter and St Paul, the rope with which Judas hanged himself and St Luke's portrait of Christ.

A description of the Coronation of Pope Innocent V in February 1645 was made by John Evelyn. 'The streets this night were as light as day, full of bonfires, canon roaring, fountains running wine, all in excess of joy and triumph.' Evelyn enjoyed the Roman Carnival on 13 February, and visited the Catacombs of Domitilla, Hadrian's Villa, and the Villa d'Este at the Tivoli, built in 1560.

The road to Rome from the north lay by way of Perugia or Siena, and from Florence the journey took three days. Both roads were considered by the travellers as being reasonable. Already in the seventeenth century curiosity not only to see the antiquities but also to acquire them and bring them back to stately homes in England and Scotland, brought distinguished travellers to Rome and Naples. Sir Andrew Balfour in 1660 and Sir John Clerk in 1697 extended their tours of the Low Countries, Germany and Switzerland southwards into Italy. The Second Marquess of Annandale's Grand Tour took over three years, from 1717 to 1720. He returned home with over 300 paintings and drawings, portfolios of engravings, a whole library of books and many classical marbles. 'It would be endless', he wrote in his notebook, 'to give an account of the statues, Bas-relieves and Paintings of Rome – the number is incredible to one who has not been there.'

In the Palazzo Muti, off the Piazza dei Santissimi Apostoli, is a plaque that commemorates that Henry IX was there proclaimed King of Great Britain and Ireland. His famous brother, proclaimed King Charles III, was born in the palazzo in 1720 and died there in 1788. The court of Bonnie Prince Charlie in exile drew many sympathetic visits from Jacobite supporters amongst travellers on the Grand Tour to Rome.

Reports quoted 60 travellers in 1718 clustered round the two coffee houses there, 40 in 1734, 40 again in 1753, and 50 in 1787. Making allowance for the other main towns on the itinerary, Florence and Naples, there must have been nearly five hundred milords in circulation at any one time in the eighteenth century.

By the time that Joseph Spence had bear-led his young milords on his three Grand Tours, the population of Rome had grown to 150,000. His usual route was from Loreto, through Foligno, Spoleto, Terni, Narni, Otricoli, and Città Castellana into Rome. His friend Mr Edward Holdsworth, another poet, had been robbed at night of his clothes, watch, diamond ring and money. 'The Italians', Spence noted, 'love to pick pockets and pilfer everything they can steal slyly.' This is still the case. 'In mid summer the '*mala aria*', the bad air, lies over Rome,' he continued. Certainly spring and autumn are the best times to visit the Eternal City, to avoid the heat and the overcrowding of the tourist influx. Spence goes on to say, '*This* is the place where Julius Caesar was stabbed by Brutus, at the foot of *that* statue he fell and gave his last groan, *here* stood Manlius to defend the Capitol against the Gauls, and *there* afterwards was he flung down *that* rock for endeavouring to become Tyrant of his country'. Spence and his young charges visited one of the two Opera houses every night during the winter of 1741, as well as seeing three or four '*burlettas*', 'mock operas meant only to play the fool with the more serious ones'. At the Teatro Aliberti a few steps from the Piazza di Spagna, the centre for all the travellers, he saw the Pretender and his son reading his opera-book. The custom was to sup in the theatre box with dessert and sweetmeats. All stage parts were played by men, the Queen and all the ladies of the play were eunuchs as the Romans thought it indecent for a woman to appear on stage. The Carnival of Rome in the Corso was adjudged number two in Italy after that of Venice, and the Punchinellos, Pierrots, Punches and Harlequins dressed as devils and conjurers, the Barbary horse races in the streets, confetti and sweet throwing, and the gondolas on wheels (floats) were great attractions.

Walpole wrote, 'The English are numberless – schoolboys just broke loose or old fools that are come abroad at forty to see the world and to see Rome while it yet exists. Between the ignorance and poverty of the present Roman everything is neglected and falling to decay, the villas are entirely out of repair, the palaces so ill-kept that half the pictures are spoiled by damp, and the few ruins cannot last long. I am far gone in medals, lamps, idols, prints and all the small commodities to the purchase of which I can attain. I would buy the Coliseum if I could . . .'

Angelica Kauffman, the Anglo-Swiss painter, spent many years in Rome, and she and Nathaniel Dance, the portrait painter, met James Boswell on his Grand Tour in the winter of 1765. The young (24 year-old) roisterer wrote in his diary of Angelica, 'B. quite in love'. 'B.', however, met up with John Wilkes, recruited a young French art student called Guillaume Martin to pimp for him, and 'resolved to have a girl every day'. The Scottish Antiquary Colin Morison conducted Boswell on a six-day course in 'Antiquities and Arts' including the Capitol Hill, the Forum, the Coliseum, the Palatine Hill and the Baths of Diocletian. He was painted by Gavin Hamilton; 'make it full size and neglect nothing. As I'm to have a picture, don't mind the price' – which was £200! He also met Pompeo Batoni, the

Italian portrait painter, who during his lifetime painted over 300 travellers on the Grand Tour. On 13 May he dressed in silks and was presented to Pope Clement XIII. He also encountered all the members of the Jacobite Court in exile. During Holy Week, Boswell thoroughly enjoyed himself – and left Rome with a dose of clap.

What a contrast between the young rake and Edward Gibbon, who wrote 'I can neither forget nor express the strong emotions which agitated my mind as I first approached and entered the *eternal* city! It was at Rome on the 15th of October 1764 as I sat musing amidst the ruins of the Capitol while barefooted Fryars were singing vespers in the Temple of Jupiter that the idea of writing the decline and fall of that city first started to my mind.' Mr Byres, a Scots antiquary, was his guide during his stay.

Indeed, during the eighteenth century, resident Anglo–Scots antiquarian guides, such as Colin Morison, James Russell, Abbé Peter Grant and Gavin Hamilton, were available to any visitor for a fee. These local antiquarian guides became art dealers supplying wealthy tourists such as the Dukes of Northumberland, Grafton, Hamilton, and Dorset. Andrew Lumsden estimated that one could live modestly in Rome for £75 a year, but Mrs Forbes thought differently. 'The expense of coming and of living here being not at all so easy as I imagined.' That was in 1768. 'The luxuries of life such as coaches, plays, operas and wine are cheaper, but for the necessarys they are to the full as dear as at home.'

After Bonaparte's downfall – Rome was attacked in 1798 by the French army and in 1809 Pius VII was in captivity – two of the earliest travellers were Matthew Todd and Captain B. They stayed at the Albergo Locando Damon, via della Croce 69, where Todd counted twelve for dinner including seven English. At St Peter's he was enchanted with the good singing but 'disgusted with the bargaining and greed'. They walked around the Pantheon (then undergoing repairs), to the Flavian amphitheatre, Constantine Arch, the Vatican and its library, had ices at the coffee houses and watched the fashionable drive down the rue de la Course (Corso) filled with carriages from 11am until sunset. Then they took the *diligence* to Naples just before Napoleon escaped from Elba. After Waterloo, the English Society was back in force. Lady Frances Shelley took lodgings at La Grande Bretagne, as did the beautiful Lady Jersey. She met the Duchess of Devonshire, Lady Westmoreland, Prince Henry of Prussia and Prince Altieri. She had a three-quarter hour audience with the Pope (who had been freed two years before when the Papal States were restored to the Vatican), but the Garde Suisse, the chattering Cardinals and the ludicrous ceremony of pulling up the Pope's petticoats dismayed her.

At the age of 44, our greatest painter, J.M.W. Turner, made his first visit to Italy. Despite a tour to France and Switzerland in 1803, it took another sixteen years before Thomas Lawrence, who was painting Pius VII, urged his friend to join him. Crossing into Italy by the Mont Cénis pass, via Turin, Lake Como and Milan, he arrived in Venice. Thence via Loreto to Rome, where including a visit to Naples and Vesuvius in eruption, he made nearly 1,500 pencil sketches. His visit to Rome itself came half-way through his professional career and marked a turning point in his art. 'The Passage of Mont Cénis', 'The Coliseum', 'The Roman Campagna', and 'Rome from the Vatican' are some of his masterpieces created on that Grand Tour.

William Hazlitt drew less inspiration. 'In Rome', he wrote in 1824, 'you are for the most part lost in a mass of tawdry, fulsome *commonplaces*. It is not the contrast of pig-styes and palaces that I complain of, the distinction between the old and new . . . [but] an almost uninterrupted succession of narrow, vulgarlooking streets where the smell of garlick prevails over the odour of antiquity . . .'

The irascible architectural genius John Ruskin, visiting Rome in 1840, wrote in his book *Praeterita*, 'A great fuss about Pope officiating in the Sistine Chapel. Advent Sunday. Got into a crowd and made myself very uncomfortable for nothing: no music worth hearing, a little mummery with Pope and dirty cardinals. Outside and west façade of St Peter's certainly very fine: the inside would make a nice ball-room but is good for nothing else.'

The Dickens family, although grieviously disappointed by St Peter's and the Coliseum, hired a carriage for the Roman Carnival in 1845. They donned wire masks, decorated themselves with nosegays and threw sugar plums and confetti with enthusiasm on the Corso. They stayed at the Hôtel Meloni where Mrs de la Rue, his protégée, had a seizure in the night. The Dickens and the de la Rues stayed throughout Holy Week, and the *Letters of Charles Dickens* include a vivid description of their stay.

Three American visitors to Rome in the mid-nineteenth century recorded their views. Bayard Taylor walked in the ruins of the Coliseum and watched the orange groves gleaming with golden fruitage in the Farnese gardens. George Stillman Hillard visited Rome in 1847 and met many artists dining at the Lepri in via dei Condotti, and taking coffee at the Caffè Greco in the same street. He found the Rome of the day with narrow, dark and gloomy streets without sidewalks, frequently crooked, not kept clean, and with an air of mouldiness and decay. He visited the Shelley and Keats tombs in the Protestant cemetery and took part in the carnival, either watching from a balcony, or riding up and down the Corso in a carriage, or mingling on foot with the crowds. '*Beefsteak et pomme de terre*' was the Roman nickname for English visitors who had taken over entirely the Piazza di Spagna.

Mark Twain conscientiously visited all the major sights and measured them on foot. (The Coliseum 1600' long, 750' wide, 165' high.) Finally he wrote, 'Michael Angelo Buonarroti — I do not want him for breakfast — for luncheon — for dinner — for tea — for supper — for between meals. In Genoa he designed everything, in Milan he or his pupils designed everything: he designed the lake of Como: in Padua, Verona, Venice, Bologna — in Florence, he painted *everything*, designed *everything*. In Pisa he designed everything but the old shot-tower. He designed the piers of Leghorn and the customs house regulations of Civita Vecchia. But here in Rome, here it is frightful. He designed St Peter's, he designed the Pope, the Tiber, the Vatican, the Coliseum, the Capitol, the Tarpesian Rock, the Barberini Palace, St John Lateran, the Campagna, the Appian Way, the Seven Hills, the Baths of Caracalla, the Claudian Aqueduct, the Cloaca Maxima — the eternal bore designed the Eternal City and unless all men and booksellers lie, he painted everything in it.'

VISITING ROME TODAY

WHERE TO STAY

John Murray's late nineteenth-century *Guides* recommended several good hotels for the travellers in Rome. One was the Angleterre, now the **D'INGHILTERRA**, via Bocca di Leone 14 (Tel. 672161), between the Colosseum and the Stazione Termini. The Brownings stayed here in 1846, Henry James a little later, and even earlier the King of Portugal and entourage took suites here on a visit to meet the Pope. The **ALBERGO CESÀRI**, via di Pietra 89a (Tel. 6792386), is close to the Pantheon and Piazza Navona. Built in 1787 it has harboured Stendhal, Mazzini and Garibaldi in its past. The **ALBERGO SOLE AL PANTHEON**, 63 Piazza del Pantheon (Tel. 6780441) overlooks the Pantheon and is the oldest hotel in Rome (once known as Albergo Montone), having been built in 1467. Ariosto, author of *Orlando Furioso*, lodged here in 1513 and visited Pope Leo V. So too did Pietro Mascagni who composed his opera *Cavalleria Rusticana* here. In a small piazza with a large fountain, the charm of the Renaissance still lingers.

The **GRAND HÔTEL DE LA VILLE**, via Sistina 69 (Tel. 6733), is near the Spanish Steps. John Mayne and his Irish family stayed here in

1 Vatican City   2 Sistine Chapel   3 St. Peter's Basilica and Square   4 Castel of Saint Angelo   5 Villa Borghese

6 Villa Medici   7 Hôtel d'Inghilterra, Via Bocca di Leone 14   8 The Spanish Steps   9 The Grand Hôtel de la Ville, Via Sistine 69

10 Via Veneto   11 The Albergo Sole al Pantheon, Piazza del Pantheon 63   12 Pantheon

13 The Albergo Cesari, Via di Pietra 89a   14 Trevi Fountains   15 Quirinal   16 The Quirinale, Via Nazionale 7

17 Piazza della Repubblica   18 Museo Nazionale Romano   19 Mausoleum of Augustus   20 Palazzo Venezia

21 Church of Santa Maria Maggiore   22 The Capitol Hill   23 Roman Forum   24 The Coliseum   25 Arch of Constantine

26 Palatine   27 Baths of Caracalla   28 Catacombs

1814. The **QUIRINALE**, via Nazionale 7 (Tel. 4707), is between the Stazione Termini and the Piazza Repubblica. It dates from the mid-nineteenth century, and Verdi stayed here in 1893 for the première of *Falstaff*.

In the post-railway period several 'Grand' Hotels were opened in Rome. **LE GRAND HÔTEL ET DE ROME**, via Vittorio Emanuele Orlando 3

(Tel. 4709), was opened in 1894 near the station. It is the most elegant hotel in Rome (which is saying a lot), ideal for the wealthy modern milord and his lady. The restaurant **LE RALLY** and a café **LE PAVILION** are added attractions. Other late nineteenth-century hotels include the **ESPERIA**, via Nazionale 22 (Tel. 4744245); the **EDEN**, via Ludovisi 49 (Tel. 4743551); the **MASSIMO D'AZEGLIO**, via Cavour 18 (Tel. 460646), opened in 1875, full of nostalgic comfort and an excellent restaurant; the **FLORA**, via Vittorio Veneto 191 (Tel. 497821), and the **HASSLER-VILLA MEDICI**, Piazza Trinità dei Monti 6 (Tel. 6792651), which dates from 1885, near the Spanish Steps. Both the Flora and the Hassler have superb views of Rome.

WHERE TO EAT

To feed Rome's three million occupants there are several thousand restaurants, trattorie and osterie, and a few still exist that served the early travellers. **DELLA CAMPANA**, vicolo della Campana 18 (Tel. 6567820), was an albergo in 1518 in the Campo di Marzo district. Try their '*stufatino al sedano*' (celery and meat stew). The **HOSTARIA DELL' ORSO**, via dei Soldati 25 (Tel. 6564250), was an inn in 1300. St Francis of Assisi, Dante, Rabelais, Montaigne and Goethe have all eaten and stayed here. Now very elegant and expensive. At night try their '*canneloni Hostaria*' or '*paparelle al porcini*'. The **BRASERA MENEGHINA**, via Circo 10 (Tel. 808108), was a taverna in 1673 in a former monastery. A speciality is '*rostin negaa*', veal chops in white wine. The **RISTORANTE G. RANIERI** (originally Osteria del Passeto), via Mario de' Fiori (Tel. 6791592), near the Spanish Steps, was started in 1843. Their '*lasagne verdi*' topped with cheese and their '*zabaglione*' with pineapple slices are commended. The original Giuseppe Ranieri, a Neapolitan, was chef to Queen Victoria. On the menu today are '*mignonettes à la Queen Victoria*'. The restaurant **MASSIMO D'AZEGLIO**, via Cavour 18 (Tel. 460646), is sited within the hotel of that name. Founded and run for over a century by the Bettoja family, it specializes in game dishes and '*cannelloni d'Azeglio*'. **ROMOLO**, via di Porta Settimiana 7 (Tel. 588284), dates from the seventeenth century and is sited in a courtyard near the Aurelian Wall in the Trastevere sector. Raphael's mistress, la Fornarina, lived here and the poet Trilussa dined daily. '*Fettuccine*' or '*scaloppine al marsala*' are favourite dishes. **ANGELINO A TOR MARGANA**, Piazza Margana (Tel. 6783328), is sited in Goethe's historic eighteenth-century inn, and was once a centre for writers and painters. It is a classic Roman *trattoria* with a good eggplant '*parmigiana*'. **IL FEDELINARO**, Piazza di Trevi 95, near the famous fountain, was founded in 1835 as a simple *trattoria*, which it still is. The veal '*piccata*' is praised. The **RISTORANTE ULPIA**, Foro Traiano 2 (Tel. 689980), was founded in 1805. The house speciality is '*fettuccini Ulpia*'. Late at night there is music and dancing. **DA PANCRAZIO**, Piazza del Biscione 92 (Tel. 6561246), is part of Pompey's ancient theatre, and as a *trattoria* dates from the eighteenth century. Try their '*risotto alla pescatora*' (seafood and rice). **LA SACRESTIA**, via del Seminario 89 (Tel. 6797581), dates from the early nineteenth century and is near the Pantheon. Their '*tagliatelle alla sacrestana*' is a speciality. **IL BUCO**, via Santo Ignazio 8 (Tel. 6793298), was opened in 1891 by Raffaele Masini, and has traditional Tuscan cuisine and wines including '*bistecca alla fiorentina*'. The **AL FICO VECCHIO** (Fig Tree), via Anagnina 134 (Tel. 9459261), in the Grottaferrata section of Rome, was a tavern in the seventeenth century, and Jacob Phillip Hackert painted it in 1789. Run by the Ciocca family, '*rigatoni al Fico*' (ham, tomatoes and cream) is a speciality. Try the local white wine of Grottaferrata. The **ANTICO FALCONE**, via Trionfale 60 (Tel. 353400), belonged to Pope Alexander VI's treasurer, Rodrigo Borgia. The building dates from 1480, and the inn from the eighteenth century. Here you will find good Roman cooking including '*penne all' arrabbiata*'. Murray commended its '*trippa*' and '*testicciuola*' (fried lambs' brains) in 1846.

The oldest cafés in Rome are the **CAFFÈ GRECO**, via dei Condotti 86, dating from 1760, and famous as the rendezvous for musicians and painters all over the world; **DONEY**, via Veneto 145; and the **CAFÉ DE PARIS**, No. 90 in the same street. **BABINGTON'S TEA ROOMS**, Piazza di Spagna, were founded by Anna Maria Babington in 1896, for tea, muffins and scones.

Amongst the many popular dishes, Roman cuisine has half a dozen specialities including '*fettuccine al burro*' (noodles with cream and Parmesan cheese), '*spaghetti alla carbonara*' (mixture of bacon, cheese, eggs, and garlic on top of spaghetti), '*bucatini all' amatriciana*' (pasta with hot sauce), '*abbacchio*' (sucking lamb in white wine), and '*saltimbocca*' (slices of veal and ham cooked in butter with Marsala wine sauce). The local wines from the Castelli Romani include Velletri, Marino, Colli Albani and Frascati. The best wines from Latium often appear as '*vino da tavola*'. Look for Cerveteri white and red, red Cesanese, and red and white Fiorano.

WHAT TO SEE AND DO

The main **TOURIST OFFICE** (EPT) is at via Parigi 5 (Tel. 463748), half a kilometre northwest of the station behind the Museo Nazionale Romano in the Piazza della Repubblica. Ask for their brochure *Here Rome*. The *Carnet di Roma e del Lazio* lists the month's activities. There are EPT branches in the Termini station and at Fiumicino airport.

Public transport in Rome, including taxis, is efficient. Do not attempt to drive. The two Metro lines A and B criss-cross the city, but bus is the better system. If you can, walk!

Although John Murray recommended a minimum stay of one week in Rome, the major sights can be seen in three or four days. However, careful planning is essential since on Mondays all museums are closed except the Vatican, and most churches are closed in the afternoon. The EPT have very sensibly devised three Roman itineraries which take in all the ten main sights. A hotel based in the centre of the old city (the medieval quarter) reduces travel time.

The famous Trevi fountains are in the centre of Rome. To the east are the EPT, Museo Nazionale Romano, the Termini station and the church of Santa Maria Maggiore. To the south is the Palazzo Venezia, the Capitol (and its museums), the Roman Forum and the Coliseum. To the west is the Pantheon, and across the Tiber St Peter's, the Vatican and the Castle of St Angelo, and back over the river, the Mausoleum of Augustus. To the north are the Villa Medici, the huge gardens of the Villa Borghese, the Via Veneto and the Spanish Steps (Keats-Shelley memorial). One could spend a week in Vatican City and St Peter's and another week examining the antiquities around the Capitol, Forum and Coliseum. Let alone the baths, catacombs, basilicas, picture galleries, markets, mausoleums, piazzas and twenty or so elegant palazzi. Of all the Italian cities Rome demands the greatest amount of pre-planning. A two-hour tour by ATAC sightseeing bus, 3.30pm from Piazza dei Cinquecento near the station, will show the first-time visitor all the key sights, albeit briefly. Then one can decide which areas to investigate, as Joseph Spence and Dr John Moore would have done two and a half centuries ago!

The travellers went to the theatre or opera every evening. In Rome the open-air summer opera is at the Baths of Caracalla, and from November to May the opera is at the **OPERA HOUSE** at Piazza Beniamino Gigli 1 (Tel. 461755). The **TEATRO GOLDONI**, vicolo dei Soldati (Tel. 6561156), has English language performances. The

FANTASIE DI TRASTEVERE, via di Santa Dorotea, is a folklore restaurant on the west bank of the Tiber giving a dramatic meal and performance (Tel. 5892986).

The main events on the Roman calendar are the children's Feast of the Epiphany on 5–6 January in the Piazza Navona; the feast of St Joseph on 19 March in the Trionfale district; Holy Week – on Easter Sunday the Pope blesses the crowds in St Peter's Square; the April spring festival around the Trinità dei Monti church; the Art Fair in the via Margutta (spring and autumn); the Feast of St John on 23–24 June in the San Giovanni district; the summer Tevere exhibition on the banks of the Tiber with musical and dance events; the Feast of Noantri in mid-July in Trastevere; the major summer Festival of arts, concerts, dance and folklore; the Feast of the Assumption on 15 August; the Feast of the Immaculate Conception on 8 December in Piazza di Spagna; and Christmas Day, when the churches have cribs and processions and the main streets have decorations.

The main excursions from Rome are to Ostia Antica, the ancient Roman port 25 kilometres to the southwest, and to Tivoli, 31 kilometres east of Rome (the Villa Adriana and the Villa d'Este are major attractions). There Mariana Starke in 1803 praised the **RISTORANTE SIBILLA**, via della Sibilla 50 (Tel. 20281) which is still excellent. It dates from the eighteenth century; try the trout from the Aniene River and the white San Gimignano wine. Other excursions include Castelgandolfo, the Pope's summer resort; Cerveteri, 44 kilometres away, to see the Etruscan necropolis; Nemi, to see the museum of Roman ships; and Frascati to see the villas and drink the celebrated wine.

NAPLES

an earthly Paradise

Since the capital of the region of Campania is well over 200 kilometres south of Rome, it is surprising how many of the travellers on the Grand Tour visited Naples and its superb bay, climbed Mount Vesuvius, and explored the macabre ruins of Pompeii. This was their last stop, and usually they returned the way they came, on the coast road through Gaeta and Latina. Now a modern airport, Capodichino, or the Autoroute A2, or trains called the Tirrenica and the Dorsale, make travel to Naples easy. Moreover

Naples, though second to Genoa in freight, is a larger sea-passenger port, with hydrofoils, ferry-boats and cruise liners.

Of all the travellers' views on Naples there are three that stand out. John Ruskin in the mid-nineteenth century wrote, 'Naples is certainly the most disgusting place in Europe'. Nugent in 1778 described it as 'the pleasantest place in Europe, air pure, serene and beautiful', and young Mrs. Anna Jameson visiting in 1826 wrote that 'it has all the allurements of the Syren and all the terrors of the Sorceress'.

In AD305 the Emperor Diocletian executed San Gennaro (Saint Januarius). The martyr, who became patron saint of Naples, lies buried in the funeral catacombs of La Sanità, one kilometre north of the Museo Archeologico. The annual Feast of the Miracle of St Januarius takes place on the first Saturday in May and on 19 September. The Saint's blood in two glass ampoules is kept dry in a flask in the cathedral. If it fails to liquefy on those two days disaster will come to Naples. In 1527 that happened, and 40,000 people died of the plague. In 1836 a cholera outbreak killed 24,000 people.

The sunny climate of Naples brought rich Roman citizens such as Virgil, Augustus, Tiberius and the revolting Emperor Nero to winter here.

On his way south from Rome in 1595, disguised as a 'poor Bohemian', guarded by 60 musketeers against 'banditti', Fynes Moryson reached Naples. He described the area as 'an earthly Paradise'. He drank the Falernum wine from Pozzuoli, praised by Horace, and noted 'foure publike houses called Seggii in which the Princes and Gentlemen have yeerely meetings and there is also the daily meeting of the Merchants. Almost every house hath its fountains of most wholesome water: the street chaires instead of coaches called Seggioli di Napoli with windows in sides, two porters carry these chairs by two long staves.'

From Capua along a broad road to Naples came John Evelyn, admiring the vines festooning the fruit trees, the rice fields and sugar cane. Even in February Evelyn noted the crops of melon, 'charries' and 'abricots'. The Spaniards had ruled Naples since 1501 and he visited the riding school of the resident Spanish Viceroy. Evelyn stayed at the Three Kings Inn with 'maraculously cheape fare', comprising '18–20 dishes of the most exquisite meate and fruites'. He visited the High Castle of St Elmo, the magnificent cathedral and the Castello Nuovo with four thick towers by the sea. Capra and Ischia were 'doubtless one of the most divertisant and considerable vistas in the world'. He also reported, 'Mount Vesuvius was smoaking and through the foggy exhalations and impetuous noise and roaring, one of the most horrid spectacles in the world. The Neapolitans a cheerful people, good horses, invented sedan chairs, women were libidinous, the country people jovial and musical with guitars and fiddles.' Carnival took place on 6 February and was attended by thirty thousand local prostitutes and 'registered sinners'. The journey continued by *felucca* north to Baia.

The seventeenth-century Neapolitan baroque painter, Salvator Rosa, was admired by eighteenth-century travellers, though his macabre and desolate landscapes with scenes of witchcraft, *banditti* and savage battles are not to everyone's taste! Lady Mary Wortley Montagu thought the Kingdom of Naples appeared gay and flourishing, the town so crowded with people that she could only obtain a very sorry lodging. She found the nobles' entourage 'disagreeable and incommodious in the grandeur of the equipage, two coaches, two running footmen, a gentleman usher and two pages'. Thomas Gray noted, 'the streets are one continued market, thronged with populace so much that a coach can hardly pass. The common sort are a jolly lively kind of animals, more industrious than Italians usually are: they work till evening then take their lute or guitar (for they all play) and walk about the city or upon the seashore with it to enjoy the fresco.'

In 1734 King Charles III of Spain made Naples the capital of the Kingdom of the Two Sicilies.

Joseph Spence stayed at the Tre Ore auberge. He paid twelve *carlini* a day for chamber and food, and his hired coach cost him the same. Eight years before, in 1732, there had been another disastrous earthquake and 30 English ladies and gentlemen had hurriedly to get on 'shipboard' to escape. Several thousand houses were destroyed. 'Naples', he wrote, 'is the land of earthquakes, and so the most agreeable place in the world is one of the most dangerous to live in. It is one of the most delicious sea-ports in the world, lies down a sloping ground, all in a large half-moon to the sea. In one side of it about six miles on the left hand from Naples is Vesuvius, and on the right the grotto of Pausillipo and the tomb of Virgil. The people of Naples think Virgil was a schoolmaster, a conjurer, or a Saint or a Sorcerer . . . Good Lachryma Christi wine grows on the mountains.' Naples then had a population of 500,000, was 18 miles in circumference, and boasted not only 300 princes, but also dukes *senza numero*.

Spence was not impressed with the antiquities, commenting 'neither the pictures nor the churches seem extraordinary'. He visited the Palace of the Viceroy of Naples, Count de Harrach, the Marquis Marino's Palace, the Court of Caraffa, the Terminalis catacombs that ran for three miles, the marble statue of Jupiter, and the new opera theatre opened in 1737, with six rows of boxes, thirty boxes in a row.

Other mid-eighteenth-century travellers commented on the waterfront '*lazzaroni*' – hordes of poor people living on their wits, the streets full of prostitutes plying for trade, soldiers, priests, barrow boys, street musicians, and sailors all jostling each other. The *tarantella* was a 'low dance consisting of turns on the heel, much footing and snapping of the fingers'.

James Boswell, aged 24, arrived in Naples over carnival time. 'My blood was inflamed by the burning climate and my passions were violent. I indulged them.' With John Wilkes as his companion he dined, drank, laughed and ascended Vesuvius, heaved up by five men into the sulphurous smoke, coughing and spluttering. Wilkes hired a country house a mile from Naples after spending six weeks in the city with his mistress Madame Corradini. He wrote of the garlanded vines, the fireflies, the mosquito nets and the sights. He watched the Miracle of San Gennaro being performed in 1765 before a large and hysterical crowd. 'The women shrieked hideously, beat their breasts and tore their hair.'

The young boy-king of Naples was introduced to Edward Gibbon by the distinguished English envoy Sir William Hamilton. From 1764 to 1800 the Sessa Palace was the home, and the local court for travellers to attend, of this antiquarian. He climbed Vesuvius 26 times, and married a beautiful young woman – a syren who entrapped distinguished sailors. Perhaps Gibbon realized that when he wrote, 'Naples, whose luxurious inhabitants dwell on the confines of paradise and hellfire'?

At a private ball at Mr (as he was then) Hamilton's in 1778 there were 'Minuets, country-dances, reels and Strathspeys'. Another Scot who took up residence in Naples was James Clarke, who from 1768 to 1799 showed travellers the sights and arranged for them the purchase of prints and paintings. John Robert Cozens and Thomas Jones painted many Neapolitan landscapes in this period.

Lady visitors to the Court of Naples (and to the Hamiltons) were Mrs Anne Damer, an accomplished sculptress who later made a bust of Nelson; Lady Anne Miller, who subsequently wrote a book about her Italian adventures; and Mrs Hester Thrale, newly married to her second husband, the music master Gabriel Piozzi. If the Hamiltons' large palace was full, distinguished English travellers were put up at the Hôtel Crocelle or Auberge Reale. Philippina Lady Knight and her daughter Cornelia found Naples so economical that they stayed for a year in various hotels in the Chiazza, a quarter made smart by the seventeenth-century Spanish viceroys.

Forsyth, in 1800, before his capture and imprisonment in the north, wrote that 'Naples in its interior has no parallel on earth. The crowd in Naples consists in a general tide rolling up and down and in the middle of this tide a hundred eddies of men. Here you are swept on by the current, there you are wheeled round by the vortex. A diversity of trades dispute with you the streets. You are stopped by a carpenter's bench, you are lost among shoemakers' stools, you dash behind the pots of a macaroni stall and you escape behind a lazzarone's night basket. In this region of caricature every bargain sounds like a battle.'

The *Juvenile Traveller* noted that in Naples there were more religious processions than anywhere else in Italy, as the people there were very superstitious. There were 30,000 *lazzaroni* with no habitation or support, who slept under porticos or in piazzas, in huts, caverns and caves, who were fed bread and soup by the monks in the convents. These poor wretches carried loads, went on errands, fished – anything to keep themselves alive. The travellers predictably called them 'poor and idle'. The Neapolitan nobles and gentry kept only men servants, who swept, made the beds and cooked.

Every traveller visited the opera at the San Carlo theatre. Dr Burney wrote that 'the actors seem in a perpetual brawl'; the audiences talked, kissed and flirted, gambled and threw orange peel at all and sundry. William Beckford noted 'Every Lady's box is the scene of tea, cards, cavaliers, servants, lapdogs, abbés, scandal and assignations.' The grandest opera house in Italy was hung with mirrors and the boxes were illuminated from top to bottom.

Many Italian noblemen, such as the Duke of Monte Leone, the Prince of Francavilla and Gaetano Filangieri and his sister Principessa Ravashieri di Satriano, delighted in providing entertainment for the visiting English and Scots milords.

Naples for a century and a half was a most entertaining place at which to complete the outward-bound leg of the Grand Tour. The carnival especially was a great event with music, feasts, masquerades, diversions, even weddings, and processions to the seraglio-mosque with the gentry masked, and adorned in rich dresses and glittering jewels. During the evening on the Corso by the seaside one saw painted, gilded, varnished carriages drawn by spirited prancing horses, many footmen, and the haughty princes, dukes, counts and their ladies surveying each other's splendour.

But of all the travellers to Naples, Mark Twain was the most eloquent. 'To see Naples as we see it [in 1867, aged 32] in the early dawn from far up the side of Vesuvius, is to see a picture of wonderful beauty. At that distance its dingy buildings looked white, and so rank on rank of balconies, windows and roofs, they piled themselves up from the blue ocean till the colossal castle of St Elmo topped the grand white pyramid and gave the picture

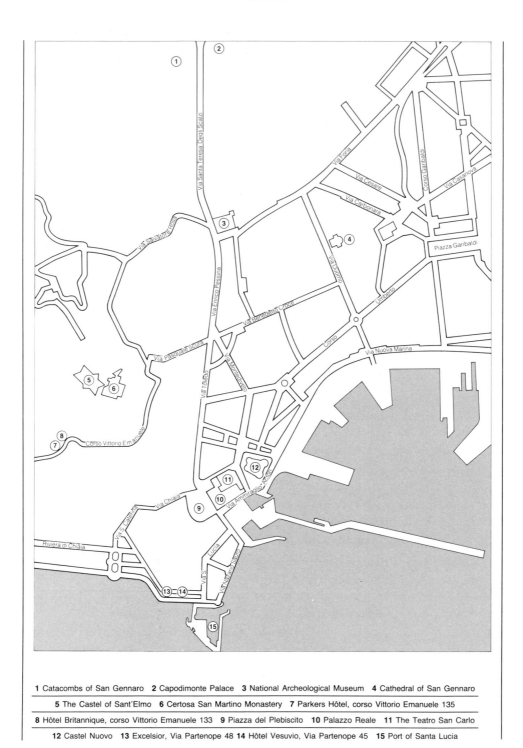

1 Catacombs of San Gennaro   **2** Capodimonte Palace   **3** National Archeological Museum   **4** Cathedral of San Gennaro

5 The Castel of Sant'Elmo   **6** Certosa San Martino Monastery   **7** Parkers Hôtel, corso Vittorio Emanuele 135

8 Hôtel Britannique, corso Vittorio Emanuele 133   **9** Piazza del Plebiscito   **10** Palazzo Reale   **11** The Teatro San Carlo

12 Castel Nuovo   **13** Excelsior, Via Partenope 48   **14** Hôtel Vesuvio, Via Partenope 45   **15** Port of Santa Lucia

symmetry, emphasis and completeness. And when its lilies turned to roses, when it blushed under the sun's first kiss — it was beautiful beyond all description. One might well say, then, "See Naples and die".'

VISITING NAPLES TODAY

MODERN NAPLES

Modern Naples, with a population of one and a quarter million, is not a tourist city in the way that Rome, Florence and Venice are. Parts of the city are very sleazy indeed, others are mildly dangerous, particularly at night, and pickpocketing and minor thieving are rife. It is unpleasant to drive a car in Naples because of the crowded roads and ferociously competitive drivers. It is not a cultural city, although it boasts the second finest opera house in Italy and, in the National Archaeological Museum, one of the finest classical collections in the world. Its cooking is based on pasta and seafood, and its wines rank low in scale compared to most other Grand Tour cities in Italy.

In the last decade the city fathers have initiated a programme of cultural revival after the air raids of 1943 and the severe earthquake of 1980. The Teatro San Carlo has been restored to its eighteenth-century elegance, and its 250th anniversary was celebrated in 1987 with a gala performance of Donizetti's *Robert Devereux*. The theatre Mercadante, the triumphal Roman arch in front of the Castel Nuovo, the castles of Sant'Elmo and Ovo, the buildings round Monte Sant'Angelo, the Piazza of San Domenico Maggiore and parts of the rather drab University have been refurbished or restored.

Naples is unique in Italy, indeed in the world. The Bay of Naples, seen from the sea, is superb. Stendhal called the Via Veneto in 1817 the 'busiest most joyous thoroughfare in the entire universe'. And so it is. The Quartiere Spagnuoli, the Spanish Quarter, is the European Casbah. And there is always nearby Pompeii, Herculaneum, the heights of Vesuvius and the isle of Capri.

WHERE TO STAY

John Murray's guides of 1853 and 1892 recommended a number of good hotels that still exist and have since been modernized, which will suit the modern traveller on a grand tour today.

Once known as the tramontano, **PARKERS HÔTEL**, corso Vittorio Emanuele 135 (Tel. 685866) is an excellent old-fashioned hotel on a hillside avenue. It is currently being refurbished. The **HÔTEL BRITANNIQUE**, with three stars, corso Vittorio Emanuele 133 (Tel. 660933) is nearby, owned by the Swiss Loliger family. It was known early in the nineteenth century as the Pension MacPherson. The restaurant serves delicious home-cooked meals. Both hotels have lovely views of the Bay. The five-star **HÔTEL EXCELSIOR**, via Partenope 48 (Tel. 417111) is on the waterfront, with views of Vesuvius and Santa Lucia. So too is the five-star **HÔTEL VESUVIO**, via Partenope 45 (Tel. 417044), coloured pink and white with a dramatic view and a roof-top garden restaurant. They both date from the end of the nineteenth century.

WHAT AND WHERE TO EAT

Most of the best Neapolitan dishes contain fish or seafood. '*Spaghetti alle vongole*' (clams), '*alle cozze*' (mussels), '*aragosta*' (crayfish), and '*polipi*' (octopus), are some of the good regional dishes, as well as '*fritto misto di mare*' (seafood, squid and prawns, first boiled, then deep fried) and '*pesce spada*' (swordfish). '*Zuppa di cozze*' or '*cozze al limone*' are dishes based on mussels. '*Sartu*' is a mixture of ground beef, eggs and liver covered with '*mozzarella*' (white cheese). Naples has many local pizza dishes including '*pizza alla napoletana*'. '*Pizzaiola*' is fresh tomato sauce with oregano or basil and garlic. '*Crocche*' is a potato dish and '*mozzarella in carrozza*' is a grilled buffalo cheese sandwich.

There are many bayside restaurants to choose from in the port of Santa Lucia. **GIUSEPPONE E MARE**, via Ferdinando Russo, is an established traditional seafood place. Try their bass '*alla riva fiortia*' with local wine from Ischia or the slopes of Vesuvius. In the city is **DANTE E BEATRICE**, piazza Dante 45. Try the '*pepata di cozze*' (mussels in pepper broth). At **PIZZERIA BELLINI**, strada Sta. Maria Constantinopoli 80, try '*fettucine alla Bellini*' or '*linguine al cartoccio*' (seafood, pasta in pepper and tomato sauce); and at **LE ARCATE**, via Aniello Falcone 249, the '*zuppa di pesche*' is excellent. These are three old-fashioned, reliable Neapolitan restaurants where the modern traveller is unlikely to be disappointed.

The local cuisine has a few meat dishes such as '*rigatoni*' with meat sauce, and '*cannelloni alla Sorrentina*'. Besides *mozzarella* cheese, there are '*scamorza*', '*fior di latte*' and the smoked '*provoloni*'. Pastry dishes include the famous '*fogliatelle*' (pastry filled with candied fruit), and seasonal cakes such as Easter '*pastiera*', Christmas '*struffoli*', Lent '*sanguinaccio*', and All Saints' Day '*torrone*'. And, of course, Neapolitan ice-creams.

The Romans, and particularly Horace and other poets, lauded the wines of Campania Felix, the volcanic hills surrounding Naples; and especially Falernum and Caecubum. The vines were called Aglianico, Greco and Fiano. The modern Falerno del Massico DOC is a strong fruity red wine, as are Gragnano and the red Taurasi from Aglianico. The Mastroberardino wine growers produce excellent Fiano and Greco di Tufo white wines. Lachryma Christi is usually white (the tear of Christ) and white wines from the little islands of Ischia and Capri go very nicely with seafood dishes.

WHAT TO SEE AND DO

The main **TOURIST OFFICES** are at piazza Gesù Nuovo (Tel. 323328), and via Partenope 10 (Tel. 406289), as well as in the main railway station in the east of town. *Qui Napoli* is a bilingual monthly guide to local events.

The two most important museums are the National Archeological Museum at the piazza Museo, which is near the piazza Cavour, ten minutes' walk from the station, and the Museum and National Gallery of Capodimonte, which is one kilometre due north of the Palazzo Reale in the park of the same name. The former, a huge red building built in 1585, houses the masterpieces of Pompeii and Herculaneum in spite of the fact that several travellers and Sir William Hamilton 'exported' many antiquities. Sculptures, bronzes, ceramics, paintings, mosaics and jewellery make this museum, despite damage in the 1980 earthquake, one of the richest in the world. The latter was originally a royal palace, built in 1738, and it has a superb picture gallery with works by Bellini, Titian, Masaccio and Mantegna. A Breughel and a Caravaggio are notable. The gallery is on the second floor and the Royal Apartments on the first floor. Both are closed on Mondays.

The other main sights are the thirteenth-century moated Castel Nuovo of Charles of Anjou, with the 1443 Triumphal Arch, Palatine Chapel and Barons Hall which overlooks the port and is a few minutes' walk east of the Palazzo Reale; the Opera House of San Carlo; the hidden thirteenth-century cathedral with the Capella del Tesoro

garden full of all variety. Here lived the duke with his Swiss guards after the frugal Italian way selling what he can spare of his Wines of the cellar under his house with wicker bottles dangling over the chiefe entrance into the Palace.' The Palazzo Vecchio was grim, but a repository of admirable antiques, particularly Michelangelo's statue of David. In the loggia dei Lanzi he admired Donatello's statue of Judith and Holofernes, inspected the Grand Duke's stables and zoo, the San Lorenzo church with the famous Medici statues and tombs, the Santa Maria Novella, and factories for making silk damask and velvets. None of the sixteenth- or seventeenth-century travellers mentioned the fate of Savonarola, the fanatical Dominican friar who in 1494 welcomed the French King Charles VIII into Florence, burned the trappings of 'vanity' in the Piazza della Signoria, only in 1498 to be burned at the stake himself. The last powerful Medici prince died in 1609, 33 years before Evelyn's visit.

'You cannot imagine any situation more agreeable than Florence' wrote Lady Mary Wortley Montagu, 70 years later. 'It lies in a fertile and smiling valley watered by the Arno, which runs thru' the city and nothing can surpass the beauty and magnificence of its public buildings, particularly the Cathedral whose grandeur filled me with astonishment. The palaces, squares, fountains, statues, bridges do not only carry an aspect full of elegance and greatness but discover a taste quite different from public edifices in other countries.' Her favourite was the Medici's Venus in the Galleria. Florence in the early eighteenth century had a good opera, and one evening in 1725, twenty English visitors were noted there, although according to Lady Mary the opera was 'not as fine as for voices and decorations as Venice'.

The poet Joseph Spence bear-led his young charges on three occasions to Florence, and preferred to stay at the Aquila Nera, 'well entertained and much cheaper than at Mr Collins'. One winter in the 1740s they stayed for the carnival, and noted a cruel sport. From a float, fishing rods baited with sugar almonds were extended, with two or three small boys nibbling at them, hooked and played as fish. Nevertheless, Florence, then a city of 70,000 souls, was 'a most agreeable place to live in the vale of Arno, one of the finest cities for buildings, statues and pictures in Italy'. They visited the Great Duke's gallery 'above a hundred times', noting 'what a fund of entertainment does one single collection there sometimes afford one'.

Horace Walpole admired the fine unfinished palace of the Strozzi, and declared himself 'fond of Florence to a degree, the most agreeable of all places. Our little Arno is not boated and swelling like the Thames but tis vastly pretty, [and] being Italian has something visionary and poetical in its stream.' His friend Thomas Gray admired the 'peasant girls in the market place, gold and brocaded petticoats, scarlet stockings, real pearl earrings, necklaces of immense size and their braided hair interwoven with coloured cords . . .'

At the end of the eighteenth century Lord Hervey was the English Minister, and he entertained Arthur Young to dinner. There he met Lord and Lady Elcho, Lord Hume, the Beckfords, the Charteris and fifteen other English families, since none of the Florentine families ever received guests for dinner, only having card parties or 'conversaziones' with lemonade, coffee, tea or ice-creams. Young looked at the Aquila Nera, the Vanini, and the Scudi di Francia inns, but decided on lodgings at the del Sarte Inglesi, in the via dei Fossi. The botanist Sir James Smith, visiting Florence in 1793, stayed at the Vanini, enjoyed delicious Florentine wine, and for four rooms paid six paols or three shillings daily. Besides the main sights of the Galleria, Piazza Reale and the cathedral, Smith went to the Grand Duke's Museum of Natural History and botanical gardens. He paid three paols to attend the very good musical opera, and at the comic opera found many women singers in men's clothes.

A decade later Mariana Starke praised the Florentine wines, vino Santi, Aleatico, Montepulciano and the local chianti. She, and later John Mayne, stayed at Schneiders' hotel called 'Armes d'Angleterre'. Matthew Todd in 1814 described his visit to Monsieur Anthony Schnaidriff's hotel thus, 'most excellent hotel, capital bed, carpeted room, sent for a barber to cut our hair, took a hot bath and had some tea, half a bottle of port and retired to rest'.

Before he visited Florence, Lord Byron wrote 'I have not the least curiosity about Florence. I must see it for the sake of the Venus, the fall of Terni and then return to Venice via Ravenna and Rimini.' During his visit in May 1817 he completely changed his mind. After composing his poem *Lament on Tasso* he wrote in his usual staccato fashion (note his interest in mistresses!): ' I went to the two galleries from which one returns drunk with beauty – the Venus is more for admiration than love – but there are sculpture and painting – Mistress of Raphael, a portrait, the mistress of Titian, a portrait – a Venus of Titian in the Medici gallery – *the* Venus – Canova's Venus also in the other gallery – Titian's mistress in the Pitti Palace gallery – the Parcae of Michael Angelo – the Antinous – the Alexander – the Genius of Death in marble . . . There are not many English on the move, and those who are, mostly homewards.'

Another distinguished visitor to Florence was J.M.W. Turner, who spent Christmas of 1819 there and visited again briefly in 1827. Many painters came to Florence in the eighteenth and nineteenth centuries, although usually Rome, Naples and Venice were their main targets. They included Joshua Reynolds, Inigo Jones and Richard Wilson.

Charles Dickens, his wife, and the de la Rue family were greeted on their arrival in the spring of 1845 by Lord and Lady Holland, who invited the English residents including Mrs Trollope and her son Augustus, the painter George Watts, and Walter Savage Landor, to meet the great 'Boz' at their beautiful villa, Careggi di Medici. The Landor's villa was on the nearby heights of Fiesole.

After their six-month honeymoon in Pisa, Robert and Elizabeth Browning arrived in Florence thinking that it would be less expensive and the climate better. Initially, in April 1847, they stayed at the Hôtel du Nord and soon joined the coterie of English and American writers, artistes, and painters including Hiram Powers the sculptor, George Stillman Hillard from Boston (who wrote a book entitled *The English in Italy*), Buchanan Reid, poet and painter (who wrote *Six months in Italy*), the journalist George Curtis, the Hoppners, Thomas Trollope (elder brother of Anthony) and his wife Theodosia, and William Wetmore Story, a rich Bostonian sculptor. Then the Brownings took an apartment in Casa Guidi at the corner of the via Maggio and via Mazzetta. Elizabeth wrote, 'I have seen the Venus, I have seen the divine Raphaels. I have stood by Michael Angelo's tomb in Santa Croce. I have looked at the wonderful Duomo. At Pisa we say "How beautiful", here we say nothing: it is enough.' In 1848 she wrote *Casa Guidi Windows* and her son was baptized at the Lutheran chapel. She was painted by Buchanan Reid, and sketched by Thackeray and others including E.F. Bridell, Field Talfourd and Michele Gordigiani. At Bagni di Lucca she wrote her famous *Sonnets from the Portuguese*. By 1850 there were no less than 15,000 English and American residents in Florence, reducing to 13,000 by 1914, and 2,000 in 1986.

Bayard Taylor, one of the American visitors, stayed at the Hôtel Leone Bianco and ate for 25 U.S. cents a day at the cafés and trattorias. The most popular with the foreign artistes was del Cacciatore. Taylor's farewell to Florence echoes the feelings of many visitors – 'stand with me on the heights of Fiesole and let us gaze on the grand panorama around which the Apennines stretch with a majestic sweep, wrapping in a robe of purple air, through which shimmer the villas and villages on their sides. Florence lies in front of us, the magnificent cupola of the Duomo crowning its clustered palaces. We see the airy tower of the Palazzo Vecchio and the long front of the Palazzo Pitti with the dark foliage of the Boboli Gardens behind!'

After the arrival of the railways in central Italy, Mark Twain arrived from Venice, and promptly got lost in the streets of Florence and was arrested by the local militia! Although he thought Florentine mosaics were the choicest in the world, and he wept on the tombs of Michelangelo, Raphael and Machiavelli, he dismissed the River Arno as a 'great historical creek with four feet in the channel and some scows floating around', adding, 'My experiences of Florence were chiefly unpleasant . . . these dark and bloody Florentines . . .' Twain stayed at the Hôtel de l'Europe, which John Murray's guide rated as excellent, together with the Balbi-d'Italie, the Nord and the York. In Florence in the mid-nineteenth century there were English bankers, wine merchants, a circulating library, physicians, grocers and booksellers. No wonder that Queen Victoria stayed at the palace at Fiesole in 1894 and was entertained by the Crawfords, sketched and visited the English cemetery to see Elizabeth Barrett Browning's grave, and saw many other distinguished English and American residents.

VISITING FLORENCE TODAY
WHERE TO STAY AND EAT

Many of Florence's hotels are converted from fifteenth- and sixteenth-century palaces. The **HÔTEL PORTA ROSSA** (Red Door), at via di Porta Rossa 19 (Tel. 287551) was, according to the Datini archives, a well-known albergo in 1386, and certainly dates from the thirteenth century when merchants trading in English wool lodged there. Part of the hotel is a tall thirteenth-century tower. Throughout the nineteenth century John Murray's guides praised it as 'economical, with French and German spoken'. It is a nostalgic place, much appreciated by Lord Acton, the doyen of Anglo-Florentine society, and Balzac and Stendhal. It has three stars, is quiet and central, but has no restaurant. The four-star **ANGLO AMERICANO**, via Garibaldi 9 (Tel. 282114), dates from 1780 when it was two linked villas. It is quiet and dignified, with an excellent restaurant, most appropriate for modern-day English and American travellers.

The Swiss hotelier Gerard Kraft linked the two old hotels De la Ville and Italie and called them the **EXCELSIOR ITALIE**. Archive data shows that the former was housed in 1427 in the present building. This five-star CIGA-owned luxury hotel in the Piazza Ognissanti 3 (Tel. 264201), has one of the best restaurants in Florence, and the well-known Donatello bar.

Known as the Continental Royal de la Paix in the eighteenth

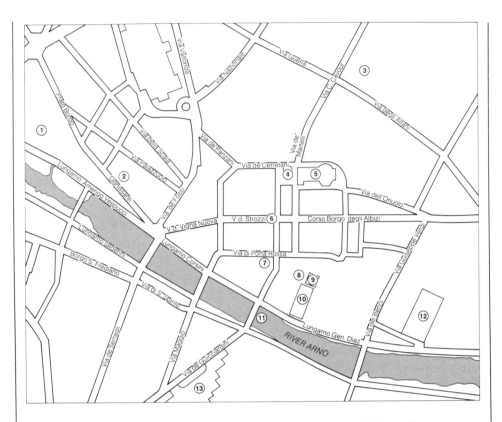

1 The Anglo Americano, Via Garibaldi 9   2 Excelsior Italie, Piazza d'Ognissanti 3   3 Galleria dell'Academia

4 Baptistry   5 Cathedral of Santa Maria del Fiore   6 Hotel Porta Rossa, Via di Porta Rossa 19   7 Piazza della Repubblica

8 Piazza della Signoria   9 Palazzo Vecchio   10 Galleria degli Uffizi   11 Ponte Vecchio   12 Church of Santa Croce

13 Palazzo Pitti

century, the five-star **GRAND HÔTEL** stands on a piazza corner overlooking the Arno at Piazza Ognissanti 1 (Tel. 278781). It is a CIGA hotel, quiet, sumptuous and elegant, and it has a distinguished restaurant. The **GRAND HÔTEL BAGLIONI** and the **GRAND HÔTEL VILLA CORA** both date from the late nineteenth century. The former is in the centre of town, the latter on a hill south of the Arno overlooking Florence. The Cora is housed in a Renaissance palace built for the Napoleons. Its restaurant, the **TAVERNA MACHIAVELLI**, has many specialities including '*costata*' (grilled veal fillets cooked in olive oil), and '*triglie*' (red mullet).

The most appropriate Florentine restaurants for the modern traveller are the **PAOLI**, founded in 1827, via dei Tavolini 12, between the Duomo and the Piazza della Signoria. Try their '*fettuccine alla Paoli*', or '*rognoncino trifolato*' with '*piselli alla fiorentina*'. The **BUCA LAPI**, via del Trebbio, near Piazza Sta. Maria Novella, is a cellar restaurant founded in 1880. Try their '*pâté di fegato della casa*', '*bistecca alla fiorentina*' (very good local beef steak) and '*fagioli Toscani all'olio*' (beans in olive oil). The **OLIVIERO**, via della Terme 51, has '*crêpes alla fiorentina*', '*maccheroncetti alla fiorentina*', several local fish dishes including '*baccalà*' (dried cod with olive oil, garlic and pepper) and '*zuccotto*', the delicious Florentine liqueur chocolate cake. The **SOSTANZA DETTO IL TROIA**, via del Porcellana 25, was started in 1869. Specialities include '*calamari in zimino*' (squid), and '*tortino di carciofi*' (artichoke pie).

DONEY, via de' Tornabuoni 48, is one of the best restaurants in Tuscany and a smart afternoon-tea café with a wide range of Italian pastries. Originally known as Café Donin, 150 years ago, then Doney et Neveux, it is still one of the social landmarks in Florence. By contrast, **VECCHIA FIRENZE**, Borge degli Albizi, has a long established reputation for value-for-money meals for artisans and students. Try their '*minestra di fagioli*', '*ribollita*', '*arista*' (roast pork), or '*trippa all' fiorentina*', then *pecorino* cheese, and gallo nero chianti to drink.

WHAT TO SEE AND DO

A hundred years ago John Murray's guide suggested a minimum stay of a week in Florence to do justice to the divine and beautiful city. Certainly try to allow four days, perhaps alternating each day an ecclesiastical sight in the morning and a classic museum (not Monday) in the afternoon, refreshed in between at Doney's or at the old Café Giubbe Rosse or Gilli's in the Piazza della Repubblica.

The main **TOURIST OFFICES** in Florence are the AAT at via de' Tornabuoni 15 (Tel. 2165440), and EPT, at via A. Manzoni 16 (Tel. 2478141), 700 metres east of the Duomo. They have two useful monthly papers, *Welcome to Florence*, and *Tempo Libero* (*Time Off*).

Apart from the Pitti Palace in the Boboli Gardens, a few minutes south of the River Arno across the fabled Ponte Vecchio, the essential sights are on the north bank, easily reached on foot. The main railway station, Santa Maria Novella, and the neighbouring Air Terminal for Pisa airport, are both 700 metres west of the Duomo.

The Duomo, the Cathedral of Santa Maria del Fiore, was begun in 1296, and finished in 1436, and is the same size as St Paul's in London. From the gallery there is a magnificent panorama of Florence, as there is from the nearby noble Giotto's Bell Tower, with 414 steps up to the top! The Baptistry doors by Pisano and Ghiberti are world-famous, as are the thirteenth-century frescoes on the inside of the dome. The cathedral museum has Michelangelo's 'Pietà' and works by Donatello, *the* Florentine sculptor. It is a few minutes' walk south to the main square, the elegant Piazza della Signoria, now being excavated for Roman remains. If you stroll down the via del Proconsolo you come to the Palazzo del Bargello, the thirteenth-century Governor-Constable's palace, which is now the Museo Nazionale containing the best of Florentine sculpture, with Michelangelo's 'David', 'Brutus and Bacchus', and Donatello's 'Marzocco and David'.

The Palazzo Vecchio is on the south side of the Piazza della Signoria. The thirteenth-century Old Palace with its bell-tower is one of the top museums in Florence, with Michelangelo's 'Victory Group' and paintings by Vasari and Bronzino. Adjacent on the river side is the Galleria degli Uffizi, Vasari's 1560 Renaissance palace where the powerful Medicis had their offices – or '*uffizi*'. Every traveller to Florence over four centuries visited the '*uffizi*' and often spent several months, looking at a different series of masterpieces each day! The Botticelli 'Birth of Venus' and 'Primavera', Leonardo's 'Annunciation' and 'Adoration of the Magi', Raphael's 'Leo X' and 'Two Cardinals', Titian's 'Flora' and 'Venus of Urbino' are just a few of the hundreds of masterpieces to be seen.

The other major art gallery north of the river is the Galleria dell' Accademia, 60 via Ricasoli, and also worth visiting is the adjacent Museum of St Mark, a former monastery. Both are in the northeast sector of Florence, 500 metres from the Duomo. In the former are major works by Michelangelo and in the latter Fra Angelico (1387–1455), one of the greatest Florentine painters, along with Giotto di Bondone (1267–1337), Masaccio (1401–1428), and Sandro Botticelli (1445–1510).

The famous Pitti Palace, 300 metres southwest of the Ponte Vecchio, houses no fewer than five quite different museums. The Palatine Gallery on the first floor is the best known gallery in this fifteenth-century Renaissance ducal palace built for the Medicis by Brunelleschi. Look at Titian's 'La Bella' and portrait of Pietro Aretino, and Raphael's 'Woman with a veil' and two Madonnas – del Granduca and della Seggiola. Both the Uffizi and the Pitti have excellent collections of the Dutch and Flemish schools, particularly Rubens, Rembrandt and Van Dyke.

Apart from the Duomo the most interesting churches are the Santa Croce (with cloisters), 400 metres east of the Uffizi, the Santa Maria Novella, 300 metres northwest of the Duomo, the Santa Maria del Carmine (frescoes), 400 metres west of the Pitti Palace, and the Medici chapel and San Lorenzo church, 250 metres northwest of the Duomo.

Fortunately the retreating German commander spared the fourteenth-century covered Ponte Vecchio for posterity. It must be the handsomest, most interesting river bridge in Europe. On its first floor is the Vasari Corridor which used to link the Uffizi with the Pitti Palace. Guided tours are possible from Room 25 in the former.

Amongst Florence's 400 palaces the following in particular must be mentioned: the Medici Palace 1460–1540, now known as the Palazzo Medici-Riccardi; the Strozzi Palace (with a small museum) begun in 1489; and the Palazzo Davanzati (now the Museo della Casa Fiorentina Antica). Houses with a significant historical interest are Casa Buonarroti, via Ghibellina 70, a small Michelangelo museum; Dante's house at via Santa Margherita 1; and Casa Guidi, Piazza San Felice 8, where the Brownings lived.

The most handsome square is the Piazza della Signoria, where in June each year the savage medieval football game of *callio storico* is played with a wooden ball by two teams each of 27 players. This is one of several highlights; others include the *Scoppio del Carro*, on Easter Sunday, when a large cart laden with fireworks is brought to the Piazza del Duomo and then literally exploded! The Festa del Patrono for St John the Baptist, patron saint of Florence, takes place on 24 June with fireworks and parades. In May there is the Cricket Festival when they are sold in decorated cages along the paths of the Cascine Park and in September is the Festival of the Rificolone with a children's procession carrying multicoloured paper lanterns.

There are three musical festivals during the summer. Maggio Musicale (May–June), Estate Fiesolana (June–August) at the Roman Theatre in Fiesole, and the Musica nelle Piazze held on Thursday evenings throughout the summer. Information can be obtained from **TEATRO COMUNALE**, corso Italia (Tel. 216253). There are also two film festivals each year (25 May–8 June) at the Forte Belvedere, and film documentaries in December.

Some of the best cafés are in the Piazza Repubblica and Piazza della Signoria, and the smart evening strollers take their '*passeggiata*' in the via del Calzaioli. The via de' Tornabuoni is the Bond Street of

Florence, harbouring Gucci, Ferragamo and Saint Laurent. Open markets are to be found at San Lorenzo, Parco delle Cascine, Mercato Nuovo and Piazza Ciompi.

The best local expedition is to Fiesole (population 15,000) on a hill eight kilometres east of Florence. See the Duomo, Roman theatre and Bandini Museum, and villas occupied by Charles Dickens, Shelley and other writers. Prato is 20 kilometres northwest of Florence. Despite being a textile town of 160,000 population, it has a cathedral with frescoes by naughty Fra Filippo Lippi, the thirteenth-century Imperial Castle, and the orange-tree-lined Piazza del Comune. The legend of 'Doubting Thomas' lingers on. The Virgin's Holy Girdle is a relic to be found in the chapel within the cathedral.

TURIN

the royal city

Heading south from Geneva or Lausanne, or east from Chambéry, the eighteenth- and nineteenth-century travellers had to visit Turin *en route* for Genoa, la Spezia and Florence. Under the name of 'Taurini' the Romans had built a fine town which, despite rule by the House of Savoy and occupation by the French crown, was rebuilt on a regular plan in the seventeenth and eighteenth centuries. The Romans influenced the grid-iron street pattern, and later the Savoyards and French left their imprint and helped establish Turin as the intellectual centre of Italy. Bombardment in World War II failed to destroy the old town, which huddles round the Duomo San Giovanni. From 1720 the royal family of Sardinia resided at Turin, as did the royal family of Italy from 1861 to 1945. The city is at the crossroads of northwest Italy. Mont Blanc and the Valle d'Aosta lie 113 kilometres to the northwest, Susa and the French border 53 kilometres to the west, Milan 140 kilometres to the east, Lakes Maggiore and Como 180 kilometres to the northeast, and the Italian Riviera lies to the south.

Thomas Coryat admired the delicate straw hats worn in the area, 'some have one hundred seames made with silke, prettily woven with silver, many flowers, borders and branches, valued at two duckatons'. He noticed the 'vines growing up high poles or railes, wallnut trees and early Rie', but suffered 'Great distemperature in my body by drinking the sweete wines of Piemont . . . grievous inflammation in face and hands! Advice – mingle their wine with water.' Very early in the seventeenth century Thomas found

Turin 'incompassed with hils, in a plaine, well walled, foure faire gates, a very strong citadel with 500 pieces of Ordinance: town built of brick in square form'. The sights to see were, he reported 'the Dukes Palace with a goodly [picture] gallery made of tall whitestone, the Cathedral Church of St John with its Quire, and the Tabernacle with its high Altar and Pulpit'. He then rode by coach to Siena. All the main roads in northern Italy were commended, particularly those in Lombardy and Piedmont.

A century later, in 1716, Lady Mary Wortley Montagu lodged in the Piazza Reale *en route* from Genoa to Mont Cénis and the Alps. 'Processions and masses are all the magnificence in fashion here' she wrote, 'the Holy Handkerchief [presumably she meant the shroud], churches, Kings palace and those of La Venerie and La Valentine are very agreeable retreats.'

The Earl of Essex was Ambassador in Turin in 1733, and noted 'The finest opera that ever was heard, and vast deal of company; there were 32 English here'. On Joseph Spence's third Grand Tour, six years later with young Lord Lincoln, they spent several months living in the Ecole Militaire in the Accademia Reale, where milord learned to ride, fence and dance. The Oxford professor of poetry was delighted with the 'delicious city, neat and beautiful' which by then had a population of 70,000, and a circumference of three miles.

Lord Lincoln wrote home, 'Turin is the most regular and prettiest city perhaps in Europe, ramparts, vistas, the Strada del Po their best street, but the Strada Novella with its stuccoed houses looks better. Tis of great length and terminates one way in the Porta Nuova and the other in the Kings Palace, with delightful walks on all sides. From the ramparts you can see the Alps, rugged and all covered with snow, and on the other side the most beautiful hills, sprinkled with little country seats, vineyards, fine clumps of wood and the Po running at the bottom of them..' The young milord rode at 8am, danced at 10, fenced at 11 and dined at 12.30. Lincoln went to the 'assemblies' every night, and met 'all the best company at Turin'. He visited the University, the Duke's Palace (where he admired the staircase by Don Filippo), the Royal Academy, the Duke of Savoy's palace with its 60 busts, and all the other museums and palaces.

The next year Horace Walpole and Thomas Gray stayed in Turin for two weeks in November. They went to the Teatro Regio to see the *Damned Soul*, to the Opera, and to a playhouse to see a set of strolling players. Italian comedy, Walpole wrote, was 'the devil of a house, the devil of actors'. He attended the assembly '*conversaziones*', and played at ombre, pharaoh and Tarot with 78 tall painted cards. These two travellers stayed at the Auberge Royale in a handsome avenue. Gray thought the opera was excellent, and in

1741 attended the carnival, with balls and masquerades every night. Laurence Sterne admired the city on his brief visit in 1762, but Edward Gibbon was less enthusiastic when he went there in 1764, even though Montesquieu described Turin as 'the finest village in the world'. The historian wrote, 'These palaces are cemented with the blood of the people. In a small poor kingdom like this they must grind the people in order to be equal with other crowned heads. In each gilded ornament I seem to see a village of Savoyards ready to die of hunger, cold and misery.' He found the Court old and dull, punctilious in etiquette but lacking true politeness.

James Boswell met John Wilkes in Turin in January 1765 after being carried over the mountains in the 'Alps Machine', a sort of cord and board chair carried by six porters. Boswell predictably met the notorious Madame de St Gilles, and at the Opera pressed his urgent gallantries on *three* Countesses. Despite this he was presented at Court to King Charles Emmanuel of Sardinia.

Thomas Nugent's *European Guide*, dated five years later, noted that Turin was one of the finest cities 'for the magnificence of its buildings, the beauty of its streets and squares and for all the conveniences of life'. The best inns were the Duke of Florence and the Spit, but Arthur Young in 1786 preferred the Hôtel Royal and the Angleterre, also called the Bonne Femme. Young visited the herb market, preferred the Strada della Dora Grossa to the Strada di Po, and bought books from Signora Briolo the bookseller. In the sensibly built King's Palace he admired the collection of paintings by Lorenzo Sabattini, Guido, Carlo Cignani, Gerard Dow, Saffa Ferrata, and Van Dyke.

Mariana Starke praised Turin and commended the Albergo dell' Universo, L'Europa, the Pension Suisse and L'Angelo. Lady Emma Hamilton passed through Turin on her Grand Tour with Gavin Hamilton, the painter, to meet Sir William Hamilton in Naples. A young travelling Scotsman, Joseph Forsyth, was arrested by Napoleon's police in Turin in May 1803 and spent the next eleven years in French captivity. There he wrote a book called *Remarks on the Antiquities of Rome*.

Lady Frances Shelley on her third Grand Tour stayed at the Hôtel de l'Europe in 1833, 'a charming residence, the picture galleries are excellent, the Cabinet of Natural History well arranged'. Lady Foster, who lived in the nearby Vigna del Duco, explained to her the mysteries and intrigues of the Cicisbeism social customs. On her return to Italy as a widow in 1840, Mary Shelley wrote, 'All Italian travellers know what it is after toiling up the bleak bare northern Swiss side of the Alps to descend towards ever-vernal Italy. The rhododendron was thick, bushes in full bloom first adorned the mountain sides, then pine forests, then chestnut groves. The mountains were cleft into woody ravines, the waterfalls scattered their spray and their gracious melody, flowery and green, clothed in radiance and gifted with plenty, Italy opened upon us.'

VISITING TURIN TODAY

WHERE TO STAY AND EAT

John Murray's guide-book recommended a stay of two days at Turin plus six days if gentle excursions were made to Lanzo, Sacra di San Michele, Racconigi, Ivrea and Aosta. The best café in town was the San Carlo; the best restaurants Le Indie and Il Pastore. In 1842, Turin chocolate was reckoned to be the best in Italy and the '*pane grisino*', long thin wands of bread, were said to be very good. But avoid poultry in the spring!

At the end of the nineteenth century John Murray commended several hotels including the two-star **DOGANA VECCHIA**, via Corte d'Apello 4 (Tel. 6511963), and the **EUROPA**, Piazza Castello 99 (Tel. 6544238). Mariana Starke had earlier suggested the two-star **UNIVERSO**, corso Peschiera 166 (Tel. 6336480). Some modern travellers may prefer the four-star **VILLA SASSI** (which has an excellent restaurant) housed in a seventeenth-century villa at via Traforo del Pino 47 (Tel. 5890556).

The **DEL CAMBIO** restaurant, Piazza Carignano 2 (Tel. 6546690), is undoubtedly the oldest and most elegant place to eat in Turin; it has white and gilt walls, crystal chandeliers and gilt mirrors. Ask for the Turin speciality '*agnolotti piemontesi*' (ravioli stuffed with lamb and cabbage) or '*costolette alla fagiolini*' with truffles. Try one of the regional wines – Arneis, Barbaresco, Barbera, Gavi or Tunina. Your aperitif choice is easy – either Carpano, Martini or Cinzano vermouths blended in Turin, or even sparkling Asti Spumante.

The two most elegant cafés in Turin are the **SAN CARLO** and the **BARATTI AND MILANO**. The modern traveller should try them both and ask for the Turin pastries called '*bocca di Leone*' and the delicious *panini* bread. Other dishes to ask for are '*bagna caoda*' (a hot dip of anchovies, spices and garlic fried in olive oil), '*bugie*' (fried sweets), '*torta di nocciole*' (hazlenut cake), and '*bignole*' (cream puffs). Turin's famous chocolates are called '*gianduiotti*'.

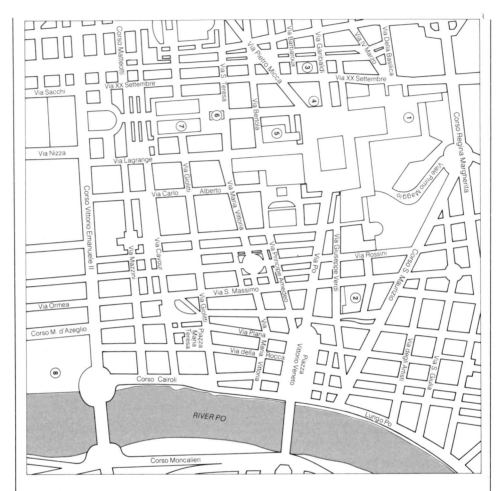

1 Duomo San Giovanni and Capella della Santa Sindone 2 Mole Antonelliana 3 Dogana Vecchia, Via Corte d'Apello 4

4 Europa, Piazza Castello 99 5 Science Academy Building 6 Piazza San Carlo 7 Teatro San Carlo 8 Parco del Valentino

WHAT TO SEE AND DO

The capital of Piedmont, nestling under the Alps, has now become a highly industrialized city. It has a population of over a million and is the home of the Italian car and tyre industries, and Italian vermouths, and is the guardian of the Turin Shroud. The mighty River Po starts in the French Alps, bisects Turin, and travels due east to the Adriatic south of Venice.

Start your sightseeing of Turin from the **CAFFÈ TORINO**, Piazza San

Carlo 204, the large main square of the old town, half-way between the main railway station (1868) and the Duomo San Giovanni. Turin is a dignified, cultured city with a large university, many antiquities and bookshops, well known newspapers including *La Stampa*, and eight theatres and concert halls.

The summer festival, *I Punti Verdi*, of music, theatre and dance takes place in various parks from 14–24 July. A classical concert season is given in the autumn, (*Settembre Musica*), and from October to March the Teatro Regio has a season of opera, ballet (Turin Dance) and concerts. During April the *Mostra Mercanto dell'Antiquariato* is held at the Palazzo Nervi. Contact the **ASSESORATO PER LA CULTURA**, via San Francesco da Paola 3 (Tel. 8397956), or **UFFICIO ATTIVITÀ PROMOZIONALI**, Teatro Regio, Piazza Castello (Tel. 549126). The **TOURIST OFFICE** (EPT) is at via Roma 222 (Tel. 535181), in the Piazza San Carlo, and also at the Porta Nuova railway station (Tel. 5313270).

The Guarini-designed Science Academy Building (closed Mondays) is in the northeast corner of the Piazza San Carlo. This seventeenth-century Palazzo houses four good collections: the Egyptian Antiquities (second only to Cairo); the Galleria Sabauda (with seventeenth-century Bolognese and Milanese paintings, plus Piedmontese works of the fifteenth and sixteenth centuries); the Dutch and Flemish collections, which are probably the finest in Italy (Van Eyck, Memling and Van der Weyden); and the Gualino Collection of paintings, sculptures, plate and furnishings. In the via Magenta, one kilometre away on the west side, is the Municipal Gallery of Modern Art, and in the Palazzo Madama, near the Duomo in the Piazza Castello, is the Museum of Ancient Art. In the Royal Palace, next to the Duomo, is housed the Royal Armoury, one of the most comprehensive collections in Italy.

For ultra-modern travellers in this auto-city, the Museo dell'Automobile Carlo Biscaretti di Ruffia in the Corso Unità d'Italia in the south of Turin, covers three acres and houses many hundreds of Turin-made cars and tyres.

Most of the prinicipal sights of Turin are near the elegant via Roma, which bisects the old town. Turin has twelve kilometres of shopping arcades and the two most important areas are the via Garibaldi between the Piazza Statuto and the Piazza Castello, and the Corso Vittorio Emanuele II running past the main railway station.

One of the major sights is the Holy Shroud, housed in Guarini's 1668 Capella della Santa Sindone. Although now generally accepted as a medieval fake, the shroud arrived in Turin from Chambéry in 1578 and has been seen by millions of the faithful in the last four centuries. The Renaissance cathedral was built in the fifteenth century for Cardinal Della Rovere. An essential visit. So too is the inside of the Basilica of San Lorenzo, another seventeenth-century Guarini creation.

In February, at Venaus, the Sword Dance takes place with skilful jugglers in period costume performing with large swords. At nearby Ivrea, carnival week includes parades, the battle of the oranges, and historical tableaux. In April, at San Georgio di Susa, is the Feast of St George with tableaux and sword dances, and in May at Scalenghe is the May Tree ceremony.

The best views of Turin are from the Mole Antonelliana between the Duomo and the River Po. This eccentric folly, 183 metres in height, was started in 1863 as a synagogue, but is now a two-storey Greek temple crowned by a lighthouse. By lift one can ascend to the observatory on top. (Closed Monday.) Along the west side of the River Po are the Botanical Gardens and Parco del Valentino, extending for nearly two kilometres. The medieval village (Borgo Medioevale), seventeenth-century Castello del Valentino and New Theatre are all in the park.

So take Murray's advice of 150 years ago. Spend two or three days in Turin, and longer if you wish to explore the mighty Basilica of Superga, Juvara's masterpiece, built in 1731 and now reached by cable car. A longer stay would also allow visits to the majestic abbey of the Sacra di S. Michele alle Chiuse, the castles of Aglie and Moncalieri, the palace of Venaria Reale, and the hunting lodge of Stupinigi on the outskirts of the city.

MILAN

'La Grande'

The capital of Lombardy, situated by the fertile tributaries of the River Po, has always known prosperity. By tradition Milan is a trading centre, and the Lombard bankers and money-changers were famous throughout Europe in the Middle Ages. Even now the city has 432 banks (812 in the district as a whole). The Viscontis and the Sforzas were the controlling families of Milan in the thirteenth to sixteenth centuries. The last of the line, Ludovico, married Beatrice d'Este and sponsored Leonardo da Vinci. No wonder that Fynes Moryson, having walked 90 miles from Genoa, described the city as

'La Grande': it was 'large, populous and rich, [with] low built bricke houses, nice town gates of rounde forme. The great and stately Il Domo of white marble was supported by one hundred pillars.' He also admired the church of St Lawrence and the vines of Lombardy outside the town.

Thomas Coryat arrived in 1610 via Buffolero and Novara from Ticino, part of Switzerland. He recorded meticulously the facts and the sights. The town wall was 24 feet broad, 64 feet high and had ten gates in its seven-mile circumference. 'The Citadell is the fairest in Europe, seems rather a towne, incomparable strength, built with bricke, covered in fair tile, moated around, two mills, one for grinding, one for gunpowder manufacture, great ordinance with sixteen feet brass cannon. The population of 300,000 needs 120 schools and 168 churches (in five categories). The magnificent Hospitall with 112 chambers relieves 4,000 poor people. The main trades are embroiderers, cutlers making hilts for swords and daggers, and silkemen.' Coryat described in detail the Church of St Ambrose, St Barnabas, the Cathedral Church of our Lady (built in 1386), the Monastery of the Ambrosian monks, the palace of the Viscounts of Milan, and the Church of the Augustinian monks.

Over the Simplon on mules came John Evelyn and his guide, fending off bears, wolves and wild goats, passing over roaring cataracts, along precarious ledges cut out of the rocks, and through narrow passes between fallen mountains. In 1645 the Spaniards ruled Milan, but Evelyn still went to the Opera and admired the snow-white statues on the enormous cathedral, though he did not like its Gothic design.

Joseph Spence recorded that there were 35,000 printed books and 15,000 manuscripts in the Ambrosian library, and that the Grand Hospital looked after 12,000 bastards (with ten new ones each week). He admired the Treasury in the Duomo (the latter, 'length 500', breadth 300', height 400''), the Biffi statue and the Count d'Arese's gallery with works by da Vinci, Arpino and Guido. Spence noted that the women of Milan 'never walk the streets, [but] look out of wooden latticed windows (of a jealous nature), their hair with two long braids behind, drawn round a silver bodkin on the top of their heads, wear two-three red rose-buds, a sprig of jessamin and a little cap with short red ribbons' – sounds enchanting! He also admired the six-month clock, rare cloths from the Indies, and the collection of emeralds in Settala's gallery.

On the last of his continental journeys Laurence Sterne was well received in Milan, where he enjoyed a brisk flirtation with the celebrated Marchesa Fagniani. John Wilkes travelled the same route in 1764 through Milan and Parma to Bologna where his mistress Madame Corradini was awaiting him. In January 1765 James Boswell inspected the Duomo and the Ambrosian library, and 'made a perfunctory inspection of pictures, palaces, churches and cathedrals'. It is doubtful whether he ignored the well-dressed Milanese women, attired 'with skilful abandon', or the many obliging pimps offering women of whatever colour and country wanted. There were numerous beggars even at the Palazzo Simonetto, two miles outside the town, where the traveller was advised to hear the famous echo. Like Joseph Addison half a century earlier, Boswell fired his pistol into the air and counted 58 echoes.

The first traveller to be struck by the quality of music to be heard in Milan was Arthur Young. At the Opera House, completed in 1778 ('most noble theatre, largest and most handsome ever seen, with 6 rows of boxes, 36 boxes in a row') he sat in the pit on a broad easy sofa ('good space for one's legs') and paid two and a half livres to hear the Impresario in *Augusta* by Cimarosa, 'a pleasing quintetto'. Young stayed at the Albergo del Pozzo, but reckoned the Reali and the Imperiali to be the best in town. His room, dinner and supper cost him six livres a day (six livres Milanese = one ecu = four shillings in English money in 1786). He was waited on by men, and outside an itinerant band of musicians gave a 'seranade to the illustrissimi, excellentissimi, noble Signori Inglesi'.

In 1797 the French Army entered Milan under a rain of flowers, and it became the capital of the Cisalpine Republic and later of the Kingdom of Italy. Napoleon was crowned there in 1805, and Marie Henri Beyle (alias Stendhal), who spent several years in Italy and met Lord Byron, was captivated by the town's liveliness and gaiety. Mariana Starke advised that the best hotels at the time were the Gran Bretagna, Croce di Malta and the Suisses, but Catherine Wilmot stayed at the Albergo Reale.

John Mayne thought the Teatro della Scala was second only to Naples' San Carlo Opera. There were 70 performers, the horns were good, but the audience was noisy. The men talked business in the pit, and the army officers were drunk, played cards and drank coffee during the performance. Mayne, in 1814, encountered numerous parties of strolling players in all parts of the town, two or three singers accompanied by guitar, violoncello and violins singing overtures of opera music with great spirit.

Two years later Lady Frances Shelley on her first Grand Tour arrived via Lodi from the southeast. She thought the Milanese women were particularly pretty. 'They wear their hair dressed in plaits held by silver pins.' She and her husband saw and heard Winter's *Mahomet* at La Scala and reported that 'the music is beautiful and the singers good'. She visited the Forum Bonaparte – a Triumphal Arch on the Corso, and saw the carnival 'in all its splendour and gaiety'.

Percy Bysshe Shelley was quite disillusioned with the Milanese – men and women – but Lord Byron, writing to John Murray, found 'Milan is striking, the Cathedral superb, the city altogether reminds me of Seville . . . the Brera gallery has some fine paintings, the il Guercino (1590–1666) of Abraham putting away Hagar and Ishmael, the Carlo Borromeo (canonized in 1610) chapel in front of the altar at Milan Cathedral . . .' The inns, however, were 'not up to much . . .'. Writing to Augusta Leigh, Byron described his journey: 'The Simplon is the most superb of all possible routes, navigated Lago Maggiore, went over the Borromean Islands, fine but too artificial, the lake is beautiful as indeed is the whole country from Geneva hither and the Alpine part most magnificent'. What delighted the noble poet most was a manuscript collection he discovered in the Ambrosian library of original love letters and verses of Lucretia Borgia and Cardinal Bembo, and a lock of her hair!

Dickens visited Milan briefly and rushed excitedly to La Scala, only to find the performance 'execrable'. He wrote, 'It is so strange and like a dream to me to hear the delicate Italian once again – so beautiful to see the delightful sky and all the picturesque wonders of the country'. Mary Shelley returned to her beloved Italy in 1840 and on her visit to Milan stayed at the Hôtel de la Ville, run by a Swiss with a pretty English wife. She looked at Leonardo's fresco expressing 'majesty and love'. She saw the Petrarch relics in the Ambrosian library, heard *Templano* played at La Scala and condemned the horse-dealing and stock-jobbing carried on in the pit. She visited a silk manufacturer and saw the looms at work, describing the sight as, 'cloth of glass, spun glass ideal for curtains and hangings, all bright yellow and white'. Bayard Taylor heard Rossini's *William Tell* at La Scala and wrote afterwards, 'overture very beautiful, the rest unworthy'. He was depressed by the 'bevies of priests in their cocked hats and black robes, mournful to see a people oppressed in the name of religion'.

John Ruskin was in Milan a few years later, and surprisingly had some nice things to say. 'I like this Milan as I always did – it is far more Italian in the people than Florence. The women wear the black veil and are pretty coiffées, the men are honest and busy – the air is cool. I saw the Mont Rosa, Finster Aarhorn, the Simplon, St Gothard, Jungfrau all clear this morning at five.'

Mark Twain and his companions arrived by the new train to Milan from Genoa in 1867. He fell in love with the Duomo. 'At last a forest of graceful needles, shimmering in the amber sunlight, rose slowly above the pigmy housetops – the Cathedral. What a wonder it is! It was a vision, a miracle – an anthem sung in stone, a poem wrought in marble.' Then aged 32, he visited what every modern traveller should visit – the Duomo, La Scala (largest theatre in the world), the Ambrosian library (MSS by Virgil, annotations by Petrarch, drawings by Michelangelo), the huge Roman amphitheatre (flooded for spirited regattas), the endless gardens and shrubs. There is, however, no need to go to a public bath-house, with three people in *one* tub – and no soap! He did appreciate the Asti wines.

VISITING MILAN TODAY

WHERE TO STAY AND EAT

In 1842 John Murray wrote that the best hotel in Milan was **DE LA VILLE CHEZ BAIRR** (an Englishwoman who had married the owner). Located between the Duomo and La Scala, at via Hoepli 6 (Tel. 867651), this distinguished old hotel, now agreeably modernized, but with tapestries, old clocks and a fine collection of china, must commend itself to the modern traveller. Its **VIVERO** restaurant will proffer Milanese cuisine. The **MARINO ALLA SCALA** originally (pre 1842) Il Marino, Piazza della Scala 5 (Tel. 867803), has a profusion of antiques, chandeliers and velvet curtains. The third choice is the **HÔTEL CAVOUR**, via Fatebenefratelli 21 (Tel. 650983), which was John Murray's second choice in 1899. Again close to the Duomo and La Scala. The composer Verdi was ill in 1901 in the **GRAND HÔTEL ET DE MILAN**, via Manzoni 29, another distinguished old hotel founded in 1860. The final one in the selection is the **HÔTEL MANIN**, founded in 1848.

The **BETTOLINO** restaurant was started in 1750 and is the second oldest in Milan. The **BOEUCC** dates from 1800, and the **DIANA** and the **TRATTORIA DELLA PESA** are pre-1900. The **SAVINI RESTAURANT**, Galleria Vittorio Emanuele 11 (Tel. 898343), was founded in 1867 and is in the centre of the glass arcade opposite the Duomo. Under the crystal chandeliers ask for 'risotto alla Milanese', 'costoletta alla Milanese', or 'taglialine alla Savini' (prosciutto, peas and cream). The wines to ask for are Oltrepo Pavese Rosso to wash down their 'osso bucco' (a Milanese speciality).

The **BRASERA MENEGHINA**, via Circo 10 (Tel. 02808108), is installed in a former monastery in the ruins of a Roman amphitheatre. Since 1673 it has been a tavern, and it is now the oldest in Milan and a

1 Pinacoteco di Brera **2** Hotel Cavour, Sempione Park, Via Fatebenefratelli 21 **3** Gallery Poldi Pezzoli **4** Teatro alla Scala

5 The Marino, Piazza della Scala 5 **6** Hôtel de la Ville, Via Ulricho Hoepli 6 **7** Duomo

quality restaurant. Try their 'risotto alla milanese' or 'rostin negaa' (veal chops cooked in white wine) and the Grumello dry red wine. Traditional dishes to ask for are 'riso giallo' (rice with saffron) and 'cassoeula' (pork and cabbage).

GIANNINA, via Amatore Sciesa 8, and TAVERNA DEL GRAN SASSO, Piazzale Principessa Clotilde 10, are two more very old traditional restaurants. BIFFI, in the Galleria Vittorio Emanuele, is in the most popular arcade in Milan and was John Murray's No.1 restaurant choice a century back. It is still very popular. Try their 'risotto alla milanese', and ask for a bottle of ruby red Sassella, one of the best Valtellina wines. The BOTTEGA DEL VINO SCOFFONE, via Victor Hugo 4, is a tavern dating from 1700 which offers a huge range of wines as well as food. Try their Lugana white or Sforzato red.

WHAT TO SEE AND DO

The nineteenth-century traveller to northern Italy was advised to spend four days in Milan. The twentieth-century visitor should try to reserve two or three days, more if the fashion capital of Italy seduces you. On the via Monte Napoleone and the via Montenero, between the Duomo and the Piazza San Babila are the most elegant boutiques in the country, including Monitor and Fiorucci; Peck, at via Spadari 9, built in 1894, is the equivalent of Fortnum and Mason.

An essential sight is the Duomo with its gilded Madonnina, 108 metres up. Started in AD1386, it now has a total of 96 gargoyles, 135 spires and 2,245 statues, and can absorb up to 40,000 worshippers. Across the piazza is the Museo del Duomo which documents the history of the cathedral, and nearby is the famous Teatro (and Museo) alla Scala, which seats nearly 3,000 people. The theatre was demolished in World War II and rebuilt in 1948. In the foyer are statues of Rossini, Donizetti, Bellini and Verdi wearing his top hat. The opera season is mid-December to May. Seat bookings are difficult, and reservations must be made well in advance. La Scala has a summer season of recitals, operettas and concerts. The Conservatorio Teatro Lirico and the Piccolo Teatro are the other theatres/concert halls of note. Read about their performances in the *Corriere della Sera*, the Milan-produced national newspaper.

The two most important art galleries, which should not be missed, and which were often mentioned by the travellers, are the Pinacoteca Ambrosiana, Piazza Pio XI 2, and the Pinacoteca di Brera, via Brera 28. The former has mainly Lombard and Venetian schools from the fourteenth to eighteenth centuries. Leonardo's 'Portrait of a Musician' and Caravaggio's 'Basket of Fruit' are notable, as are Raphael's cartoons.

The Ambrosian library containing Petrarch's notes is in the same building, a palace built in 1609. In the latter go and see Piero della Francesca's 'Sacra Conversazione', Raphael's 'Betrothal of the Virgin' and Mantegna's 'Dead Christ'. Venetian painters include Bellini, Tintoretto and Titian. Many seventeenth-century Milanese artists are represented, including Morazzone, Cerano and Procaccini. Two other galleries of note are the Modern Art, via Palestro 16, and the Poldi Pezzoli, via Manzoni 17. The Ambrosiana is closed on Saturday, the others on Monday.

Apart from the Duomo, the other important churches to visit are the Santa Maria delle Grazie in the Piazza of that name, and the Sant'Eustorgio, corso di Porta. In the former is Leonardo's famous 'Last Supper', painted in 1495–97.

Milan is built in a series of circles, radiating outwards from the Duomo. The Brera is 600 metres north, the Ambrosio 800 metres west, and the huge fifteenth-century Sforza castle, the large Sempione Park, and the Sta Maria delle Grazie are one kilometre west-north-west from the Duomo.

The **TOURIST OFFICE** (EPT) is in the via Marconi, in the Piazza del Duomo (Tel. 809662). Their booklets include *Tutta Milano*, *Milano Giovane* and *Milano Mese*. Local transport is by Metro (two lines) and frequent trams and buses. The main railway station, the Centrale, is two kilometres northeast of the Duomo, with the large public gardens half-way between the two.

The Corso Vittorio Emanuele near the Duomo is the great Milan rendezvous for shopping and eating. The most elegant shops are in the via Monte Napoleone and via Manzoni. (The word 'milliner' derives from Milan – the city of fashionable clothes!)

At Epiphany, early in January, the Procession of the Three Kings takes place, a grand costumed folklore parade through the city, and in May at Legnano is the double event – Saga del Carroccio, a pageant, and Palio delle Contrade, with processions and horse riding displays. In June is the festival of the Navigli, a canal festival. Finally, in early December, there is the Fair of Oh Bei! Oh Bei! around the Basilica of Sant' Ambrogio.

Milan makes an appropriate centre for visits to the other five principal Lombard towns – beautiful Bergamo with its hilltop old walled town, the Carrara Academy and eighteenth-century travellers' inn, the Agnello d'Oro; Brescia, with its two cathedrals, Queriniana library and Tosio-Martinengo Gallery; Cremona, Virgil's home and birthplace of the famous violin-maker Stradivari and the composer Monteverdi; Mantua, with its Gonzaga Palace and St Andrew's Basilica (Tom Coryat in 1610 called Mantua 'that sweet paradise'); and finally Pavia with its fourteenth-century Charter House (ten kilometres north) and University, and twelfth-century church of San Michele.

A folklore festival is held here called Settembre Pavese. Lady Mary Wortley Montagu, worldly Grand Traveller, found Brescia so beautiful that she retired there in 1746, grew vines, fished, and played whist with the local priests.

GENOA

'Genova the Superb'

At first sight one would not credit Genoa, one of the four ancient Italian marine republics, as being of much interest to the original travellers, let alone those of today. Equidistant from Milan, Turin and the French border, it has been owned or occupied by the Romans, the Spaniards, the French, the Austrians, and more recently, the Germans. Most of the famous Genoese, including Christopher Columbus and Andrea Doria, have been admirals: the most notable exception is Giuseppe Mazzini, the Genoese patriot who took refuge in London in 1837 before becoming dictator of the Roman Republic in 1848. Rubens, Van Dyck and Puget lived and worked in Genoa in the seventeenth century, and many of their paintings are still to be seen in the local museums. Most of Genoa's 30 palaces date from the fifteenth and sixteenth centuries, and the via Aurea (now renamed via Garibaldi) was *the* street of the palaces. Despite World War II bombing of the harbour, the old town of Genoa still retains a great deal of charm.

Fynes Moryson, on his Grand Tour of 1595 wrote, 'Mountains without wood, Sea without fish, Men without faith, Women without shame, the white Moores, Genoa the Proud'. He admired the great antiquities, the 'Pallaces' of marble, narrow streets paved with flint, the houses of freestone five or six storeys high, and windows 'glassed', which in those days was rare in Italy. Genoa's mild climate was praised for its 'summer flowers in December'. Moryson then walked 90 miles to Milan!

John Evelyn in 1641 stayed at an inn run by Mr Zachary, an Englishman. He wrote, 'Never was any artificial sceane more beautiful to the eye of the beholder . . . so full for the bigenesse of well designed and stately Palaces. But Genoa was more stayn'd with horrid acts of revenge and murder than any one place in Europ, or haply the World . . .' In the Palazzo Doria were 'whole tables and beadsteads of massy silver besides many of them set with Achates, Onyxes, Cornelians, Lazolis, Pearle, Turquizes and other precious stones: The Pictures and Statues innumerable. Orange-trees, Citrus and Pomengranads, Fountaines, Grotts and Statues amongst which one of Jupiter of a Colossal magnitude. The mole a stupendous feat of engineering, the pharos a Lanterne of incredible height, new town walls made with herculean industry.'

Early in the eighteenth century Joseph Addison recorded that the 'Genoese are extremely Cunning, Industrious and enured to hardship'. Lady Mary Wortley Montagu visited Genoa several times. Her social rank and knowledge of the language meant that she was accepted into society, attended the '*conversaziones*', and commented about the strange '*Cizisbei's*' customs. She thought the Strada Nuova 'perhaps the most beautiful line of buildings in the world'. She admired the vast palace of Durazzo, the two Balbi palaces linked by a magnificent colonnade, the Palace of the Imperiale at San Pier d'Arena, and the Palazzo Doria Tursi with rich furniture, 'of most elegant taste'. The painting galleries were visited. Her favourites were paintings by Guido and Correggio, but she thought the pencil drawings by Raphael, Paulo Veronese, Titian, Carracci and Michelangelo should be seen. The black and white marble churches of St Lawrence, the Annunciation, and the Jesuit St Ambrose were also appreciated. James Howell found Genoa full of beggars and the Genoese dialect the worst in Italy. Later on, Mrs Piozzi found the beggars aggressive, although she had great sympathy for the Turkish prisoners in the harbour hulks.

The *Juvenile Travellers*, the collective précis of six distinguished eighteenth-century travellers, pulled no punches about the Genoese 'gloom and sadness of countenance' . . . 'they cherish a disdainful pride and love of show that dazzles strangers, confers no real happiness. The Genoese trade in money, lend huge sums to foreign merchants, export dried mushrooms, silk flowers, gold filigree, but local silks and velvets are well manufactured.' They were considered reserved, pompous and ignorant. They did not speak Italian but a jargon of Genoese dialects, a corruption of pure Italian. The ladies wore no jewels, dressed in black with ugly cotton veils, seldom read, but gamed and had a superstitious devotion to their saints!

Henry Swinburne in 1770 called Genoa the city of palaces, and Lady Pomfret thought that it had a noble beauty, magnificence and politeness of society. Sir James E. Smith found the Hôtel Gran Cervo excellent in 1793, and admired the usual tourist antiquities and the magnificent buildings, declaring Genoa altogether a 'superb neat town, noble port, ships, wealth and populousness'. The two streets Balbi and Nuova 'composed of the most sumptuous palaces in Europe, pillars and cornices of marble, spacious courts, arcades and galleries'. He praised the opera and the 'rich treasures of paintings' of Genoa.

The American Bayard Taylor's visit in 1840 produced a poetic vision. 'Genoa, like some grand painting of a city, rising with its domes and towers and palaces from the edge of the glorious bay shut in by mountains – the whole scene clad in those deep delicious sunny hues which you admire so much in a picture. The City of Columbus deeply tinctured with the magic of history and romance of heroic Admiral Andrea Doria.. the Doria palace fit to be a monarch's residence.' Taylor encountered a 'religious festa, [with] banners from the windows, floated across the streets'. He slowly moved on with the procession through the city and noted 'the choirboys and nuns proceeded the friars in black and white robes carrying the statue of the saint with a pyramid of flowers, crosses and blazing wax tapers while companies of soldiery and monks followed. Behind them came the band playing solemn airs which alternated with the deep monotonous chanting of the friars. The whole scene dimly lighted by the wax tapers produced in me a feeling nearly akin to fear, as if I was witnessing some ghostly unearthly spectacle.'

The Dickens family arrived by sea from Nice and San Remo. They rented the decaying pink Villa Bella Vista, and 'Boz' watched the marriage brokers, sedan chairs and the squalid mazes, and admired the regilded Church of the Annunziata. After three months the family moved to the Palazzo Peschiere (Fishponds), with a Spanish Duke on the floor below. Despite the charms of Mrs de la Rue, *The Chimes: A Goblin Story* was written in Genoa and published at Christmas 1844. Dickens 'came to have an attachment for the very stones in the streets of Genoa and to look back upon the city with affection as connected with many hours of happiness and quiet'.

Mark Twain liked Genoa. 'Early in the bright summer morning the stately city rose up out of the sea and flung back the sunlight from her hundred palaces – sumptuous inside but very rusty without and make no pretensions to architectural magnificence: "Genoa the Superb" would be a felicitious title if it referred to the women!' . . . 'The Genoese live in the heaviest, highest, broadest, darkest, solidest houses one can imagine . . . but Genoa's greatness has degenerated into an unostentatious commerce in velvets and silver filigree work . . .'

VISITING GENOA TODAY

WHERE TO STAY

Today there are very few old hotels in Genoa, although half a dozen were built in the post-railway period in the late nineteenth century. The **ADLER ROYAL**, built in 1890, is now modernized, as is the three-star **AQUILA REALE**, both at via Arsenale di Terra 5 (Tel. 261641). The original Astoria Isotta is now the **NUOVA ASTORIA**, four-star, Piazzale Brignole 4 (Tel. 873316). The **BRISTOL PALACE**, four-star, via 20 Settembre 35 (Tel. 592541), and the **VITTORIA E ORLANDINI**, via Balbi 33 (Tel. 261923), both date from 1880.

1 Hôtel Adler Royale, Aquila Reale, Via Arsenale di Terra 5　**2** Museo Durazzo Pallavicini　**3** Museo Bianco

4 Museo Doria Tursi　**5** Saint Lawrence's Cathedral　**6** Teatro Carlo Felice　**7** Bristol Palace, Via 20 Settembre 35

Two nineteenth-century restaurants are the **ANTICA OSTERIA DEL BAI**, via Quarto 12 (Tel. 387478), where Garibaldi used to dine, and the **CICCHETTI**, via Gianelli (Tel. 3316410), which dates from 1860.

Genoa's cuisine is similar to that of Nice but obviously more Italianate: '*pesto*' is a sauce of cheeses, basil and garlic cooked in olive oil; '*burrida*' is a fish stew; '*cappon magro*', a fish dish; '*totani*' is octopus; '*trippa*' is tripe; '*polpettone*' a meat and vegetable loaf; '*lumache*' are snails; '*ripieni*' is stuffed zucchini; '*cima*' is a veal dish; '*pansotti*' is ravioli with spinach sauce; and '*pandolce*' is the sweet cake of Genoa. '*Torta pasqualina*' is a puff pastry with vegetable filling. The local white wines

147

are Polcevera, Cinqueterre and Coronata. Restaurants serving Genoese food include **VITTORIO AL MARE**, Belvedere Firpo 11 on the waterfront; **PICHIN**, at the Piazza Fontane Marose; **TRATTORIA DEL MARIO**, Piazza Bianchi in the port; **GRAN GROTTO**, via Fiume 11; and **PICCOLO**, via Casaregis 33.

WHAT TO SEE AND DO

After the advent of the railways, John Murray's recommended north Italian tour of three months suggested four days in Genoa. For the modern traveller three will suffice, and the Tourist Office has a detailed tour.

A boat trip round the harbour past the Lanterna lighthouse takes an hour, although like all modern ports that of Genoa has lost much of its character. Twenty-five kilometres of quays service the annual docking of 8,000 ships, and ferries sail to Sardinia, Sicily, Barcelona and Tunis.

Take a walk down the golden streets of via Garibaldi (Aurea that was) and via Balbi to view the score of palaces, many of which are now museums. The Cataldi, Doria Tursi, Bianco and Rosso are in the former, and the Reale (originally the Durazzo), the dell'Università and the Pallavinici in the latter. They are usually closed at weekends or on Mondays, but *always* enquire at the **TOURIST OFFICES** at via Roma 11 (Tel. 581407), or in either of the two railway stations, Principe and Brignole. The Palazzo Spinola, the National Gallery, at Piazza Pellicceria 1 (closed Monday) is at the east end of the via Garibaldi. The Gothic black and white marble St Lawrence's Cathedral is also rich in seventeenth-century and eighteenth-century Genoese paintings, and has a notable treasury. It lies just west of the Palazzo Ducale in the centre of the old town. Do not be surprised to see many works by the famous Flemish painters Rubens, Van Dyke, Gerard David and Provost in the palace-museums and churches amongst the Genoese artists Magnasco, Cambiaso and Strozzi.

The narrow alleys of the old town are called '*carrugi*', and harbour many little food shops called '*Torte e Farinate*' producing fried fish and savoury pies and the local speciality of '*farinuta*' (chick pea paste cooked in olive oil). The harbour, like all commercial ports, can be dangerous, so you are advised to take care in the daytime and not go there at night.

The prettiest square in Genoa is the Piazza San Matteo, the brashest is the Piazza di Ferrari, and the most interesting church is the Santa Maria di Castello, once a crusader hostel and church, with cloisters, courtyard, chapels and gardens. A funicular railway from Largo Della Zecca (via Cairoli) takes one up 350 metres above sea level to Righi. The view of the city, harbour and Mediterranean are superb. Look for the line of eighteenth-century forts of Richelieu, Quezzi, Diamente, Sperone, Tenaglia and Belvedere.

The original Opera House, the Carlo Felice, where Paganini played so often is in the course of being renovated. The Teatro Margherita and the Teatro Comunale have three-month opera seasons in the winter. During the summer there is also a ballet festival at Nervi, the eastern seaside suburb of Genoa.

The main fair of Genoa is that of Santa Agata, which John Evelyn noted during his visits in the early seventeenth century. May sees the fish festival at Camogli, when fried fish is offered to the passing crowds. In late June is the Palio of St Peter, a historical regatta in San Pietro alla Foce. The Feast of our Lady of Montallegro, with fireworks, takes place in July at Rapallo. Two festivals take place in August: the ceremony of Christ of the Deep, which takes place underwater, and the Wedding Cake of Fieschi.

Excursions west and east along the Italian Riviera from Genoa are pleasant and easy by train, bus or rented car. Rapallo, Sestri and La Spezia are to the east, Savona and Imperia to the west. Mussolini made the trains run on time. This no longer holds good – but they are remarkably cheap!

BOLOGNA

'the learned city'

Situated on the trade routes between Venice and Florence, Milan and Ancona, the city of Bologna, capital of the province of Emilia Romagna, has earned many different reputations. Its university was founded in the eleventh century and is the oldest in Europe: in the thirteenth century it had 10,000 students, mainly studying law and theology. One professor, Novella d'Andrea, was so beautiful that she had to give her lectures from behind a curtain to avoid distracting her students! The year of 1988 was the nine-hundredth anniversary of the founding of the University, and the city has always been known as 'La Dotta' (the learned).

During the eighteenth and nineteenth centuries, Bologna's Opera House was rated by the English milords as the best in Italy, ahead of Naples, Milan and Rome – it was truly a 'city of musick'. In 1733 no fewer than 32 of the milords were observed on one evening at the Opera. For several centuries the Bologna festival 'Octave of the Sacrament' ranked with Rome's Holy Week and the Venice Carnival. More prosaically, Bologna has earned another nickname – that of 'La Grassa' (the fat) – from its well-fed citizens and its wide variety of culinary delights, including sausages. Dr Johnson, conversing with James Boswell in 1791 remarked, 'You may advise me to go to live at Bologna to eat sausages. The sausages there are the best in the world: they lose much by being carried . . .' In the twelfth and thirteenth centuries the artistocratic families vied with each other to build the highest mansion-towers ('bella figura'). Over 200 were built, and the two tallest survivors, Asinelli and Garisenda in the Piazza di Porta Ravegnana, earned it yet another name – the city of the leaning towers.

Fynes Moryson encountered the militia, reporting that 'souldiers demanded a curtesie of us which we gladly gave them'. He admired the University, Senate House, and windows of 'oyled' paper, and noticed that the monks turned the monasteries into Temples of Bacchus, so much wine did they imbibe. The local Acqua della Porretta was a medicinal water famous since 1375, and the eel and pike stews were good. During the Renaissance period the princely court of the Bentivoglio patronized the arts, and the great thirteenth-century Bolognese painting school was in full flow.

Crossing the high Apennines in 1645, John Evelyn made his second visit to Bologna, praised the twelfth-century 156 foot high Torre d'Asinello (actually now 334 feet high), the arcades and the University, and then headed north by canals and coach to Ferrara on his way to Venice. A century later Thomas Gray, the poet, found the city smoky and of melancholic appearance, and the Auberge Al Pelegrino mean and dirty. But he approved of the countryside, extolling the 'fields planted with rows of Elms, Mulberry, Olive Trees and vines up them'. The next year Joseph Spence's notes read, 'Pelegrino auberge. Each chamber a paol a day, eating on the same conditions as at Milan. Coach twelve paols a day, though I believe you may have one for ten. Breakfasts a paol a head. N.B. the Venetian zechins are of more value than any other.' In his diary, Spence commented that Bologna was 'very populous with 120,000 inhabitants, streets built with piazzas on each side, making for dry walking in winter and cool in summer'. He watched the riderless horse races from the Grand Palace and made an excursion to the cascade of Terni, dating from 271BC.

Spence found the inhabitants and their manner of life preferable to anywhere else in Italy except Genoa! 'They've a very good opera and a public assembly every night in the year which is called the Casino, but infinitely finer and more lively than that of Siena.'

James Boswell travelled from Parma to Bologna, and thence to Modena and Florence, and by his lights quite behaved himself. John Wilkes travelled in 1764 from Turin, Milan and Parma to Bologna, where he met his mistress Gertrude Corradini; their reunion was rapturous! Arthur Young recommended three inns; I Tre Maurretti, the Pellegrino and the San Marco. In the Zampieri Palace he praised the Guidos, the Guercinos and Albano paintings, and visited the Ducal Palace and the Institute laboratories (in the University). The Church of San Dominico which contains a Guido was his favourite.

The *Juvenile Travellers* – the consortium of travel writers – noted the many art collections, the valuable library in the celebrated University, and the skilled artisans, the '*orfèvres*' and weavers of gold lace, silks and velvets. Along the banks of the Remo were situated no less than 400 silk mills. Bologna supplied Europe with sausages and macaroni from her 40,000 small farmholdings, and liqueurs and essences were also made.

The Marquis Albergati entertained many of the visiting milords in the 1780s in his beautiful villa; but William Beckford found Bologna 'sadly out of humour, an earthquake and Cardinal Buoncompagni having disarranged both land and people'. Mariana Starke thought that one of Annibale Carracci's pictures could vie with the finest productions of Raphael while it surpassed them all in beauty of colouring. The Guido Reni, Guercino, and the Carraccis were praised by most visitors and can be seen today in the National Picture Gallery, 56 via delle Belle Arti.

'Bologna', wrote Lord Byron in 1818, is 'celebrated for the production of Popes – Cardinals – Painters – sausages and a waxwork anatomical gallery' (housed in the Poggi Palace, sponsored by Pope Benedict XIV in 1742). Matthew Todd stayed at the Locando San Marco where he and Captain B. had a good supper, comfortable beds and a room with a fire. He praised the lions of the town, the churches and the two fine picture galleries of Hercolanee and Marroscalete.

On his way to Venice in 1844, Charles Dickens found traces of 'Milor Beeron', dead twenty years back. 'Boz' noted the ancient town arcades, the rich churches with their drowsy masses and tinkling bells, and the zodiacal sundial on the wall of the Basilica di San Petronio. He found Emilia slightly depressing, especially 'the sombre colonnades' of Modena, deserted, grim Ferrara, and the neglected cathedral in Parma. George Stillman Hillard,

151

Bostonian traveller in 1847, admired the University, the Palace of Rossini, the Arcades, and above all, the genius of Guido's 'Victory of Samson'.

VISITING BOLOGNA TODAY
WHERE TO STAY

The **ALBERGO AL CAPPELLO ROSSO**, via di Fusari 9 (Tel. 261891), was in business in 1375, making it one of the oldest hotels in Italy. The cardinal's 'Red Hat' was a favourite of Nicolo Albergati, Bishop of Bologna in the fourteenth century, and of Pope Paul IV in 1555, besides wealthy businessmen from all over Europe in the Middle Ages. It is small, central, discreet and now modernized, with a good restaurant. Four-star comfort – ideal for the modern traveller.

The old San Marco is now the modern four-star **HÔTEL INTERNAZIONALE**, via dell' Indipendenza 60 (Tel. 245544). A rich red-coloured corner building, it is modernized but has no restaurant. The modern four-star **PULLMAN-BOLOGNA**, near the station at viale Pietramellara (Tel. 558568), was previously the Bologna, before that the Etape, and before that the Albergo della Pace e Pellegrino, three centuries back. The elegant **CORONA D'ORO**, via Oberdan 12 (Tel. 236456), and the **REGINA**, via dell' Indipendenza 51 (Tel. 236817), both date from 1890, as does the **GRAND HÔTEL BAGNIOLE**, via dell' Indipendenza 8 (Tel. 225445), near the station.

WHERE TO EAT

The restaurant **AL PAPPAGALLO**, Piazza della Mercanzia is one of the oldest in Bologna, well known for its '*crespelle farcite alla mortadella*' (cheese pancake), and frothy purple Lambrusco wines.

The traveller should try these traditional restaurants serving typical Bolognese dishes. **TAVERNA 3 FRECCE**, Strada Maggiore 19, located in a thirteenth-century building, the **ANTICA OSTERIA ROMAGNOLA**, via Rialto 13, and the **ANTICA TRATTORIA DEL CACCIATORE**, seven kilometres outside Bologna at Casteldebole. The **ROSTARIA ANTICO BRUNETTI**, 5 via Caduti di Cefalonia is in a twelfth-century tower, and the restaurant dates from 1873. Their '*gramigna verde alla moda dello chef*' (green spaghetti with a sausage sauce) washed down

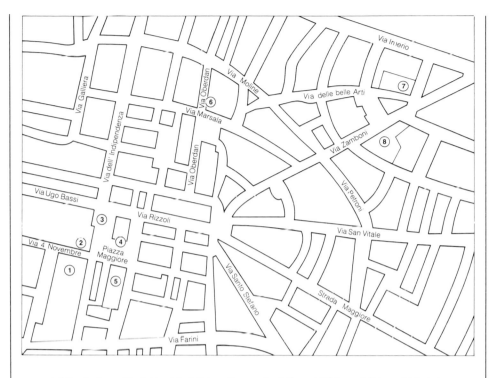

1 Al Capello Rosso, Via de Fusari 9   **2** Palazzo Communale   **3** Piazza del Nettuno   **4** Palazzo del Podesta

5 Basilica of Saint Petronius   **6** Corona d'Oro, Via Oberdan 12   **7** Museo Pinacotera Nazionale   **8** University

with a bottle of Lambrusco di Sorbara is a real treat. **AL CANTUNZEIN**, 4 Piazza Verdi, was a tavern for insolent *voiturins* and postilions. It faces the Teatro Comunale in a piazza of Renaissance buildings. The **SAMPIERI** is in a sienna-hued fifteenth-century palazzo and is noted for its '*tortellini*'. Other regional dishes are '*lasagna*', '*spaghetti alla bolognese*', '*mortadella*' pork sausage, '*zampone*' and '*crostata*', a fruit-filled pastry. The best local wines are Albana, dry white and young; Sangiovese di Romagna, a dry red; and the sparkling dry red Lambrusco. The best-known *rosticceria* gourmet food store is **A.F. TAMBURINI**, via Drapperie 2/C.

WHAT TO SEE AND DO

One of the major curiosities of Bologna is the 35 kilometres of brick and marble arcades that line the main streets. One long portico of four kilometres starts in the centre and gently ascends the hill of San Luca. The city is five-sided, with a tree-lined ring-road surrounding it. The main **TOURIST OFFICE** is in the Palazzo del Podestà in the Piazza del Nettuno (Tel. 239660), facing Giambologna's powerful statue of Neptune (now being repaired), much admired by the travellers group of the eighteenth century.

Padua is 115 kilometres to the north, Florence 105 kilometres to the south, the comic opera republic of San Marino 100 kilometres to the southeast, and Parma 102 kilometres to the northwest. The River Reno is a few kilometres to the west of the city, watering the fertile plains of Emilia Romagna. The city now has a population of half a million, and there is much to see. John Murray, a hundred years ago, suggested a stay of three days plus excursions to Rimini, San Marino, Forli, Faenza and Modena. Modern communications by road and rail are excellent, and Bologna now has its own airport. The railway station is in the north of the town, one kilometre from the centre, which includes the Palazzo Comunale with its superb staircase, the Palazzo del Podestà (Governor's Palace), the 1566 Neptune's Fountain and the Piazza di Porta Ravegnana, with the two famous leaning towers, one of which you can climb. The two major churches are the Gothic-style Basilica of St Petronius, begun in 1390, with a superb doorway, frescoes, mosaic pavements and tombs (including Napoleon's sister), and St Stephen's Basilica (Santo Stefano) a short walk east from the centre.

The leading museums are the **PINACOTECA NAZIONALE**, via delle Belle Arti 56, near the University, and the **MUNICIPAL ARCHEOLOGICAL MUSEUM** next to the Basilica of St Petronius, via dell' Archiginnasio 2. In the former, do look at the Bolognese artists' works: the three Carracci brothers, Vitale de Bologna, Guido Reni, Tibaldi and the Crespi brothers. The Renaissance wing includes the Tuscan school of Raphael, Parmigianino and Perugino. This is one of Italy's best galleries. The latter has a good collection of prehistoric, Etruscan and Roman finds. (Both are closed on Mondays.)

The University is now clustered around the Palazzo Poggi on via Zamboni, ten minutes' walk northeast from the centre. Recently formed colleges include John Hopkins, Indiana University, Brown University and Dickinson College.

In the twentieth century, 'Red Bologna' was yet another nickname bestowed on the city, headquarters of the Partito Comunista and other 'progressive' parties, probably inspired by the very large student population.

In May the procession takes place of the Madonna of St Luke. The International Fair and Food Fair is held in early June, the Shoe Fair in early March, and the Fashion Show in late November. Bologna no longer has a famous Opera House (Rossini spent many years teaching at the Music Conservatory), but is now the Italian centre for 'new-wave' music inspired by the students. The Teatro Comunale has an opera and drama season. Ask for the booklet *A Guest in Bologna* from the Tourist Office, which lists all the music and theatre performances.

Bologna has as much to offer as any small city in Italy – leaning towers, basilicas, ochre porticoes and galleries, excellent food and wine.

VERONA

city of Montagues and Capulets

To be more precise, Romeo's family were the Montecchi and Juliet's the Capuleti. The former supported the Pope and the latter Emperor Frederick Barbarossa, and the setting for *Romeo and Juliet* was Verona in 1302. Now, nearly 700 years later, Verona has a population of 270,000 and ranks with Padua and Vicenza as important towns in the Veneto region. It is 50 kilometres west of Vicenza and 114 kilometres west of Venice. Lake Garda is but 25 kilometres to the west. Catullus was born in Verona, and there are more Roman remains there than in any other town in Italy, except, of course, for Rome.

Thomas Coryat in 1610 pinpointed the key features for the modern traveller to note in Verona. 'The red marble town' is still accurate, although purists insist that pink and ochre feature amongst the palazzi and town houses. Across the River Adige which winds serpent-like through the town, Coryat counted 19 watermills and 4 bridges, but now there are 15. The two castles of St Felix and St Angelo were made of white marble. The marvellous town walls, six to seven miles in length, were 40 feet high with brick battlements and five carved gates. Now there are still three kilometres of wall on the west and south flanks of the town, with four gates. The great first-century Roman arena and amphitheatre could hold 23,000 people, and in Verona's famous summer opera festivals over 20,000 visitors can be seated. Thomas praised the Palace of the Scaligers (the Princes of the Scala in the period 1260–1387, when Verona's fame was at its greatest). He measured the Piazza delle Erbe, the old Roman forum where chariot races were run, as 67 paces by 45. The Duomo, Cathedral of our Lady, the Palace of Count Augustinius Justus, the fountains and the market place, all came in for praise. Coryat travelled from Venice, by 'barke' to Padua, thence to Vicenza (famous for its number of Counts and Knights), and from Verona on to Bergamo for St Bartholomew's Fair.

When the eighteenth-century travellers visited Verona it had been under Venetian rule since 1405. Pisanello (1387–1451) founded the Veronese School of Art, to be followed by Liberale da Verona, Morone, Francesco Buonsignori and Girolamo dai Libri. Joseph Spence in 1740 met the Marquess Scipio Maffet, sponsor of the new Opera House, Teatro Filarmonico. Edward Gibbon noted its 'boasted amphitheatre', William Beckford also surveyed it and wrote 'recollections of perished ages', but Arthur Young was more observant. The buildings he praised were St Michael Michieli, the Rotunda of St Georgio, the chapel of the Pellegrino family in the Bernardine church and the two Palazzi of Bevilaqua and Di Configlia.

Lord Byron visited Verona in the rains of autumn which sweep the Lombard plains, but the romantic fell in love with the town. 'Amphitheatre is wonderful, beats even Greece . . . Juliet's tomb (1303) plain, open and partly decayed, an open granite sarcophagus with withered leaves in it in a wild and desolate conventual garden, once a cemetery. Of the other marvels of this city, paintings, antiquities, all, excepting the gothic tombs of the Scaliger princes, pleased me.'

A few years later John Ruskin, notoriously difficult to please, wrote of 'passing thru the beautiful cities of Bergamo, Brescia and Verona past the shores of Lake Gard and thru Venetian territory'. John Murray's *Travel Guide* of 1842 noted that Verona had a population of 50,000. 'Le Due Torri was a remarkably good and comfortable inn, table d'hote at one o'clock a most convenient hour.' La Torre di London and Il Gran Parigi were two other reasonable alberghi. The fruit and flowers of the region were excellent, and visitors should see the 'real schistous petrified fishes of Monte Bolca!'

VISITING VERONA TODAY
WHERE TO STAY AND EAT

Modern travellers should endeavour to stay at the **HÔTEL DUE TORRI**, Piazza Sant'Anastasia 4 (Tel. 34130). It belonged to the Scaliger princes of the thirteenth century. Some of its famous visitors include Mozart, Goethe, and the Emperor Alexander I of Russia who stayed there in 1822 for the Congress of Vienna. Quite simply it is one of the most interesting and superb hotels in Europe, with genuine antiques and oil paintings of the seventeenth and eighteenth centuries. It also has a classic restaurant. The **GRAND HÔTEL**, Corso Porta Nuova 105 (Tel. 22570), was part of the Reichenbach Palace and is situated on the tree-lined boulevard between the Roman arena and the station. It dates from the late nineteenth century, the era of the new railways, and Verona is an important railway junction. The **ACCADEMIA HÔTEL**, via Scala 12 (Tel. 596222), dates from the same period.

The **RISTORANTE 12 APOSTOLI**, vicolo Corticella San Marco 3 (Tel. 24680) is near the main Piazza delle Erbe. Well over 200 years

1 Church of San Zeno Major   **2** The Cathedral   **3** Hotel Due Torri, Piazza Sant' Anastasia   **4** Grand Hotel

4 Piazza delle erbe   **5** Juliet's Tomb   **6** Palace of the Scaligers   **7** Roman Arena   **8** Corso Porta Nuova 105

old, it is now owned by the Gioco brothers. Try their salmon baked in a pastry shell with garlic and scallops, or their '*costelleta 12 Apostoli*'. Local wines are dry white Soave, red Valpolicella and Bardolino. The **RISTORANTE ARCHE**, via Arche Scaligere 6 (Tel. 24415), is on the same street as Romeo's house and opposite the tombs of the Scaligeri princes. It has been run by the Gioco family since 1879 but dates from even further back. Adriatic fish is the speciality, including '*zuppa di pesce*' and spaghetti with scampi.

WHAT TO SEE

John Murray's northern Italian tour of 1899 suggested a stay of three days at Verona and one at Vicenza. Certainly modern Verona has sufficient sights to justify such a visit, particularly at carnival time. The last Friday of Holy Week sees the Bacchanalian Carnival of the Gnocco celebrated in Verona. The opera, ballet and music festivals, and Shakespeare plays performed at the Teatro Romano, are in mid-summer and draw many visitors.

The Roman amphitheatre and arena are in the centre of the old town in the Piazza Bra, with the River Adige less than ten minutes' walk west (to the Ponte Scaligero) and east (to the Ponte Aleardi). The amphitheatre is 152 metres long, 128 metres wide and 30 metres in height, the second largest in Italy. It is closed to the public on Mondays.

One of the two most attractive piazzas in the old town is the Piazza delle Erbe with fountains, Roman statues, a Venetian column with the winged lion of St Mark, palaces, old houses, the 1370 Gardello Tower, and the thirteenth-century palace of the Capulets. The other is the Piazza dei Signori, with the statue of Dante, who lived in Verona, the twelfth-century Town Hall, the Lamberti Tower, Law Courts and thirteenth-century Venetian Governors' Palaces. These two piazzas, and that of Mazzanti, are situated ten minutes' walk north of the arena, in the loop of the river. The Tombs of the Scaligers (Arche Scaligere) are sited between their palace and their church. The massive fourteenth-century fortress of the Scaligers (Castelvecchio), once the seat of the ruling Della Scala family, has been restored and is now a major art museum with Veronese and Venetian schools well represented. It is closed on Mondays. It overlooks the Ponte Scaligero, bombed by the Germans in World War II but now restored.

The cathedral in the Piazza del Duomo, the Churches of San Zeno and Sant'Anastasia, and the Basilica of San Fermo (eleventh century) should also be visited. Other sights are Juliet's tomb in the Capuchin cloisters, the Roman theatre over the river, the Roman castle of St Peter, and the gardens of Giardino Giusti dating from 1580, with their quiet grottoes and cypresses. In April at Negrar is the 'Palio de Recioto', when the local wine is offered to the public. In February is the Bacanal del Gnocco, when 'gnocchi' (small dumplings) are given to the crowds.

The **TOURIST OFFICE** at via Dietro Anfiteatro 6 (Tel. 592828), is two minutes' walk west from the arena. So if you believe in the romantic story of the young lovers of Verona, do visit this beautiful pink town.

VENICE

the 'Gem of the World'

With the possible exception of Paris, more writers and poets have extolled the romance of Venice than any other city. They include William Shakespeare, Byron, Shelley, Wordsworth, Charles Kingsley, Dickens, Henry James, Thomas Mann and a score of others including George Sand and John Ruskin. Petrarch, writing in the fourteenth century, described the English noblemen at the Venetian Court, as 'comrades and kinsmen of their King', and in the fifteenth century Venetian galleys traded with the English ports and English traders sent their ships to Venice to buy salt. English trading links with Venice were strong, and reinforced the desire of the early travellers to visit the city on their Grand Tours. The Winged Lion of Venice ruled the Mediterranean, and Shylock's ducats made the city the third most prosperous in Italy.

Two sixteenth–century visitors have recorded their impressions. Fynes Moryson stayed at a 'Dutch Inne', liked the bread 'pan-buffello' and the fish, noted that the Italians were 'sparing in diet', and that the 'winds make the ayre very wholesome, [which] agrees with strangers' complexions'. He admired the public libraries, the clock of St Mark's, the Armory (called by later travellers the Arsenal), the Mint House and the sinister prisons in the Palace of the Duke. At that time in 1595 there were 20,000 families living in Venice, including the Jewish quarter Il Ghetto. There were thirteen places called *traghetti* 'where Gondole boats attended'. Four hundred years later very little has changed.

A decade after Moryson, Thomas Coryat from Somerset and William Lithgow of Lanark visited Venice on the Grand Tour. To the former it was the 'Gem of the World', and he listed the attractions: '200 churches (143 pairs of Organs), 54 Monasteries, 26 Nuneries, 56 Tribunals (places of Judgement), 17 hospitalls, 165 marble statues, 27 public clocks, 10 brasen gates, 114 Bell-Towers, 155 wells, 185 delectable gardens, 10,000 Gondoliers, 450 bridges, 120 palaces, 174 courts'; and he over-estimated the population at 500,000. Moreover he listed the thirty leading Venetian families, and the Venetian wines, both in order of importance!

Lithgow, a dour Calvinist lad who hated Catholicism and was as restless as Coryat, noted at Venice the 'desparate villians armed with a privy coat of mail and a little sharp dagger called a stilleto, between eleven and two in the morning they lurked in the lightless calles'.

The travellers brought back tales of the wonders of Venice, but also of the perils and dangers of this beautiful city on the frontiers of east and west. John Evelyn met Asians, Levantines, Turks, Armenians, Jews, Persians, Moors, Greeks and Slavs. He visited the Turkish *bagnio* and caught a violent cold, lodged near the Rialto, and at the Opera saw Monteverdi's *Coronation of Poppea*. Every traveller described the gondolas. To Evelyn they were 'very long and narrow, having necks and tailes of steel, somewhat spreading at the beake like a fishes tail and kept so exceedingly polish'd as to give a wonderful lustre'. He found the Venetian aristocracy aloof and reported that the 'proud dames wore very high heeled shoes, complicated coiffeur and dress, stalking half as high more as the rest of the world'.

Then, as now, the splendours of the Venetian Easter Carnival were recounted by all the travellers, just as they were visually safeguarded for ever by Canaletto and Guardi. Evelyn on Ascension Day in June 1647 watched the Doge's espousal of the Adriatic in the gloriously painted, carved and gilded *Bucentora*, 'environed and followed by innumerable galleys and boats filled with spectators, some dressed in masquerade, with trumpets, music and cannon.' Of the carnival he wrote, 'the universal madnesse of this place during this time of licence with the barbarous custom of crowds in antique dresses hunting wild bulls about the streets and piazza with extravagant music and a thousand gambols . . .'

The Venetian women were thought to be the most beautiful in Italy. Thomas Coryat was amazed at the veiled women, with 'hair died faire or whitish, but bare breasts, backes also naked even to the middle, hobling, vaine on Chapineys, very high shoes even half a yard high'. He saw the praetors in their red chamlet gowns, the courtesans with their ruffianos and the mountebanks in St Mark's Square. Venice had by now acquired a reputation as 'the brothel of Europe'. Besides the *prete*, the *pantaleone*, there were the *putanas* [ladies of shame and whores], 'many of them Greeks'.

Our plump foppish Cambridge poet, Joseph Spence, thought 'the Venetian ladies have a gay air, fresher complexions, and a great deal of freedom in their behaviour and manner of talking. The Venetians [are] divided between debauchery and devotion, the most melancholy and the most gay place in the world. In the carnival they give a loose for all their passions . . . only half-mad; mountebanks, ballad singers, rope dancers and conjurors.' Spence and young Lord Middlesex in Venice in the cold winter of 1732 were wrapped around in furs, shoes and stockings lined with squirrel skins. Nevertheless Venice was a fine city, floating upon the waters, gondolas best contrived for swiftness and the 'snuggest things'.

Nine years later Lady Pomfret together with Lord Lincoln arrived from Bologna; Lord Elcho, Mr Dashwood and Mr Naylor visited the Arsenal – a favourite then and now, built in 1104 and guarded by two towers, with Greek or Norse lions and Baroque statues. At the height of the Venetian empire, the Arsenal could build and equip a small armed, oared galley in one day! Then the travellers went to Murano to see the glass-making process and that of 'false lapis-lazuli', with broken glass and filings of brass thrown into a furnace. Spence and his protégé later travelled by boat on the Brenta Canal 'the most pleasant way of travelling I ever knew'. However, most of the travellers remarked on the smells from the Venetian canals carrying ordure, dead animals and the victims of the Council of Ten. 'Stinkpot' was one phrase used.

James Boswell in July 1765 wrote in his diary, 'To St Marks Church. Old mosaic. Luckily, a solemn service.' He 'intrigued with Madame Michieli. All the liberties exquisite. Another pox.' When in Venice . . . In the same year Edward Gibbon noted 'stinking ditches dignified with the pompous denomination of canals – a fine bridge spoiled by two rows of houses on it, and a large square decorated with the worst architecture I ever yet saw.'

To the relatively well-off travelling milord, life in Venice was remarkably cheap. Arthur Young stayed at Signore Petrillo's inn and paid eight pauls a day (then three shillings and four pennies) for dinner, supper, a bed with fine sheets, and neat furniture, which was quite rare in Italian inns. The opera cost three pauls, a gondolier would attend for six pauls a day. 'Thus for seven shillings and three pennies a man lives well at Venice and keeps his servant. No question but a man may live better at Venice for 100L [pounds] a year than at London for 500L.'

Just before the end of the eighteenth century Venice lost its independence to the French, and in the following year, 1798, it was ceded to Austria rather contemptuously by Napoleon, who had little regard or esteem for the place or its occupants. 'I want no more Inquisitors, no more Senate. I will be an Attila for the Venetian state.' He looted many of the Venetian art treasures, and these are now in the Louvre.

For centuries, travellers, and indeed the Venetians, have expected Venice to vanish below the waves, and floods are frequent. Having studied the paintings of Venice by Canaletto, Lady Frances Shelley arrived there the year after Waterloo. 'Exactly what I expected, falling fast into decay, looks wretched and poor, canals choked up, stench at low water dreadful.' Lady Frances studied her elegant counterparts in Venetian society. 'A Venetian Lady's day – she rises at twelve when the cavalier servant (i.e. Cicisbeo) attends her to Mass: few read anything except their prayer book. The lady strolls around the Piazza San Marco, pays or receives visits, dines between three and four, undresses and goes to bed completely. At eight pm she arises for her toilette, spends three to four am at the theatre and the casino or during the summer in the cafes on the Piazza.'

Florian's Café, established in 1720, was a favourite of Byron and Shelley and their assorted ladies, despite the cholera epidemic. Byron's 'amours' included the Countess Querini-Benzoni, the blonde lady in the gondola, and the 22 year-old married lady with great black eastern eyes and a variety of subsidiary charms, a mighty and admirable singer. In Venice, Byron finished his *Manfred* and started *Don Juan* from a lodging house in the Frezzeria, off the Piazza San Marco. Later he moved to the Villa Forcarini at La Mira on the Brenta River having swum from the Lido to the entrance of the Grand Canal. The Shelleys lost two of their children in Venice. Clara died in 1818 and Allegra in 1822. Mary wrote *Mathilda* and her husband *Julian and Maddalo* whilst there.

Byron had written in his diary, 'Venice is not a place where the English are gregarious – their pigeon houses are Florence, Naples and Rome'. To Elizabeth Barrett Browning, however, Venice *was* one of her 'pigeon houses'. 'Venice', she wrote in 1851, 'is quite exquisite: it wrapt me round with a spell at first sight and I longed to live and die there – never to go away. The gondolas and the glory they swim through and the silence of the population, drifted over ones head across the bridges and the fantastic architecture and the coffee-drinking and music in the Piazza San Marco.' The widowed Mary Shelley stayed at the 'new' Hôtel d'Italia and paid nine pounds a month for lodging and board as the Hôtel Leone Bianco was too expensive. Her two gondoliers, dressed in livery, Beppo No. 303 and Marco No. 307, cost her four pounds a month. John Ruskin stayed at the Hôtel de l'Europe and was horrified by the new railway built in 1846 and by the new gas lamps along the Rialto. 'Venice is lost to me', he wrote three years later, '. . . whereas Samuel Rogers says "there is a glorious city in the Sea" a truthful person must say "There is a glorious city in the Mud". It is startling at first to say so, but it goes well enough with marble. "Oh Queen of Marble and Mud".' The *Stones of Venice*, which he wrote, is still one of the classic books about the city.

The American travellers came with the new railways. To Henry James, Venice was a vast museum. 'There is nothing left to discover or describe, originality of attitude is utterly impossible.' George Stillman Hillard lodged in the Piazza Grassi at a hotel called the Emperor of Austria (who dominated Venice from 1814 to 1848). The rich Duchess Maria Louisa of Parma stayed there at the same time with an entourage of 28 people and 5 dogs. Mark Twain stayed at the Grand Hôtel de l'Europe and counted the 1,500 Tintorettos and 1,200 paintings by Palma. He visited the Bridge of Sighs, St Mark's Square and church, admired the Bronze Horses and the famous Lion of St Mark's and noted there were 1,200 priests out of a population of 100,000. He wrote 'Her glory is departed and with her crumbling grandeur of wharves and palaces about her she sits among her stagnant lagoons, forlorn and beggared, forgotten of the world . . . In the treacherous sunlight we see Venice, decayed forlorn, poverty stricken and commerceless forgotten and utterly insignificant. But in the moonlight her fourteen centuries of greatness fling their glories about her and once more she is the princeliest among the nations of the earth.'

VISITING VENICE TODAY

WHERE TO STAY

Towards the end of the eighteenth century, the Serenissima Repubblica boasted four very old inns dating from the twelfth century when pilgrims from the east came to pay their respects to St Mark's remains in the Basilica. The Cappello Nero and the Orientale seem to have disappeared, or more likely, changed their names. The **ALBERGO DEL CAVALLETTO E DOGE ORSEOLO**, Calle del Cavaleto 1107 (Tel. 5200955), now a modern four-star hotel, has archive records proving its antiquity. The Orseolo family, with two Doges, owned much of Venice in the tenth century, and the dell'Ospizio delle Orsoline almshouse sheltered

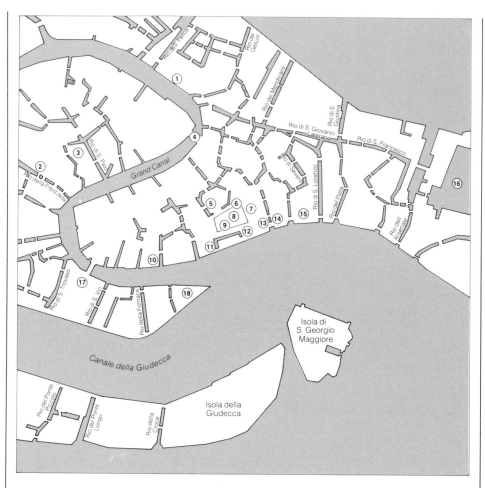

1 Il Palazzo d'Oro   **2** The San Rocco School   **3** Church of Santa Maria Gloriosa dei Frari   **4** Rialto Bridge

5 Doge Orseolo, Calle del Cavaleto 1107   **6** The Clock Tower   **7** Basilica San Marco   **8** San Marco Square

9 Caffe Florian, Piazza San Marco   **10** Gritti Palace Hôtel, Santa Maria del Giglio 2467

11 Hôtel Luna, Calle dell'Ascensione 1243   **12** Libreria Vecchia   **13** Doge's Palace   **14** Bridge of Sighs

15 Danieli Royal Excelsior, Riva degli Schiavoni 4196   **16** Arsenal   **17** Galleria dell'Accademia   **18** Santa Marià della Salute

pilgrims well before AD1305. It took its name from the Venetian cavalry who were stationed in the San Marco region for a century or so. Like the Italian dukes, the musical Strauss family and Winston Churchill who went before them, modern travellers should try Italy's oldest hotel. It is quiet, with a good restaurant, and is just two minutes' from St Mark's Square. The **HÔTEL LUNA**, calle dell'Ascensione 1243 (Tel. 5289840), is now also a modernized four-star hotel near St Mark's Square and the Grand Canal. Well before 1474, in the eleventh and twelfth centuries, it was a hostel known as *astro della notte* (the night star) for pilgrims from the east visiting the church of Santa Maria de Capite Brolli. A hundred years ago John Murray cited it as 'well managed, frequented by Germans, table d'hôte four francs, luncheon two and a half francs, rooms two-three francs'. It has a good restaurant and is near the modern waterbus services.

A Venetian entrepreneur called Guiseppe Dal Niel in 1822 rented a fourteenth-century neo-gothic palace that had belonged to the Dandolo and Bernardi families. Soon it became known as Danieli's Hôtel Royal, and was the cosmopolitan centre of Venice. George Sand and Alfred de Musset stayed there in 1833–34 (room No.10), and Charles Dickens, Wagner, Balzac and Proust, as well as Kaiser Wilhelm of Prussia, were among its distinguished guests. This opulent five-star hotel, now the **DANIELI ROYAL EXCELSIOR**, is at Riva degli Schiavoni 4191 (Tel. 26480), on the Grand Canal, with, of course, a superb restaurant.

The Gritti Palace was owned by the fifteenth-century Doge, Andrea Gritti. John Ruskin lived for a time on the top floor, and there wrote much of the *Stones of Venice*. Charles Dickens and many famous twentieth-century writers have stayed at the **GRITTI PALACE**, now a five-star hotel located at Campo Sta. Maria del Giglio 2467 (Tel. 794611). The restaurant cuisine is about the best in Venice.

On the Lido overlooking the Adriatic Sea is the **DES BAINS GRAND HÔTEL**, lungomare Marconi 17 (Tel. 765921), a huge hotel with great style, dating from the mid-nineteenth century. Thomas Mann's story *Death in Venice* was exquisitely filmed here. It has an excellent restaurant, with orchestra, and there are sandy beaches in front of the hotel. It is closed in winter.

The eighteenth-century Grand Hôtel d'Italie was purchased by the Swiss family Grünwald in 1850 and is now the sumptuous luxury five-star hotel **BAUER GRUNWALD GRAND HÔTEL**, campo San Moisè 1459 (Tel. 5207022), overlooking the Grand Canal near St Mark's. This hotel also has a superb restaurant.

Tchaikowsky composed his Fourth Symphony in 1877 at the **LONDRA PALACE**, Riva degli Schiavoni 4171 (Tel. 5200533), a five-star hotel founded in 1850. This also overlooks the Grand Canal and is known too for its **DI LEONE RESTAURANT**. The **MONACO E GRAND CANAL**, Calle Vallaresso 1325 (Tel. 700211), was known before 1893 as the Grand Hôtel Albergo di Monaco, and the smaller **PAGANELLI**, Riva degli Schiavoni 4182 (Tel. 5224324), was opened in 1874.

WHERE TO EAT

Venice boasts a number of interesting old restaurants. **ANTICA CARBONERA**, (Coal Cellars), calle Bembo 4648, near the Rialto, was used by the coal bargees whose guild was founded in 1476. They brought coal on barges from the mainland to the Rialto bridge limit. The restaurant was founded in 1773 by Lotti and Zerbone and two of its specialities are '*seppie alla veneziana*' and salmon tagliatelli. **ANTICO MARTINI**, Campo San Fantin 1983, opposite the Teatro la Fenice, has been serving good food since 1720. Their specialities are '*cannelloni alla Dogaressa*' and '*ravioli farci fromage et épinards*'. The restaurant is closed Tuesday and Wednesday lunch-time.

ANTICA TRATTORIA ALLE POSTE VECIE, Mercato del Pesce Rialto, was a trattoria well before 1793. It is in the fish market by the Rialto. Besides many fish dishes, try their '*tagliata alla Robespierre*'. Closed Tuesday. **RISTORANTE AL COLOMBO**, corte del Teatro 4619, near the Teatro Carlo Goldoni and Rialto Bridge, dates from before 1885. **TAVERNA LA FENICE**, campiello de la Fenice 1936, San Marco, in a beautiful setting, dates from 1890. Try their '*cartoccio alla Fenice*' or '*rosette di vitello à la Fenice*'.

The **VINO VINO WINE BAR**, Ponte delle Veste 2001/A near the San Fenice Theatre, has the largest selection of Italian wines sold by the glass (or bottle) in Venice. The **CAFFÈ QUADRI**, Piazza San Marco 120, was praised as a restaurant by John Murray a hundred years ago. The restaurant part closes in the winter; '*côte de veau serenissima*' and '*fettuccine à la marinara*' are specialities. Modern travellers should also consider **AL GRAPPO D' UVA** (Bunch of Grapes), calle dei Bombaseri 5093, the **TRATTORIA ALLA COLOMBA**, Piscina di Frezzeria 1665, the **LOCANDA MONTIN**, Dorsoduro 1147, and **LA VIDA**, campo San Giacomo dell' Orio, all dating back nearly a century. Some Venetian specialities to try include '*zuppa di pesce*' (fish soup), '*sogliola alla mugnaia*' (sole meunière), '*gran fritto dell' Adriatico*', and a Venetian-style '*bouillabaisse*'.

Henry James and dozens of other literati patronized the seventeenth-century **CAFFÈ FLORIAN** in the Piazza San Marco, sipping a '*cappuccino*' and listening to the music.

WHAT TO SEE AND DO

Opinions differ about the best season of the year to visit this 'Gem of the World', this 'Paradise of Cities'. Venice is overwhelmed by tourists in the three mid-summer months, and the canals stink. Mid-winter can be cold, wet and desolate. The best two periods for the modern traveller are May–June and late September–late October. Hotel prices can be exorbitant in the season, but reduce from 1 November.

The entrance to the main island of Venezia is reached by a long road and rail bridge of four kilometres from the oil port of Mestre. Cars have to be left on the artificial island of Tronchetto or in one of the garage parks in the Piazzale Roma. The visitor to Venice should be prepared to walk, although the ubiquitous gondoliers, *motoscafi* (motorboats), *vaporetti* (small steamers) and *traghetti* (ferries) will provide travellers with a variety of experiences. But be precise with your gondolier and agree your destination and fee before you step aboard. For hundreds of years travellers have been taken to the cleaners by the Venetian gondoliers – and always will be! The most useful vaporetti are Nos. 1, 2 and 5.

A **TOURIST OFFICE** is located in the Santa Lucia railway station, (Tel. 715016), another is at the bus station (Tel. 27402) in the Piazzale Roma, and there is one on the Lido Island, Viale Santa Maria Elisabetta 6 (Tel. 765721). The main office is in San Marco square, Ascensione 71 (Tel. 5226356). Ask for their bi-lingual weekly magazine *Un Ospite di Venezia*. The Historic Monuments Committee of Venice organizes daily tours from 3.30pm starting at the church of Sta. Maria della Pietà. (The six regions of Venice, the Sestieri, are Santa Croce, San Polo and Dorsoduro on the south bank, and on the north bank, Cannaregio, San Marco and Castello. Squares are called '*Campi*', and streets '*Calli*'. St Mark's is the only Piazza, although there are a few Piazzale.)

The main sights are clustered around St Mark's Square, and include the large Piazzetta, originally called Il Broglio, after the intrigues hatched there by nobles plotting and counterplotting. St Mark's Basilica was once the chapel of the Doges, and contains lovely floor mosaics, the Pala d'Oro gold altarpiece, the tomb of St Mark, the rich treasury, and the Marciano Museum. Next to it is the 100-metre Campanile or bell-tower, rebuilt in 1902, with a lift to the top to see *the* panorama of Venice. The Clock Tower, Law Courts, Correr Museum and Procuratie Nuove are also in St Mark's Square (as are Florian's and the Quadri).

The Doge's Palace, Palazzo Ducale, is on the corner of the Piazza San Marco overlooking the canal. It is best to pinpoint a few of the treasures beforehand – pictures by Bellini, Tiepolo and Bosch in the Doge's apartments, Tintoretto's 'Paradise' in the Grand Council Chamber, and Veronese's 'Europa' on the third floor in the Waiting Room. The Ballot Room houses portraits of the Doges and seascapes of Venetian naval victories. The Libreria Vecchia has the Archeological Museum and the Marciano Library in it.

Outside the Doge's Palace is the famous seventeenth-century Bridge of Sighs, named after the melancholic passage of the Doge's victims walking to death or squalor in the dungeons. Other palaces to see are the d'Oro, the Mocenigo (where Byron lived), the Vendramin-Calergi (where Wagner died), the Tron, and the Rezzonico (museum of eighteenth-century Venice). Take a guided tour of the Grand Canal from St. Mark's Square by *vaporetto*, or if you are brave enough, by gondola. Only three bridges cross the Grand Canal, the Scalzi, the superb Rialto, and the Accademia.

The Academy of Fine Arts (Gallerie dell'Accademia) is the main art gallery and museum in Venice. Deriving from the fifteenth century it is sited on the south bank near the bridge of the same name. As the pigeon flies, it is three-quarters of a kilometre from San Marco. It is closed on Monday. The Academy contains the definitive collection of Venetian paintings from 1400 to 1700, mainly Bellini, the Carpaccios, Giorgione, Tintoretto and Titian. Most of the fine Canalettos and Guardis are in the U.K. or in Lisbon, few are in Venice!

It is unclear what John Ruskin would have made of Peggy Guggenheim's collection of modern and contemporary works; it is, however, housed in a gorgeous palazzo!

The most important churches are the seventeenth-century baroque Santa Maria della Salute, ten minutes' walk east of the Accademia; San Giorgio Maggiore on the island, 400 metres south of San Marco; Santa Maria Gloriosa dei Frari, one kilometre north of the Accademia;

and SS Giovanni e Paolo, one kilometre north of San Marco. The Arsenal, much favoured by the sixteenth- and seventeenth-century travellers, is now alas closed to visitors, but one of the great Schools or 'Scuola', must be visited – the San Rocco, near the Frari church, which contains 56 superb canvasses by Tintoretto.

John Murray's guide of a century back suggested a three-day stay in Venice, more if it coincided with one of the main events. Carnival is a frenetic week in mid-February, with parades, concerts, bands and exotic masquerades; the ancient Marriage of Venice and the Sea is on 21 November; the Festa del Redentore (the Redeemer) is on 18 July; and the grand Royal Regatta on the Grand Canal is on the first Sunday in September. It looks similar to the familiar paintings by Guardi and Canaletto. In addition, the Film Festival takes place in late summer, and the Modern Art Festival in even-numbered years. La Fenice is the very pretty opera house, which has a December–May season.

An essential excursion is to Murano to see the thirteenth-century glass-making processes, the museum and the exquisite twelfth-century church of Santissimi Maria e Donato. Also to sleepy Torcello, with its Cathedral of Santa Maria Assunta, and superb Byzantine mosaics, followed by lunch at the Locanda Cipriani. Finally, if there is time, a visit to Giudecca, Burano and Chioggia islands, with lunch at El Gato on the waterfront.

If, carrying Ruskin's *Stones of Venice*, you decide to visit the 117 islands, walk across the 150 bridges, along the 160 canals and visit the 200 churches *and* 200 palaces of 'The Most Serene Republick' – in that case, like Byron, spend a month or two in Venice.

BELGIUM

'A beautiful little Kingdom'

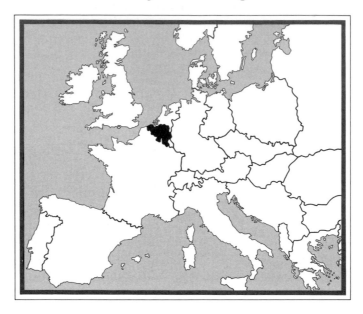

$\mathcal{U}$ntil 1830, Belgium was fought over by the French, the Spanish and the Austrian Hapsburgs, who wanted the fertile agricultural lands and the key ports of Antwerp, Ostend and Zeebrugge for themselves. Travellers on the Grand Tour in the sixteenth, seventeenth and eighteenth centuries were always attracted to Antwerp. John Evelyn, there in 1641, observed 'there was never a more quiet, clean, elegantly built and civil place than this magnificent and famous city of Antwerp'. The Spaniards had sacked the town in 1576 and it had been ruled by them since 1633. But Antwerp had recovered to become a rich medieval Burgundian court, sophisticated enough to encourage Flemish artists such as Jan Breughel, Jordaens and Peter Paul Rubens. Evelyn admired that 'sumptuous and most magnificent Church of the Jesuits built by Pieter Juyssens, being a very glorious fabrique without and within wholly incrusted with marble, inlayd and polished, with divers representations of historic Landscips, Flowers Etc.' The Antwerp citadel was 'the most matchlesse piece of modern Fortification in the world, ramparts and Platforms are stupendous, ravished by the delicious shades and walks ... of the magnificent and famous Citty'.

Evelyn also visited Ghent, 'a diminished city with fields and desolate pastures within its extensive medieval walls,' and Bruges 'cheezes and butter pild up like heapes of Mortar', before visiting Brussels, 30 miles inland. There he was intrigued by the 'floating dwellings kept so sweete and polite'.

In the Cour des Princes he looked at the pictures by Titian, Rubens, and young and old Breughel. Evelyn also admired a rural park 'with a heronry, cascades, rocks, grotts, fallow and red deer all bounded by a hedge of water turned up by a fontaniere'.

The War of the Spanish Succession (1701–13) made life dangerous for travellers, but Sir Carnaby Haggerston was in Antwerp for most of 1711, and the European conflicts of 1739–48 hindered but did not stop the English tourists. In the sixteenth century, Antwerp Exchange had been the money capital of Europe, but a fourteen-month siege of the town and the closing of the River Scheldt by the Spanish, by agreement with the Netherlands, put Amsterdam in the ascendant. Howell wrote, 'This goodly ancient city looks like a disconsolate widow or rather some superannuated virgin that hath lost her lover'. Once the population had been 200,000 and between 2,000 and 3,000 vessels could be seen in the Scheldt, but by the eighteenth century, Antwerp was but a shadow of its former self.

Joseph Spence bear-led his client milords to Belgium in 1739. In Antwerp they stayed four days, and Spence wrote, 'That city was the great school for the Flemish painters Rubens, and I think Van Dyck was born there. There's a great number of pieces of both their hands.' Spence listed the main sights to see – 'the Grand Carmes, Academy des Peintres, Dominicans, St Vanburgius, Jesuits church, Shooters Hall, Peeter Sayers, St Michaels, St Marys Great Church, St Jacques, the Augustins, the Reclets, and Abbey of Bernardins'. However, he thought little of Brussels, noting that 'the town has little beauty in it. There is not much to be seen at Brussels.' In Ghent they admired the Vandyck painting of St Amand and the great Convent of the Béguines housing 900 nuns. The roads between Antwerp and Brussels, Brussels and Ghent, each about 30 miles, were of superb pavé, unusual, and thus remarked upon, although in many villages the blacksmiths hung around the stage posts expecting to repair broken springs!

The eighteenth-century travellers Harry Peckham, John Alkin, and bearleader Thomas Brand (1779) all praised the religious paintings in Antwerp. Brand wrote, 'The instant I got into the cathedral I lost my breath and stood still with wonder, the superb altars, the colossal statues, the pictures, the solemnity of the people all together deprived me of all my faculties'. He went on, 'I gaped and stared at the descent of the Cross in the Cathedral by Rubens, and Christ in the Church of the Béguinage by Vandyke – either of them worth a journey from England'. Adam Walker, Viscount Perceval, noted 'Tapestry and paintings in the church denoting the triumph of Popery over Luther and Calvin'. The bankers in Antwerp were of service to Edward Mellish and Samuel Bernard, but Zachary Grey was more interested in the recipe for cabbage salad in the Antwerp tables d'hôte. Grey took a boat from Zeeland to Antwerp, which ran aground, was holed and sank, and he had to walk 14 miles to find lodgings. The Earl of Essex complained in 1773 of the journey from Ghent to Antwerp in a miserable équipage called a *carosse*, a two seater open *chaise* pulled by four pathetic horses at the rate of three miles per hour, but noted 'the most delightful inclosed country, beautiful Avenues, delightful arbours'.

Brussels housed the court of the Austrian Governor of Belgium, but that did not deter the Duke of Queensbury's party in August 1734 from going to bed drunk. His Duchess and her friends 'had to make do with two cold *black* chickens which from extream hunger they found delicious'. Philip Thicknesse, not to be outdone, claimed that the Brussels wine merchants added pigeon dung and brimstone to their wine! Robert Arbuthnot complained of the 'vile screaming' of the French opera singers in Brussels!

The British envoy in Brussels in 1786 was Lord Torrington, who complained that the British who came there were much inferior to those who made the long journey to the very superior Court of Vienna. Indeed in 1787 Brussels was 'over-run by indigent Englishmen', many staying at the Hôtel L'Impérial. Charles Spencer, fifth Earl of Sunderland 'when at Brussels . . . was so exceedingly smitten with a Miss Rockford that many of his friends were afraid he might be imprudent enough to marry her'!

Thomas Nugent's guide-book of 1778 commended two hotels in Antwerp, both in Meer Street; the Hôtel Labourer and the City of Brussels. In Brussels, the Arms of Flanders in the fish-market, and the Duke of Brabant Inn in the Koolmarkt were his favourites.

William Beckford, travelling in style on his Grand Tour towards the end of the eighteenth century, wrote of his journey from Ostend to Antwerp, 'Were anyone to ask my advice upon the subject of retirement I should tell them – by all means repair to Antwerp'. He found himself 'insensibly drawn towards the cathedral whose stupendous tower shot up 466 feet into the air. In its 212 streets and 22 squares the grass grows in deep silence. A city to fill the mind with melancholy reflection concerning the transient state of worldly glory. Only on high days of church festivals did the somnolent city come to life, a prodigious number of priests, singing psalms all the way processed to the church with wax tapers in their hands, accompanied by French horns and serpents. The streets alight with the glow of bonfires, reports of rockets, squibs and crackers.' But he was more cheerful in Brussels. 'The Grande Place of the Hôtel de Ville was one of the beautifullest squares to be found anywhere, marvellous fountains, inns and restaurants equal to the best in Europe. The Opera House built in the early 1700s one of the finest in Europe with boxes heated by individual coal fires hired by the nobility for the winter season.'

Sir James Edward Smith, travelling in 1793, arrived by postwagon in Antwerp. 'The Hôtel St Antoine a very good inn, table magnificently spread. Antwerp a place of great devotion, great gallantry, inhabitants need every sort of dissipation to make existence tolerable in so gloomy and lifeless a town. The Scheldt is a fine river but the Dutch having possession of its mouth have ruined the trade of Antwerp, inhabitants now sunk in idleness and sloth.' Smith admired the Rubens 'Descent from the Cross', St Walburgh's altar-piece and painted windows, and the magnificent size and pictures of St James' church where Rubens was buried. He visited the art dealers Van Lancker in the Place de Mer, and Pilner and Beeckmans. Smith next took the *diligence* through pretty Conti, admired the laceworks in 'Mechlin', and stayed in Brussels at the Hôtel Rouge. Brussels was 'an agreeable place for strangers, much gaiety and [the] dissipation of a court or rather of a watering place'. He admired the views from the ramparts, the Hôtel de Ville's elegant spire, the great church of the Capucins, and the Duke Charles of Lorraine's palace.

Mariana Starke's guide of 1802 noted that Brussels then had a population of 75,000 and was a cheap city in which to take up permanent residence. The best hotels were the Europe in the Place Royale, the Angleterre and the Bellevue. Messrs Pratt and Barry had a good range of English books and newspapers. The Palace of Laeken, she reported, 'is pleasantly situated, Park and Place Royale are splendid. The Tower of the Hôtel de Ville is fine, especially the Gothic arches, 364 feet high and on the summit the statue of St Michael turns with the wind.' She commended the Public Gallery of Paintings, the public library rich in illuminated manuscripts, the Church of St Gudule, and the handsome Opera House, and recommended a purchase of the town's celebrated lace. She noted that Antwerp then had a population of 50,000, reduced to a quarter from its heyday. The River Scheldt had a 20-foot tidal rise and fall, the Place de Mer was the finest street, and the docks and citadel were excellent, as were the harbour and fortifications, improved by Napoleon.

173

During the Hundred Days, Matthew Todd and his Captain visited Antwerp, and reported that they 'went to the top of the great church to look at the views, which were 'well worth the trouble of going there'. In Brussels they stayed at M. Proft's Belle Vue Hôtel. They admired the beauty and the cleanliness of the town, as well as the music played by men *and* women on violins during the three to four o'clock dinner. 'The music and singing is remarkably good and the means of easing the traveller of his small change.' They visited the Brussels China Manufactury and the Lace Manufactury, 'both extremely curious and ought to be seen by travellers. The prices of full sized veils run from 15 to 25 pounds each – not over moderate.' Lady Castlereagh and Lady Clancharty arrived at the Belle Vue Hôtel, the former proceeding to Paris to see her Lord, and the latter coming from the Hague to buy a stock of Brussels lace. They visited Louis Bonaparte's country house and grounds and went out hunting. On their way to Paris they visited Ghent, Courtrai and Lille.

Meanwhile Fanny Burney was writing her *Diary and Letters*. She watched the Duke of Wellington listening to Madame Catalini singing at a concert in Brussels attended by the Queen of the Netherlands. During the One Hundred Days, Brussels was in a nervous state as preparations were made to assemble the army of Belgians, Hanoverians, English, Scots and Welsh which eventually defeated the Emperor at Quatre Bras and Waterloo. The poet Robert Southey was there in September 1815. 'Brussels has been too much modernised, too much Frenchified in all respects.' Lord Byron's Grand Tour started at Ostend where the young lecher 'fell like a thunderbolt upon the chambermaid'. At Antwerp he and John Cam Hobhouse saw 'the famous basons of Buonoparte, as for churches and pictures I have stared at them till my brains are like a guide book'.

Galignani's guide-book of 1815 recommended the Hôtel London in Brussels, the Angleterre in Antwerp, and the Bellevue in Ostend. Harry Inglis stayed at the St Sebastian inn in Ghent, the Hôtel Harshchamp in Namur and the Holland in Liège.

Lady Frances Shelley on the Grand Tour in 1815 visited Antwerp with her country squire of a husband. Lady Frances was an undoubted snob. In her diary she wrote, 'Belgian manners are very different from French manners. The people are slow, stupid and obstinate. Their country is fertile, damp and foggy. The countrywomen wear long black scarfs over their heads which are very unbecoming.' Nevertheless, the Shelleys conscientiously saw the sights of Antwerp: Napoleon's famous naval basin where 53 sail of the line with all their guns on board could be moored; the arsenal; the rope houses; and the site for the new city on the opposite bank of the Scheldt.

They ascended the cathedral and espied Walcheren. She could not stand the 'ennuie of the coche d'eau, nor people killing frogs in the meadows' (for fricassées of course). In Brussels the Shelleys spent much of their time with the Duke and Duchess of Richmond, at whose house in the rue de la Blanchisserie the famous ball was given on the night before Waterloo.

Mrs Trollope made a modest tour of the Low Countries and Germany in 1833, with her son Henry and her daughter-in-law. On their crossing the vessel was found to be dirty and the fare both bad and insufficient. They stayed at the Waterloo Hôtel in Ostend, enjoyed walks by the sea, visited the vegetable and flower markets, attended Mass at St Peter's, picnicked, and made many excursions. She noticed the quality of the lace, a superb collection of dolls, and how the peasant women wore pairs of stays with ribs of steel, and delicate lace caps. They then travelled to Bruges by packet boat. The fine old capital city of Flanders, once the commercial depot for the Hanseatic League, had a population of 37,000 – but no fewer than 16,000 received aid from public charities. The Hôtel de Ville tower had a magnificent chiming machine, by which 'a vast variety of tunes is arranged'. The Trollopes stayed at the Hôtel de Commerce and paid two francs a head for the table d'hôte. They visited the Cathedral Church of St Sauveur and admired the rich gilded carvings, silver, tapestry, sculpture and Michelangelo's 'Virgin and Child'. They went to Notre Dame, the hospital of St John, the Jerusalem chapel, and the Wednesday market where beds, pictures, kettles, old clothes, books and fire-irons were on sale.

The Trollopes made similar thorough and enjoyable visits to Ghent and Antwerp, where they stayed at the Grand Hôtel St Antoine. In Brussels, 'one of the prettiest little capitals in Europe', they chose the Hôtel Garni. There they went to the opera, visited the cathedral, mint, and the Place Royale and dined at the Restaurant du Bois. On leaving Brussels they went to Louvain, Waterloo, Namur and Liège. Their lasting impression – 'Belgium is a beautiful little Kingdom'.

William Thackeray visited Belgium in 1840 and noted how badly the English travellers behaved to the Flemish, and how our manners suffered by comparison with theirs. Charles Dickens' first visit to Belgium took place in 1837 and his second in 1845. He arrived from Calais and travelled by postcoach to Ghent, Brussels and Antwerp with Hablot Browne. They met Charles Lever, physician to the British Legation, in Brussels. That was in 1837, and 'Boz' became a dedicated European as a result. Alfred Lord Tennyson sailed for Belgium by the *Princesse Maude* and arrived eventually at Bruges 2 August 1846. He noted a 'picturesque sunrise from the pier', and stayed at the Hôtel Fleur du Blé. The poet was tetchy and had difficulties with passports, porters, a missed coach and a 'hot nervous night'.

John Murray's guides to Belgium were full of fun. Of Bruges he quoted Southey's poem, 'Fair City, worthy of her ancient fame' ending, 'Fair Bruges! I shall remember thee!' After mentioning the English nunnery, he wrote 'Bruges is famed for pretty girls, many a fair face and pairs of black eyes peeping out from under the black hood of the cloaks worn by females of the lower orders and surrounded by primly plaited frills of a lace cap'.

Of Ghent, Murray noted that in 1297 the citizens beat off an army of 24,000 English under King Edward I. Ghent in 1840 was the equivalent of Manchester, and its history was linked with that of England. Many Flemish silk weavers living in England were refugees from Antwerp encouraged by the first Queen Elizabeth to set up in East Anglia. In Brussels the best cafés were the Suisse and des Milles Colonnes in the Place de la Monnaie, and the Café des Italiens. The city of 124,000 was described as 'Paris on a small scale. French is the prevailing language, tho many among the lower orders speak only Flemish.' Up to the Revolution, due to the cheapness of living, a large English colony appreciated the cafés, little opéra, palace garden, and miniature boulevards. Murray's recommended tour was from London to Ostend, Bruges (one and a half days), Ghent (one-two days), Antwerp (two-three days), Mechlin and Brussels (one and a half days), Waterloo, Namur, Liège (half day), Spa (health resort one day), and Aix-La-Chapelle (now not in Belgium, one day). Ships sailed from London to Antwerp on Sundays and Thursdays, from London to Ostend on Saturday, and from Dover to Ostend four times a week.

The little town of Spa is 38 kilometres southeast of Liège. King Henry VIII's physician Agostino first commended the healing mineral waters of this little town. Later, in the sixteenth century, two doctors, Paddy and Richard Andrew, visited it to study and assess the content of the waters. Their verdict was that the feruginous waters were medically effective. Spenser mentions Spa in his *Faerie Queen*, and in the early 1600s the word entered the English language with Leamington Spa, Buxton Spa etc. King Charles II visited the town and an English church was built there in 1626. Casinos appeared in 1762, and an English social club was founded under the presidency of Lord Fortrose. Travellers on the Grand Tour of Europe often included Spa in their itinerary. The Duke of Northumberland, Lord Palmerston and Lord Stewart met at the Vaux-Hall to take the peat baths. In 1723, over 100 English gentry of both sexes were recorded as taking the Spa cure during the season. After three years on the Grand Tour the young Earl of Carlisle arrived there in 1768 to find the place full of English friends. He rose at six, rode until breakfast, played cricket until dinner and then danced in the evening until he could scarely crawl home. He wrote, 'this was the life!'

By 1780 there were 15 hotels with English names in Spa, for a succession of distinguished visitors which included the Duke of Wellington and Disraeli. William Thackeray stayed at the Hôtel des Pays-Bas, and there wrote *Pendennis*.

On a visit in 1785 Lady Sarah Lennox wrote, 'If it rains, Spa is detestable. If it's fine and your health admits it, 'tis impossible to resist entering into the goodhumoured idleness of the whole place, particularly as it is easily done without expense .. My system was to *cut* all the tiresome English, to join the agreeable ones if asked; if not I comforted myself with chusing my own society among the forreigners which I always found civil, chearfull, obliging and very often agreeable.'

Now with a population of 10,000, the town is still a noted spa, with suburbs with English names such as Reid, Balmoral and Boulevard des Anglais, the same casino and several excellent restaurants. The strict mineral water regime is always accompanied by good cuisine!

VISITING ANTWERP TODAY

WHERE TO STAY

One hundred and fifty years ago Murray recommended eight hotels in Antwerp. All have changed their names or disappeared during two World Wars, but several relatively old ones remain. Three of the best are the **ROSIER**, 21 Rosier, very exclusive and expensive, (Tel. 225 01 40), the **FIREAN**, 6 Karel Oomstraat, with 12 rooms (Tel. 237 02 60), and the **RUBENSHOF**, Amerikalei 115–117 with 25 rooms (Tel. 237 07 89). The travellers visited these restaurants: **LA RADE** (near the market), 8 Ernest van Dijck Kaai, the **ROODEN HOED**, 25 Oude Koornmarkt (near the cathedral), and the **NOORDER TERRAS**, 27 Jordaenskaai (near the Schelde Museum). Ask for '*moules à l'anversoise*', mussels poached in white wine with herbs and shallots.

WHAT TO SEE AND DO

The **TOURIST OFFICE** is at 15 Grote Markt (Tel. 232 02 03), two minutes' walk from the cathedral. There are three walking tours of the old city taking in the sights mentioned by the travellers, including five churches, the Rubens and Plantin-Moretus museums, and a view of the

River Scheldt. Also consider a Flandria boat cruise, a visit to the famous Antwerp zoo, with 7,000 animals in 25 acres, and to one of the four diamond exchanges or to a diamond manufactury. The 'Diamond Centre of the World' is a title applicable to Antwerp, as well as 'City of Rubens'. Allow a day or two there, more if you use it as a base to see Mechelen's tapestry weaving, Lier's thirteenth-century Béguinage and

1 Bonaparte Dock 2 Grand'Place 3 Cathedral 4 St. Jacob's Church 5 Plantin Moretus Museums 6 Rubens House

7 Zoo Gardens 8 Rosier, 21 Rosier 9 Rubenshof, Amerikalei 115–117

the incomparable medieval city of Bruges. Even more if you are a Rubens fan. Sir Peter Paul (1577–1640) was the Flemish painter with a huge output of glorious paintings, whose Grand Tour to Italy in 1600 to 1608 had a profound effect on him. His deep Catholic faith can be seen in his paintings in the Royal Museum of Fine Arts, in the cathedral and in his 'Rubenshuis' – all in Antwerp.

VISITING BRUSSELS TODAY
WHERE TO STAY AND EAT

Few of the existing hotels in Brussels date from the early nineteenth century. Constant building and clearance schemes by the city fathers have meant that most of the old hotels have vanished. The small one-star DE BOECK'S, 40 rue Veydt (Tel. 537 40 33), the two-star AUBERGE SAINT MICHEL, 15 Grand' Place (Tel. 511 09 56), the two-star DE FRANCE, 21 Boulevard Jamar (Tel. 522 79 35), and the two-star AUX ARCADES, 36 rue des Bouchers (Tel. 511 28 76), are all central, modest and inexpensive. The HÔTEL CENTRAL, 3 rue Auguste Orts (Tel. 511 80 60) was mentioned by John Murray a hundred years ago. The five-star MÉTROPOLE, 31 Place de Brouckère (Tel. 217 23 00), the two-star ALBERT I (1910), 20 Place Rogier (Tel. 217 21 25), and the three-star PALACE, 3 rue Gineste (Tel. 217 62 00) date from the turn of the century.

One of the surprising things about Brussels is that clustered around the startlingly beautiful seventeenth-century Grand' Place are nearly 200 restaurants, brasseries and cafés literally cheek by jowl. Three of these are genuinely old – and good! They are the RÔTISSERIE VINCENT (1905), 8 rue des Dominicains, the BON VIEUX TEMPS, 12 rue du Marché aux Herbes, and the ARMES DE BRUXELLES, 13 rue des Bouchers. In the Galeries St Hubert, du Roi and du Prince there are several elegant old cafés, such as MOKAFÉ, L'ARCHDUC and AMADEUX, from which to watch the world go by. Brussels has several of the *world's* best restaurants, including the MAISON DU CYGNE, 9 Grand' Place, the CARLTON, 28 Boulevard de Waterloo, and the VILLA LORRAINE, 75 Avenue Vivier-d'Oie (to the south of the town). Some regional specialities to try include *'asperges à la flamande'*, *'carbonnade à la flamande'*, *'grilled chicorée de Bruxelles'*, *civet de lièvre à la flamande'* and *'fricadelles bruxelloises'*. Belgian beer is excellent (try 300 varieties at the CAFÉ-

BELGIUM

1 Albert 1er, 20 Place Rogier 2 Palace, 3 rue Gineste 3 Métropole, 31 Place de Brouckere 4 Brewery Museum

5 Grand'Place 6 Cathedral of Saint Michel 7 Place du Grand Sablon 8 Museum d'Art Ancien 9 Palais Royale

TAVERNE LE JUGEMENT DERNIER in the Chaussée de Haecht), and shellfish, particularly mussels and oysters, are on most menus.

There are two **TOURIST OFFICES**, one in the Grand' Place, next to the Hôtel de Ville, and the other 200 metres away at 61 rue du Marché aux Herbes. The old town, known as the Ilot Sacré, is still intact and unspoilt, except by fast-food joints. The Manneken Pis is a vulgar little black cherubic toddler who pees all day and all night, except when he is being fitted with one of his several hundred uniforms. He is located three minutes' walk southwest of the Grand' Place in the rue de l'Etuve, and is a symbol of the cheeky seventeenth-century medieval town before the EEC Commission arrived. Each 3 September, to celebrate Liberation Day of 1944, he wears the uniform of a Sergeant Major of the Welsh Guards. The Guards Armoured Division liberated Brussels, and the author's division, Eleventh Armoured, liberated Antwerp on the same day.

The Cathedral of St Michel, the elegant Place du Grand Sablon (see Lord Bruce's 1751 fountain), and above all two superb museums, the Art Ancien (with splendid Breughels), and the Royale d'Art et d'Histoire should be seen. A bus tour round the city and environs will show you the Atominium, the Royal Palaces and the many EEC buildings.

Brussels has a Métro and a good bus and tram service, and it is easy to get around in the centre. Allow two days to enjoy the city, including visits to a brewery (Gueuze, Kriek, Lambic and Faro), a lace maker, the flower market in the Grand' Place, a chocolate praline-making factory and the many shopping galleries (Louise, la Toison d'Or, Bortier, Saint Honoré and Agora). The **BREWERY MUSEUM** at 10 Grand' Place is another great attraction. For guided walks consult **ARAU**, rue H. Mausstraat 37 (Tel. 513 47 61) or the **ARTISTIC HERITAGE ASSOCIATION**, 20 rue aux Laines (Tel. 512 34 21). Brussels boasts no fewer than 100 museums, the best of which are clustered near the Place Royale. In the first week of July the festival of Ommegang takes place, when the 48 medieval Guilds put on a brave show that would have thrilled all 'Grand Tourists' except Lord Byron and John Ruskin.

THE NETHERLANDS

Land of canals and Calvinism

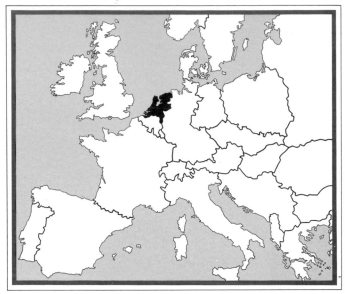

Over four centuries ago, one of the earliest Grand Tour travellers set sail with his brother Henry to Flushing and the Low Countries *en route* to Jerusalem via the antiquities of Italy. Fynes Moryson made his first Tour in 1591 through Germany and the Low Countries to Padua and Venice – on horseback. The year before, the Spaniards had occupied Antwerp, and Amsterdam as a result had benefitted considerably. His second Tour was to take him two years, and his brother was to die of dysentry in Antioch. In Amsterdam the two brothers lodged with an Englishman, 'paid for dinner and supper 20 stivers and for three pints or chopines of Spanish wine 21 stivers'. Moryson wrote, 'The narrow streetes and the buildings of brickes with two low roofes shewed antiquity. The merchants in summer meet on the Bridge on the Warmer Strat, in winter in the New Church in very great number where they walke in two ranke by couples'. In Rotterdam they lodged again at an Englishman's house and 'paid tenne stivers for supper, two for breakfast, and for beere between meals five stivers.' (The rate of exchange was then six stivers to an

182

English shilling.) On the Erasmus statue in New Kirk Street was written 'The word Erasmus in this poore house born, with Arts, Religion, Faith did much adorne.' The burghers took 'exercise in the Pecce and Crosse-bow', and they walked in the 'Hochstreet which is faire and large'. Moving on, the Morysons visited the Hague and hired a chamber for 25 stivers weekly and visited the Castle of the Counts of Holland. The week's budget included 'My beere in one weeke 14 stivers, quarter of lambe 30 stivers, a Hen 7, Pigeon 4 and Rabet 3'.

A feature of the Low Countries at this time was that expatriate Englishmen and ladies kept most of the best 'inns' for visitors on the Grand Tour to patronize.

Tom Coryat, who walked to Venice and back, visited 45 cities including 7 in the Netherlands. On his return journey through Germany, he crossed the Rhine at Wesel and visited Geldeland, 'Njmmigen', Borkum and Dordrecht (which was christened the Maiden City of Holland, famous, opulent and flourishing). There were four more rivers to cross; the Mosa, Waell, Linga and Merva, and much of Holland had been inundated in the great floods of 1420. The shape and size of the country today with its modern polders, reclaimed land, would have astonished the seventeenth-century visitors. The English influence in the country was considerable. The Dort Mint had been built by the Earl of Leicester, one of the four churches was for the English, and the main staple was 'the noble Rhenish wine', an English favourite. They visited Laudun, Middelburg (a beautiful city) and finally Flushing, which was governed by the English. Many of the 200 ships in the harbour were English traders. Then, as now, the Stadthaus had storks nesting on the roof.

Avoiding the Civil War in England, cultured John Evelyn spent many weeks in Holland as the Dutch had the best paintings, gardens, maps and book publishing – all subjects dear to his heart. In Utrecht he admired the Breughels, but at the Kermas Fair encountered 'Boores and rudeness'. In Dordrecht, 30 years after Thomas Coryat's visit, he noticed the storks building on the chimneys. His wagon to Rotterdam covered ten miles in the hour, and John amused himself 'buying landscapes and drolleries'. He admired the Groote Kirke (church), the Bourse, and of course the statue of 'learned Erasmus'. The Hague was but a pretty little village then and he commented favourably on the Renaissance ornaments, the 'close-Walkes, Statues, artificial Musique, Marble, Grotts, [and] Fountains near the Prinzenhoff'. Amsterdam was the main city, and he admired the setting and the architecture, writing that 'the streetes were exactly straite, even and uniforme, shaded with the beautiful lime trees set in rowes before every man's house, affording a very ravishing prospect. The Kaisergracht was paved with burnt bricks reclaimed from the maine sea. Everyman's Barke could anker before his very doore.' The main buildings were 'supported by piles at immense charge'. Evelyn loved the elaborately chiming Dutch bells 'a chime of Purselan dishes which fitted to clock-worke, rung many changes and tunes without breaking.'

Robert Bargrave visited Amsterdam in 1653 and lodged at the Prinsenhof, 'the noblest taverne in the world; every room is furnished with brave pictures and paved with black and white marble, especially the chiefest room which is likewise hanged with the richest guilded leather I have seen and furnished with a glorious organ.' In the strongly fortified walls a few small taverns were incorporated in the round stone towers guarding strategic canals and river approaches. The Het Rondeel (The Roundel) was a fort built in 1483, and in 1683 the first inn was established there. Now on the same site is the splendid Hôtel de l'Europe, built on 620 wooden piles and overlooking the Amstel River.

In the mid-seventeenth century, travel was difficult and dangerous. Three Anglo-Dutch Wars took place: 1652–54, 1664–67, and 1672–74, including the humiliating attack by Van Tromp (and his famous broom) up the River Medway. However, William of Orange's successful claim to the English throne in 1688 restored the original friendly relationship between the two countries, and the two rival navies joined forces to fight the French. In 1697 the Peace of Ryswyck was signed between Louis XIV and William III. The history books then produced Blenheim, Ramillies, Oudenarde and Malplaquet – Marlborough's classic victories in 1704–1709 which led to the Peace of Utrecht in 1713. Intrepid travellers took these wars in their stride. Lord Charles Somerset visited Amsterdam in 1708 and praised the Rasphouse 'where fellows that are above measure idle and debauched were forced to work' i.e. modern workfare! A large Jewish community was noted in prosperous Amsterdam, and he sampled the rich variety of church services, often three on a Sunday, although Thomas Brand, leading his first Tour, wrote of 'this vile country of canals and Calvanism'.

During the eighteenth century many travellers visited Holland and their views frequently coincided. Amsterdam throbbed with life: hundreds of street traders set their stalls around the canal bridges. Money changers clinked their black coinboxes. Passers-by were entertained by buskers, musicians and rope dancers. Booksellers' premises were frequented by the literati, who, with their wealthy friends, visited the gem-cutters, the map-makers, the optical-instrument makers and the printing houses. Quality books in the English language were for sale. The sights to see were the fourteenth-century Old Church, the fifteenth-century New Church, the Guildhall and the Synagogues. To the tulip harvest went Joseph Addison in 1710, 'enraptured by the glorious show of these gay vegetables'. Bakers turned out pies and pancakes from portable ovens. Dr Zachary Grey wrote, 'In our English House at Rotterdam for two wild ducks and two bottles of wine we paid ten shillings English Money and the Ducks (as we were credibly inform'd) cost but sixpence a piece and the bottles of wine ninepence a bottle. This was a Dutch Bill'. (British money was accepted – but at a premium!) Lady Mary Wortley Montagu wrote in 1716, 'My arrival at Rotterdam presented me a new scene of pleasure. All the streets are paved with broad stones and before the meanest artificers' doors [are] seats of various coloured marbles, and so neatly kept that I walked all over the town, incognita, in my slippers without receiving one spot of dirt!' Most travellers coming from grubby England simply could not understand the amazing cleanliness of the Netherlands.

The Hague's reputation grew, one writer describing it as 'the handsomest, the most fashionable and the most modern looking town in the Netherlands, long popular with European gents ... the Palace of Prinsmaurits Huis has a superb collection of pictures'. But gambling rooms for the gents were to be found in nearby Scheveningen, as well as a new craze for sea-bathing! Edward Wright on his Grand Tour of 1720–22 agreed that the Hague was the 'genteelest town in Holland, the most beautiful village ...' In Rotterdam he noted that everyone was 'busy all at work' including dogs and goats drawing burdens on little carriages along the streets. 'Dutch industry' he wrote, was the 'art of making their heads save their hands'. In Amsterdam the Stadthouse, the Princengracht, the Herengrat and the Keizergracht were buildings and streets to admire, the latter 'all two miles long, with parallel high well built houses with handsome bridges over the canals'.

Joseph Spence visited Helvoet (the Hook of Holland) having travelled on the *Prince of Orange* packet boat. The town was described to him as a 'ville d'harlequin' on account of the gaily coloured bricks used to build the houses. He and his charges travelled in a long cart called a *bolder-wagon*, then by a phaeton, not unlike a triumphal chariot. Nine in ten women they saw were engaged in 'work of cleanness'. Once they saw twelve storks together in one spot in an open wooden box on the top of a church! At the Hague they stayed at the Keysers-Hof and visited the Nightingale Wood, the Prince of Orange's Palace, the Voorhout, Rozelli's coffee-house, and Taxara's gardens with their statues and variety of foreign birds. He said that Rembrandt's 'Fortune Teller' should be seen, and Delft earthenware purchased. Spence visited Amsterdam which then in 1737 had 26,000 houses with a population of 400,000. The fortified town lay close to the Zuyder Zee and the sea, was seven miles in circumference, and the chief sights were the three celebrated streets, Prinsen, Heren, and Keizers, the great bridge on the Amstel, the Mall, the striking Stadthouse, the Arsenal, India House and the Jewish synagogues. The Stadthouse was reportedly built on nine thousand wooden piles, and the town had an 'old, great and venerable look'.

That satirical Irishman, Oliver Goldsmith, made his Grand Tour in 1754 aged 26, initially as a tourist, but from Geneva onwards as a 'governor'. He found Paris a city of venal hospitality, and later spent six months in Padua. At first he was enchanted with Holland, having travelled from Newcastle to La Brille, 25 kilometres south of Rotterdam, on his way to see the medical faculty at Leyden University. 'I was wholy Taken up in observing the face of the country. Nothing can Equall its beauty. Wherever I turn my Eye fine houses, elegant gardens, statues, grottoes, vistas present themselves, but enter their Towns and you are charm'd beyond description. No, nothing can be more clean or beautifull.' But a little later he commented, 'Sleepy Dutch audience at the theatre. Downright Hollanders had the manners of Frenchmen – without their liveliness of wit. The typical Dutchwoman was pale and fat, walked as if she were straddling after a go-cart.' Nevertheless he wrote verse about the country – praising its beauty.

Bawdy James Boswell arrived to visit Utrecht University in September 1763 and stayed at the Nouveau Château d'Anvers. He was so depressed by the church bells playing dreary psalm tunes that he returned to Rotterdam where he read an immensity of Greek, ate too much wild duck, and admired La Comtesse in church 'but not imprudently'. One evening at 6pm he met Madam Maleprade and wrote in his diary 'Be easy and gay. Approach not love . . .' He found the canal boats, 'treckschuyte', sluggish and tedious. Haarlem to Amsterdam took two hours, Leyden to Haarlem four hours and Amsterdam to Utrecht eight hours. It was a smooth, easy, peaceful voyage except that the Dutchmen were great pipe smokers and the cabins were full of their fumes.

Thomas Nugent's guide-book strongly recommended the English-owned houses. Many Dutch tavern-keepers were cheats, making false demands and getting the local magistrates to back them with force if necessary. Moreover, the 'Dutch gentility and nobility are not numerous – many having been extinguished in the Wars with Spain', and in Holland 'the passions of both sexes run lower and cooler than in any other country. Their tempers being not airy enough for joy, or any unusual strains . . . nor warm enough for love . . . they affected to be neat in their houses and furniture to a degree of excess.' Nugent wrote that after London and Paris, Amsterdam was the biggest city in Christendom, certainly the greatest port in the known world for trade.

Many mid-eighteenth-century travellers patronized Mrs Cator's or Pennington's hotel in Rotterdam in the Wijnhaven, provider of '*voornaam logement voor de Engelsche Lords*'. Another favourite was called the Groot Hotel van Engeland, and Mr George Crabb owned the Engelsch Logement, Mr N. Michell the Golden Stoel, and W.K. Jungh the Lord Nelson Inn. In Leyden it was the Golden Ball that was English owned, the Queen of Hungary at the Hague, the King's Head at Middelburg, and the Queen's Head and the English Bible Hotels in Warmoes Street, Amsterdam. Lodging costs were less than a third of the cost in London.

The Traveller's Guide through the Netherlands, published in 1770, noted some of the culinary delights of the country. 'The markets of Holland are better supplied and better ordered than any in Europe . . . They are very fond of pickled Herrings, Bologna sausages and other savory dishes. Their butter and cheese is very good, and the common people seldom go upon a journey without a butter-box in their pockets.'

William Beckford was tetchy at the best of times. In 1780 he was positively irascible at the amazing neatness of the houses and gardens, and the roads lined with clipped hedges for miles on end: 'endless avenues and stiff parterres scrawled and flourished in patterns like the embroidery of an old maid's work-bag'. A decade later, botanist Sir James Smith arrived via Harwich and Helvoet where a 'stout athletic damsel, whose cheeks might with more propriety be compared to the full blown peony than to the rose, conveyed our baggage on a wheelbarrow to the side of the river Maese'. On the way to Rotterdam in an open coach, sumptuously lined with red velvet and drawn by three horses abreast, Smith noticed the peasants had an appearance of ease and plenty, their clothes of dark brown, with gold filigree sleeve or collar buttons. He stayed at the Boarshead (Swineshoes), a 'very capital inn', and admired Erasmus' bronze statue and the Merchants' Exchange. Next he went to Leyden by *treckschuyt*, the horse-drawn canal boat, and to the Delft and Haarlem Fairs, each of which lasted a week, with itinerant music tabors, songs and violins. He gives us a detailed description of Amsterdam in 1793: the windmills for draining streams, the highly 'turbid and offensive' canals, the very clean pavements, the airy streets planted with trees, and the botanical gardens with many 'good' plants. He was intrigued by the druggist shop sign of a large carved head with mouth open, with a fool's cap on top, called '*de gaaper*'. He thought the many orange cockades and the fact that the Dutch wore hats in church were curious too. He admired the superb Stadthuis, the Exchange (larger than that of London), the Rembrandts and Vandykes, the organ in the New Church and the three painted windows in the Old Church. The Hague, he wrote, was 'a most magnificent village, with the well kept Prince's Museum, rich in toys, East Indies things, insects and shells good, birds uncommonly choice tho' not numerous. The principal church was lined with black escutcheons.' Smith ended his tour of Holland by noting, 'No traveller will find a dirty bed in the worst Dutch inn, except the smell of tobacco and the spitting pots on the tea table'.

The seven Grand Tourers whose comments were jointly included in the *Juvenile Travellers*, published in 1808, had much to say of the Dutch characteristics. 'The Dutch women are the nicest creatures in the world: they scower and brighten and rub not only the furniture and the inside of their houses, but the outside likewise . . . their gardens are ornamented with flowers, China vases, grottos of shellwork, and trees cut with every whimsical shape, blue tigers, red wolves, green foxes, yellow rabbits and white ravens, some designed for benches, others for fences. The Dutch are great gardeners and florists. The tulips at Haarlem are celebrated for their value and beauty. Five thousand pounds have been given for a single root.'

Dr Burney in 1815 stayed at the Queen of Hungary Inn at the Hague for one third of the price in London, but it had a communal bedroom with beds let into the walls. On the hotel barge his party enjoyed a seven course dinner of soup, pickled herrings, duck, salmon, veal, mutton, beef and vegetables, followed by desserts. Bread and beer were free, the wines cheap.

In the thirties, Bostonians Clara Crowninshield and Henry Longfellow made a tour of the Low Countries, including Amsterdam and Rotterdam. Of the former Clara wrote, 'The streets are filled with the common people in this most singular looking town, the greatest port in the world. At the corners of the bridges are stalls where fruit is sold. I saw a woman making pies and frying pancakes . . .' Above all Amsterdam was a jolly, vibrant city with musicians, rope dancers, puppeteers and buskers of all kinds entertaining the crowds, with housewives in wooden shoes washing the cobblestones outside their front doors, sailors drinking 'Genever' gin and schnapps, and noisy youngsters dancing. 'Incorrigible and lewd women' were locked up in the Spin House and made to spin for charity, 'lusty knaves' were made to work in the Rasp House, and fools and madmen were committed to the Dool-Huis.

John Murray's guide of 1836 recommended a two-week tour of Holland, starting and ending at Rotterdam and travelling via Delft, the Hague, Leyden, Haarlem, Alkmaar, Helder, Medemblik, Broek, Saardam,

Amsterdam, Utrecht and Nÿmegen. Intercity travel by barge totalled 58 hours. There were sailings from London to Rotterdam on Wednesdays and Saturdays, and on Sundays by the SS *Batavier*. A ship sailed from Hull to Rotterdam once a week.

VISITING AMSTERDAM TODAY

WHERE TO STAY AND EAT

The choice of hotels in Amsterdam is quite clear. The **HÔTEL DE L'EUROPE** (formerly the Roundel of 1683), Nieuwe Doelenstraat 2–4 (Tel. 23 48 36), the **DOELEN CREST** (formerly the old Doelen tavern of 1552), at No. 24 in the same street (Tel. 22 07 22), and the **AMSTEL INTER-CONTINENTAL**, Prof. Tulpplein 1 (Tel. 22 60 60), are three excellent five-star hotels, modernized, with good restaurants and marvellous views. The Amstel was formerly the Grand Hôtel van Amsterdam.

The most famous '*bruine kroegen*', are the **PAPENEILAND**, Prinsengracht 2 (where priests hid and drank); **CAFÉ HOPPE**, Spui 18; **DE DRIE FLESCHJES**, Gravenstraat 18; **CAFÉ CHRIS**, Bloemstraat 42; **CAFÉ PIEPER**, Prinsengracht 424; **CAFÉ JAN HEUVEL**, Prinsengracht 568; **CAFÉ SCHILLER**, Rembrandtplein 26 (1886 art-deco); **CAFÉ DE DRUIF**, Rapenburgerplein 83; **WIJNAND FOCKINK**, Pijlsteeg 31; and **'T SMALLE**, Eglantiersgracht 12. Besides a drink of Heinecken, Amstel or Grolsch local beer, try the 'Genever' gin made by Bols, Fockinck or Herman Jansen (either '*oude*' or '*jonge*').

At most of the 'brown' cafes one can get a simple regional meal in convivial surroundings. A cold fish buffet includes herrings (raw or pickled), mussels, winkles, oysters, crab, tunny fish, and smoked mackerel with soft brown bread and lots of creamy butter. *Broodjeswinkel* are the specialist sandwich shops, as a cheaper alternative to the 660 restaurants in Amsterdam.

When the railways appeared in the mid-nineteenth century a clutch of Grand Hotels were built to accommodate the travellers. Adolf Wilhelm Krasnapolsky's hotel and its restaurant **LE REFLET D'OR**, offers an excellent meal at No. 9 the Dam. The Hotel Europe's restaurant **EXCELSIOR** and the Hotel Doelen's **CAFÉ SAVARIN** are distinctly good value, as is the Grand Café restaurant **LE KLAS** in the central station, built in 1870 and offering live classical music on Sunday mornings.

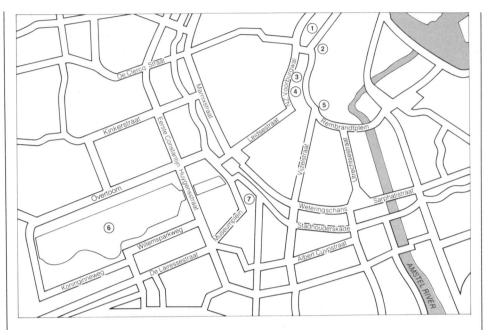

1 Nieuwe Kerk 2 Dam palace 3 Historical Museum 4 Beguinhof 5 Hôtel Europe, Hôtel Dolen, Nieuwe Doelenstraat

6 Vondel Park 7 Rijksmuseum

WHAT TO DO AND SEE

Amsterdam, population 700,000, is all things to all men (and women). For the young there are the heady excitements of bars, discos, red light areas, and the louche life to be found along the Dam. To the modern, more worldly traveller, Amsterdam has the largest historical inner city in Europe. There are 6,800 listed buildings from the sixteenth to the twentieth centuries, (No. 34 in the Begijnhof was built in 1470), mainly located along the beautiful, calm and elegant canals ('*grachts*'). These are mostly on the west side of the Amstel River, and include the Leidse, Prinsen, Keizers, Heren and Singel. The merchants' houses, on six or seven floors, with a crane on the roof to hoist up produce or goods and chattels, cluster most attractively overlooking the tree-lined *grachts*. The Jordaans quarter also should be visited. The Huguenots in the sixteenth century nurtured their gardens (jardins) and brought new skills to Amsterdam's busy commercial life.

Amsterdam houses 40 museums, more than 60 art galleries, and 32 theatres. The **RIJKSMUSEUM VINCENT VAN GOGH**, Paulus Potterstraat, has 200 paintings and 500 drawings including the 'Potato Eaters' and 'Crows in the Wheatfields'. The **REMBRANDTHUIS**, Jodenbreestraat 4–6, has a collection of drawings and etchings in the house where Rembrandt lived from 1636–58. But *the* **RIJKSMUSEUM** has a very representative collection of Dutch seventeenth-century paintings including Rembrandt's 'Night Watch' and the 'Jewish Bride', Ruisdael's 'The Mill at Wijk' and Vermeer's 'Letter Reader'. This fine museum is at Stadhouderskade 42 in the southwest of the town, between the Singelsgracht and the Vondel Park, and facing the Van Gogh Museum across Museumplein. The **HISTORICAL MUSEUM**, Kalverstraat 92, is ideal for the modern traveller – within two hours in a comfortable, well laid out setting, the development of the city over the last fifteen hundred years is shown attractively and intelligibly!

For much of the year a special museum canal boat circulates between the nine most famous museums, starting from the pier in front of the **TOURIST OFFICE** (Tel. 26 64 44) outside the Central station (VVV is their slogan). In fact canal trips (*rondvaart*) are the most attractive way of seeing the city. The one-hour trip from the Amtrak passes under many of the town's 1,000 bridges. The bus tour of the city takes about three hours, and a tram tour about two hours. Besides the two main churches – New Kerk and Old Kerk – and the floating flower market on the Singel gracht, the Dam Palace, the Anne Frank House, the Albert Cuyp market, the Jewish–Portuguese Synagogue, and the seven diamond processing houses, the most relaxing sights are the old 'brown' taverns/coffeehouses (as opposed to the modern 'white' or art-deco cafés).

The main shopping centres are Leisestraat, Kalverstraat and Nieuwendijk. Look for Delft and Makkum pottery, cigars, cheeses, flower bulbs, and of course – diamonds!

VISITING ROTTERDAM TODAY

WHERE TO STAY AND EAT

In Rotterdam the modern traveller will find only modern post-war hotels, with no charisma or history attached to them. Hitler's *Luftwaffe* destroyed many buildings: 550 hotels, taverns, brasseries and cafés in one fell swoop during 1940.

WHAT TO SEE AND DO

Rotterdam, population 600,000, is now the largest port in the world, with oil tankers and container ships filling her 100 kilometres of wharves, quays and harbours.

Only a few antiquities survived the *Luftwaffe*, and these are tucked away amid the modern glass, steel and concrete of the new buildings: the seventeenth-century statue of Erasmus is in the Grotekerkplein, next to the fourteenth-century St Laurenskerk, restored from its World War II damage; the **HISTORICAL MUSEUM** in the Schielandshuis, Korte Hoogstraat 31, still survives in its twelfth century building; and parts of Delfshaven remain, where the Pilgrim Fathers left in 1620 to found New Amsterdam. Most of the dozen museums, including the **BOYMANS-VAN BEUNINGEN**, Mathenesserlaan 18–20, with its Rembrandts, Bosch and Brueghels, are in modern buildings.

The **TOURIST OFFICE**, Stadhuisplein 19 (Tel. 413 60 00), has sight-seeing tours of the city, including visits to diamond cutters, candlemakers and corn mills, and Spido (Tram No. 5 from the station) offer a range of river and harbour trips from Willemsplein.

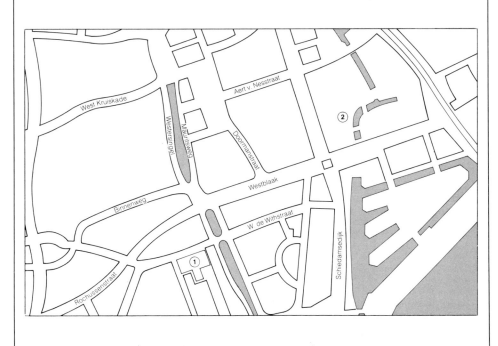

1 Museum Boymans-Van Beuningen, Mathenesserlaan 18–20

2 Historical Museum Schielandsuis Bulgersteyn, Korte Hoogstraat

VISITING THE HAGUE TODAY

WHAT TO SEE AND DO

The Hague (Den Haag), population 445,000, is only 26 kilometres northwest of Rotterdam, with Delft half-way between the two. This elegant town houses the Government. Consequently the pace of life amidst its canals, parks, and superb old buildings is quieter and more sedate. The royal family in the Palace at Noordeinde, and the many foreign embassies, lend 'ton' to Den Haag.

In the thirteenth-century Ridderzaal, or Knights' Hall, in the centre of the historic Binnenhof, the Dutch Queen presented the author with the Bronze Cross of Orange-Nassau for 'battles long ago'. On a tablet on the wall of the Knights' Court is the memorial to the infamous *England Spiel* when 54 Netherlands agents were betrayed and shot during World War II years 1942–44.

The **TOURIST OFFICE** is just outside the Central station, at 20 Kon. Julianaplein (Tel. 54 62 00), and offers town tours, bus/boat trips and a Royal Tour of the various palaces. Several eighteenth-century travellers referred to the royal palace of 'Huis ten Bosch', the house in the Hague woods. A museum bus will take you to the Madurodam (a town in miniature), the Omniversum, the Museon, the Municipal Museum (Gemeentemuseum) where the Mondrians are worth looking at, the Dutch Congress Centre, the Postmuseum and, the jewel in the crown, the Mauritshuis. This is the Royal Picture Gallery, and it has one of the world's finest collections of seventeenth-century Dutch paintings: Rembrandt, Vermeer, Hals, Potter, Fabritius, Steen and earlier works of Memling, van der Weyden and Massys. It is closed on Mondays. The St Jacobskerk in the Groenmarkt is well worth a visit. Listen to the *carillonmusick* four times a day.

The Danzkafe Sowieso is the liveliest café in town, and the thé-dansants at the Hôtel des Indes the most chic.

Scheveningen is the northern seaside resort town, now part of Den Haag. It has a casino, Kurhaus, a port used by the Norfolk Ferry Services, many fine hotels and restaurants overlooking the North Sea, and beaches for the brave.

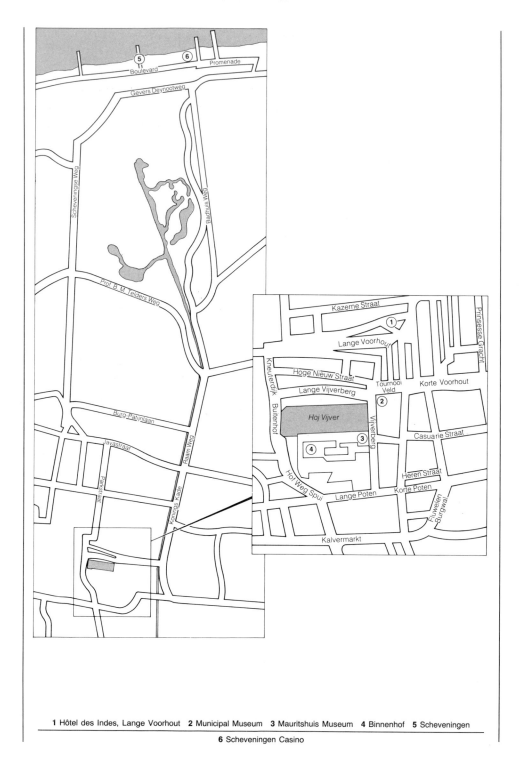

1 Hôtel des Indes, Lange Voorhout 2 Municipal Museum 3 Mauritshuis Museum 4 Binnenhof 5 Scheveningen

6 Scheveningen Casino

WHERE TO STAY AND EAT

In the Hague there are three five-star hotels dating from the late nineteenth century. The **DES INDES**, Lange Voorhout 54–56 (Tel. 46 95 53) dates from 1881, the **STEIGENBERGER KURHAUS** G. Deynoot-plein 30 (Tel. 52 00 52), dates from about the same time, and the **PROMENADE HOTEL**, Van Stolkweg 1 (Tel. 52 51 61) dates from 1874. Frederick Wirz opened the Indes with a table d'hôte of 2.50 guilders. Within a few weeks no fewer than 20,000 people had visited it, and so dinner was brought forward to 5.30pm from 6pm. The two oldest café-restaurants are the **PRINSKELDER TAVERN** (1630) at 165 Noordeindc, and the **'T GOUDE HOOFT**, 13 Groenmarkt, (the building dates from 1445 and Pieter Post opened a café-restaurant there in 1660). The former is small and discreet, the latter large and brash. The 1352 Hôtel du Vieux Doelen and the 1649 Hof van Holland have sadly both closed quite recently.

Communications in the Netherlands are so reliable, clean, fast and comfortable that excursions from Amsterdam are a real pleasure. The Grand Holland Tour by bus takes but eight hours; to the bulb fields and Keukenhof about three and a half hours; to the Alkmaar cheese market about four and a half hours. Haarlem has the excellent Frans Hal Museum, Leiden its university, Utrecht its university and a mighty cathedral, Delft its porcelain, Dordrecht its old town, and Edam its cheese. Allow a full three days to see Amsterdam as thoroughly and as enjoyably as the original Grand Tourists did in a month or more.

SWITZERLAND

'The intellectual metropolis'

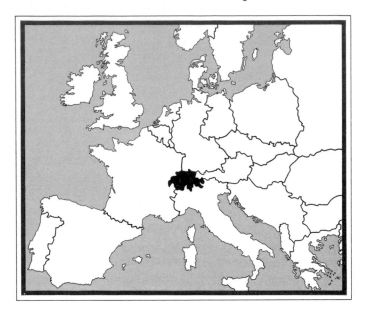

$\mathcal{T}$he travellers on the Grand Tour had to cross through this charming, small, peaceful country to reach their objectives in Italy. In the Middle Ages the route was over the Great St Bernard Pass, or down from the north through Zurich, but most visitors passed through French-speaking Switzerland, visiting the towns of Geneva and Lausanne.

GENEVA

'A very neat place'

When John Calvin settled in Geneva in 1541, his new Protestant doctrines brought fame to the city. John Knox visited him there in 1554 and became his disciple.

Fynes Moryson visited Geneva in 1595 and wrote of the 'most pleasant Hilles planted with Vines. Lower part of Which Citie vulgarly la bas rue is seated in a plaine and the rest upon a Hill. The buildings are faire and of free-stone. Citie hath defended the freedome of the Citizens and the profession of the Reformed Religion for many yeeres with great courage and piete through many miseries and practises to subdue them.' This tough, intrepid young man took everything in his stride. 'I did heare more than a hundred Woolves howling near Lanzi [outside Geneva] – made ready my carbiner to shoot at them, nothing terrified them more than the smell of powder.'

One route took the travellers on the northern shores of the Lake through Brigue to the Simplon Pass, and another took them through Geneva, then belonging to the Dukes of Savoy, to the Mont Cénis pass. Thomas Coryat in 1608 came on foot through Chambéry and was then carried part of the way – 'two slender poles through wooden rings, [at the] four corners of the chair, carried on their shoulders by two men, one before, one behind'. He admired 'the vineyards of Montmelian, the rie [rye] fields, the fast running river and lake Lezere, the goats, wilde olive trees, Hasel trees and great swarms of Butterflies. The women were very short, wore curious linnen caps called Turbents. The Swiss beds were very high. Needed a ladder to reach up into them. The diet of Swisserland was good, a great variety of dishes.' In Helvetia, the Swiss name for their own country, he visited Zurich where he saw William Tell's sword and the River Sylla 'into which the ashes of witches, Sorcerers and Heretiques are cast after their bodies are burnt'. Travellers usually noted the military preparations in the country – 'Armoury well furnished, arms for ten thousand men'. Then, as now, the Swiss believed in armed neutrality. Coryat watched archery practice and noted that the men 'wear round breeches with codpieces, the women plait their hair in two very long locks that hange down their shoulders half a yarde long, twisted with pretty silke ribbands'. In Basle the air was wholesome, the women 'beautifull and faire as any I saw in all my travels . . . the Germans drink helterskelter very socially, their glasses always full. A land of famous scholars, doctors, learned men and great printers.'

John Milton came to Geneva in 1639, Robert Boyle in 1641 and John Evelyn in 1646. The former came to meet the 'learned professor of Protestant theology Giovanni Diodati and the debauched Alexander More, Franco-Scottish professor of Greek'. The latter was not so fortunate, for he caught smallpox by sleeping in an inn bed in which the landlady's daughter had previously slept while suffering from the pox! John Evelyn found the Swiss 'of monstrous stature, extremely fierce and rude, yet very honest and trustie, their houses built strangely low for such tall people. Ordinary Swiss clownish, oddly dressed in thick blue cloth, no beggars, honest and reliable. All wore swords, well disciplined country, impregnable. This country to be the safest spot in all Europ, neither Envyed or Envying nor are any of them rich, nor poore, but live in great Simplicity and though of the fourteen Cantons halfe be Roman Catholic, the rest Reformed, yet they mutually agree.'

By the end of the seventeenth century, Richard Lassells had methodically assessed the sights of Geneva as, '(1) Great church of St Peter's Cathedral, pictures of the twelve prophets one side, twelve apostles the other (2) Steeple Bell with crucifix (3) Four good pieces of Ordnance that none may say the Church of Geneva wants Ecclesiastic Cannons! (4) The Arsenal little but well stored (5) Town House where the Magistrates sit in council (6) The library and (7) good Trouts and Capons.'

Joseph Addison spent the last year of the century in Geneva. He made a voyage round the lake and found that the 'wine is better on the south side, more sun'.

Early in the next century Henry Nassau, Viscount Boston, reported 'a great many English gentlemen in Geneva'; Lord Harrold was studying French there, and Thomas Pennant attacked those English educated at the Academy of Geneva, writing, 'They come here corrupted by the dissipation of our island, spurn at all discipline and either give themselves up to the rural sports of the country or abandon their studies for the enervating pleasures of the South of France'. Richard Aldworth with John Hervey, Earl of Bristol, William Wyndham and Benjamin Stillingfleet, founded a literary circle in Geneva and performed theatricals. 'Our countrymen flocked to see us and flattered us that we excelled the London actors.' That was in 1740–41, and Joseph Spence, bearleader, then wrote of the city, 'Geneva is a very neat place, air of liberty and happinness all over it, no beggars . . . the best houses lying on the Savoy side of the Rhône, new fortifications, garden promenade, the Great Church, Hôtel de Ville and hospital with 2,000 patients.' Horace Walpole commented on his visit to Geneva 'Many English in town, Lords Brook, Mansel, Lord George Hervey . . . Precipices, mountains, torrents, wolves, rambling, Salvator Rosa, the pomp of our park and the meekness of our palace. Yesterday I was a shepherd of Dauphine: today an Alpine savage; tomorrow a Carthusian monk: and Friday a Swiss Calvinist.' Walpole had just completed the ascent of Mont Cénis. His *chaise* (shared with Thomas Gray, the poet) was dismantled, loaded on mules, and they were carried in low arm-chairs on poles, swathed in beaver bonnets, beaver gloves, beaver stockings, muffs and bearskins. 'The dexterity and nimbleness of the mountaineers are inconceivable: they run with you down steep and frozen precipices where no man could possibly walk. We had twelve men and nine mules to carry us, our servants and baggage, and were about five hours in this agreeable jaunt.'

During the first half of the eighteenth century Geneva and the United Provinces were the only Protestant territories visited by British tourists in Europe. George Keate, who spent 1756 in Geneva, wrote and had published a *Short Account of the Ancient History, Present Government and Laws of the Republic of Geneva.*

François Marie Voltaire, French philosopher and writer, was in exile at the château of Cirey, Ferney, close to Geneva and Lausanne. To worship at his feet came many English literati. John Wilkes, patriot in exile, found Geneva depressing and the tomb of Calvin overgrown with nettles, briars and thistles. He visited Voltaire in 1764–65, as did James Boswell, then aged 24. The 70-year-old philosopher was reluctant to let these young English upstarts have access, protected as he was by his housekeeper Madame Denis. Into the 'seat of Presbyterianism' Boswell pushed his way, and made overtures not only to the distinguished old man but also to Thérèse Le Vasseur, mistress of another distinguished citizen of Geneva, Jean-Jacques Rousseau. Boswell promised to send her a garnet necklace from Italy and she later became *his* mistress. He bedded her in a series of inns between Paris and Calais. He found that in Geneva, although no playhouses were allowed, cards and gambling were permitted. He called on a banker, afterwards on a society of young folks and was amused to see card playing 'and a minister rampaging amongst them'. 'O John Calvin where art thou now?' he wrote. James toured the Eglise de St Germain, and walked on the Bastion Bourgeois, 'an excellent airy place where the Genevois assemble'.

Prices were high in Geneva since the inhabitants assumed the many English visitors were rich. To see the aged Voltaire came young 17-year-old William Beckford, who arrived in Geneva in disgrace. Ostensibly there to learn French but in reality exiled for his romantic attachment to another young man, he spent eighteen months there before setting off on the Grand Tour. Caroline Lady Holland was full of praise, and wrote in 1767 'At Geneva there appears to me to be affluence without luxury, piety without superstition, great industry and great cleanliness'.

The English enjoyed themselves in Geneva and Lausanne. Most of them were gently participating in the Grand Tour, and a leisurely few months' stay there was considered most agreeable. In 1780 Thomas Brand attended concerts in Geneva, was amazed by a solo on the double bass, but disliked the vegetarian diet given him at his lodgings. James Robson praised the performance of a comic opera, and Lord Duncannon spent 600 pounds on a sumptuous ball for 250 people. William Blackett rented a well furnished house with five very good rooms overlooking the lake. He too noted the cost of living. 'Quite a little colony of English, but provisions are exactly doubled within this few years, we cannot dine under six livres French a head.' John Baker Holroyd discovered another society 'which pleases me very much'. 'It is called the Spring because it consists of Young Women. It is held every Sunday at the house of one of the young ladies. I attend most devoutly. After cards we generally amuse ourselves with some innocent recreations . . . Blind Man's Buff, Questions and Commands etc . . . Occasionally they have balls. They are much addicted to English country dances.'

Arthur Young in 1787 was rather more scathing on his visit to both cities. 'Young Englishmen went there not merely to study French but also to play various stupid and capricious pranks and to make progress in mischief . . . Geneva with its narrow, dirty and exhausting steep streets is not considered an attractive place.' Thomas Brand, bearleader on his second Grand Tour in 1783 wrote, 'There is such a shoal of English upon the road that the like was never known'. On his third Tour in 1790 he was back in Geneva. 'Of young men here is an abundance: most of them are meer casks of British Oak imported hither to be bottled and emptied daily with the delicious wines of the Vaux and the Côte.' By 1792 Gibbon was known as the 'Grand Monarque of Lausanne', since his predilection for the Swiss was notorious. William Beckford was also back in town from Italy. His Jamaican estates had made him a very rich man. He had a yacht on Lake Geneva, a travelling ménage of 30 horses, 4 carriages, 7 musicians and many servants. As Viscount Clancarry, an Irish peer, wrote, 'a cavalcade that would astonish the princes of the present degenerate days'.

Sir James E. Smith, President of the Linnean Society, spent a month or two in the region in 1793–94. Of Switzerland he wrote, with a botanist's eye, 'Nowhere is there such a variety of magnificence harmoniously combined with so many softer charms, such lakes so beautifully bordered, such varied and luxuriant verdure: so graceful an outline, such a diversity of hill and dale, mountain and valley from the gently undulating corn-field and vineyard to the most rugged and stupendous precipice towering above the dark impenetrable forest and crowned with eternal snow.' Smith was very critical of the 'English travellers who naturally enough associate together . . . [and fail] to seek the company of the intelligent and accomplished natives'.

After Napoleon's downfall, John Mayne visited Geneva. He stayed at the Hôtel Sécheron, just outside the town, and found it full of English. The

Maynes paid six francs for three-course dinners of five or six dishes *and* soup. They found the Swiss musical, and enjoyed the public concerts and visits to the helpful music- and book-sellers. John bought a plan of the town, walked round the walls, and found the houses large, well built but dark and gloomy. However the views of Mont Blanc and the statue of J.-J. Rousseau compensated. The Maynes went to St Gervais church, 'a handsome organ well played, but the congragation kept their hats on.'

Matthew Todd and his master Captain B. were always fussy about their choice of hotels. On their arrival in Geneva in 1814 they stayed initially at L'Ecu de Genève, then at the Dejean/Dijon's Hôtel, two miles out of town, next the Hôtel de Ballance d'Ore and finally the Auberge du Falcon in Lausanne. Matthew found the Swiss to be 'a brave, just and honourable Nation'. He described two of the Swiss meals cooked for them by Monsieur Chicot *maître* of their lodgings. Almond and goat's milk soup, boiled trout with white wine sauce, roasted mutton, boiled potatoes, stewed parsnips, roasted pigeons and fruit. On another occasion they started with rice soup followed by a large trout boiled in white wine, a patty of cock's combs, boiled beef, a *fricando*, mutton chops, veal cutlets, roasted pigeons, fine custard pudding, large sponge cake, some '*pot de nuns*', asparagus, salad, cheese, apples and macaroon cakes!

Two years after Lady Shelley's visit in 1816 the first Americans came to Geneva. George Bancroft, the American ambassador in London, made a tour to be followed later in the century by George Ticknor and Fenimore Cooper. The latter in 1828 and 1832 visited Signal Hill above Lausanne and wrote, 'Whichever way the eye wanders over the wide range of hillsides, villages, vineyards, mountains and blue water, it never fails to return to this one spot – one of the nicest combinations of the great and the enchanting in scenery of any place within my knowledge'.

One of the most famous visitors to Geneva and Lausanne was Lord Byron, who with his Swiss guide and personal doctor, stayed briefly at M. Dejean's Hôtel Angleterre in Sécheron, where he signed the register 'age 100'. He then moved into the Villa Diodati where he stayed for six months. His friends John Cam Hobhouse and Monk Lewis visited him and he composed the third canto of *Childe Harold* in the villa. Percy Bysshe Shelley, Claire Clairmont and Mary Godwin were then living close by at Montalegre. The two poets met and became firm friends. The women also became involved with Lord Byron, who wrote of the 'crystal face' of the lake reflecting Mont Blanc. Mary Godwin (Shelley) started writing her novel *Frankenstein* in Geneva.

Mariana Starke's guide-book recommended Les Balances in Geneva and the Angleterre in Sécheron as being the most superior hotels. This advice was confirmed thirteen years later by John Murray's travel guide to Switzerland, published in 1838. He recommended the Hôtel d'Angleterre, owned by M. Dejean at Sécheron, La Balance, L'Ecu de Genève, La Couronne and the expensive Bergues facing the lake. Geneva then had a population of 30,000 and received 30,000 travellers each year, many of them English! The intellectual metropolis of Switzerland had much to recommend it: 'the Quartier des Bergues, the bridges across the lake at Quai des Bergues, the statue of Rousseau on the island, town ramparts and bastions erected c. 1750, the upper and lower town with narrow streets similar to Edinburgh, the Cathedral Church of St Pierre, the Museums Rath and Natural History, the Saussure and Necker art collections, with works by the Genevese painters Topfer and Guignon'. The Club Cercle de la Rive, the Museum reading room and the public library founded by Calvin were also recommended. Watchmaking started in 1587 and now employed 3,000 people making 20,000 watches annually. In Lausanne (population 14,000), the best hotels were the Faucon, the Gibbon and the Lion d'Or. The cathedral, castle, river walks and the wines of Vevay, called La Vaux, were all commended. Many years after Shelley's tragic death in Italy, his widow Mary revisited Switzerland. In 1840 she stayed at the Hôtel des Bergues in Geneva, declaring it the 'best of Swiss hotels, printed tarrif of prices fixed to the door of each room'.

The *Juvenile Travellers* book of the early nineteenth century depicted Geneva and, to a lesser extent, Lausanne as having a very pleasant atmosphere – of assemblies, many local societies, crowded churches, pretty public walks, with card parties at gentlemen's houses and bowls in the Jardin Anglais. The lake would be crowded with pleasure-boats, with music and dancing on them and many firework spectacles. The *'goûté'* was the name for afternoon tea, taken in the gardens with baskets of bread, anchovies, tarts, tea, coffee, wine and lemonade. There was much conversation as people played at cards or bowls.

VISITING GENEVA TODAY

WHERE TO STAY AND EAT

Lake Geneva is horseshoe-shaped, with Geneva (population 180,000) at the western end, on the French frontier, and Lausanne (population 130,000) on the north bank, nearly equidistant between Geneva and

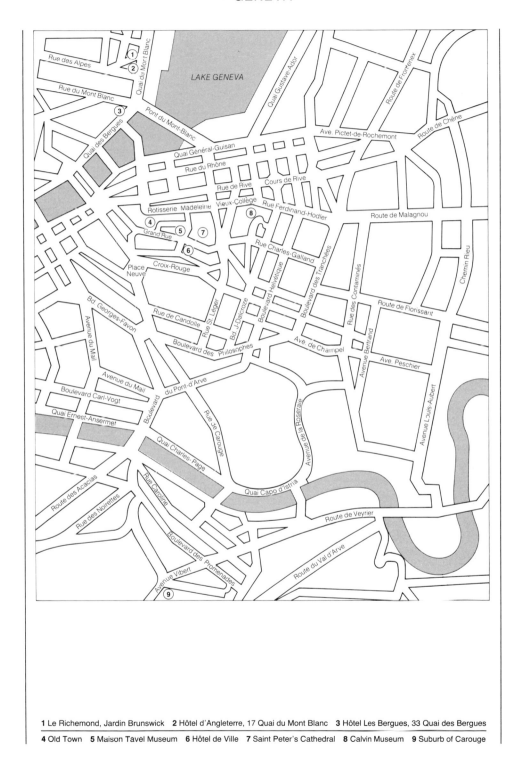

1 Le Richemond, Jardin Brunswick   2 Hôtel d'Angleterre, 17 Quai du Mont Blanc   3 Hôtel Les Bergues, 33 Quai des Bergues

4 Old Town   5 Maison Tavel Museum   6 Hôtel de Ville   7 Saint Peter's Cathedral   8 Calvin Museum   9 Suburb of Carouge

Montreux. Communications by rail, road or better still by boat are quick and pleasant. Plan to spend two or three days in Geneva. Then take the boat trip along the lake to Lausanne.

In Geneva the five-star **HÔTEL D'ANGLETERRE**, 17 quai du Mont Blanc (Tel. 32 81 800), founded in 1865, with 110 rooms, most overlooking the lake, offers the same good service proffered to Byron, Wordsworth and many others. The three-star **HÔTEL DES BALANCES**, founded about 1820, is nine kilometres along the lake road towards Lausanne, 33 route de Suisse, 1290 Versoix (Tel. 55 37 68). It has 19 rooms and was the second choice of John Murray and Mariana Starke. Both hotels have good restaurants and are thoroughly modernized and comfortable. The five-star **HÔTEL LE RICHEMOND**, founded in 1875, is in the Jardin Brunswick (Tel. 31 14 00), with 191 rooms and two excellent restaurants. But the **HÔTEL DES BERGUES**, with five stars, founded in 1834, 33 quai des Bergues (Tel. 31 50 50), overlooking the lake, is still the most expensive and the best hotel in Geneva. It is where Mary Shelley stayed. Unlike the French, most Swiss hotels have their own high class restaurants. Since the Swiss have maintained their neutrality for centuries, good hotels have survived more easily than elsewhere, and hotels in Geneva and Lausanne are very good indeed.

The restaurants in Geneva that modern travellers should visit are in the Old Town, clustered around the Hôtel de Ville on the Grand' Rue on top of the hill. The **CAFÉ LES ARMURES** was started in 1636 by Samuel Choues, and is now at 1 Puits St Pierre (Tel. 28 91 72). The **CAFÉ PAPON** was founded at the end of the seventeenth century and is now owned by M. Werner Haefliger who is proud of his Grand' Grotte dining room at 1 rue Henry Fazy (Tel. 29 54 28) (closed Monday). The **CAFÉ L'HÔTEL DE VILLE**, 39 Grand' Rue (Tel. 21 64 98), has excellent Swiss wines on sale by the glass. These three old restaurants have genuine ambience, good value menus with regional cuisine, and make a pleasant change from the expensive, classic meals at the Hôtels des Bergues, Richemond and Angleterre. The best value restaurant in Geneva is the **MANORA**, rue Terreaux-du-Temple, in the centre of town.

WHAT TO SEE AND DO

The main **TOURIST OFFICE** is tucked away in the railway station, Gare Cornavin (Tel. 45 52 00). Ask them for the weekly magazine *This Week in Geneva*, also *Weekends à la Carte*, *Excursions* and *How to visit Geneva*.

Geneva is divided by the mighty rushing River Rhône flowing southwards from Lake Geneva/Lac Léman on its long way towards Lyon and the Mediterranean. The first visual impact on arrival in the town is the unique *Jet d'Eau*. Eight tons of water are pushed up 145 metres from this unique fountain 200 metres off the Quai Gustave Ador. Six bridges straddle the Rhône. The Pont du Mont Blanc and the Pont de la Coulouvrenière carry the most traffic. The city is full of banks; Swiss, French, Arab, Japanese, American and British. The Bourse was founded in 1850 at No. 11 rue Petito. Now it is in the huge modern Confederation Centre with 76 banking members (Tel. 29 54 28).

There are 20 parks in Geneva, the famous Jardin Anglais (on the lake side from whence most of the many boats leave for excursions), the delightful Promenade des Bastions, just on the south side of the Old Town, with 40 stone carvings of the Reformers including John Knox and Cromwell, who gave Geneva its fame as a Protestant city, the Parc des Eaux Vives and La Grange, with a notable rose garden, five minutes' walk past the Jardin Anglais, and on the west bank around the official buildings of UNICEF and GATT are the Parc Mon Repos, Jardin Botanique, and Ariana. Try the two riverside walks; along the east side of the river towards the junction with the River Arve, and on the west side from the Quai du Mont Blanc following the lake for one and a half miles. Both give superb views of this great bustling commercial city, its strong flowing river and the peaceful blue lake.

All the antiquities are clustered in the Old Town which is an essential visit, and is the most interesting sector. The Grand' Rue dates from Roman times and every house, shop, and café has a tale to tell.

From mid-June to the end of September three guided tours take place from the Hôtel de Ville. On Wednesday evenings 8.30 to 10.30pm is 'Geneva during the Romantic Period' taking in the haunts of Rousseau, Voltaire, Byron and Shelley. On Monday and Thursday afternoons there is the tour of the 'Middle Ages to the Renaissance', and every evening from 5 to 7pm is the tour of the Old Town. For a cost of ten francs you will see the Zoubov collection, St Peter's Cathedral, the Church of St Germain, the Town Hall (seat of government) *and* have a free wine-tasting of local wines in the Café Hôtel de Ville. The newly opened Maison Tavel, 50 metres away, is a free museum, a beautifully laid out fourteenth-century Town House showing the history of Geneva from the fourteenth to the nineteenth centuries, as well as a second-century Roman tower. Although Geneva was for centuries a strongly fortified city, for a short period in the

French Revolutionary period it became French. Napoleon decreed therefore that it should possess and presumably utilize 'Madame la Guillotine'. The Genevese are proud that they resisted the challenge, and the macabre instrument hangs virginally in the Maison Tavel!

There are 25 museums in the city, including those of Calvin, Musical Instruments, Clock and Watch, and Natural History – most of them free of charge. Also in the Vieille Ville amongst the antique shops is the **RUSTERHOLZ CONFISEUR/TRAITEUR/TEA ROOMS**, 11 rue de la Cité, whose *chocolaterie* is worth a stop. The **AU CHALET SUISSE**, 18 quai Général Guisan has been selling lace and embroideries since 1850.

Modern Geneva with its smart hotels and restaurants is in contrast to the Old Town where you will find the rue du Purgatoire and rue d'Enfer, doubtless inspired by Calvin. The Société Biblique de Genève hovers a bit doubtfully over La Bonbonnière in the rue de Rive! Neither Calvin nor John Knox would have approved of the modern casino, 19 quai du Mont Blanc (Tel. 32 63 20), open from 9pm daily. No doubt the younger milords would have enjoyed the gaming.

Geneva is an ideal base for excursions. By boat on Lake Geneva/Lac Léman northwards to Lausanne and Montreux or southwards on the Rhône to the Verbois dam. The suburb of Carouge southeast of the town can be reached on foot. Once under Sardinian rule, the houses there still have many Italianate characteristics. Wine tours of the region can be arranged through the Tourist Office, who have produced an interesting brochure on visits to vineyards by train, bus or rented car. Visits can be made to the local watchmakers, the chocolateries, and to the International Organizations at the Palais des Nations. Also to Lord Byron's Villa Deodati on the northeastern bank of the lake, to Montalegre where the Shelleys lived, and to Ferney to see Château Voltaire where the writer lived from 1758 to 1778.

LAUSANNE

'Greatest town on the lake'

Nearly every traveller visited Lausanne on the way to or from Geneva, a day's gentle ride away along the shore of the beautiful lake. Lausanne is the pretty little country cousin, charming and unpretentious. One of the earliest visitors was the indomitable Fynes Moryson in 1595, 'through Mountains covered with Snow and thicke woods to reach Losanna. This Citie is subject to Bern as being one of the Sweitzers Cantons, but the Citizens speake French. It is seated on the North side of the lake of Losanna which is composed with Mountaines continually covered with snow which open themselves on the East Side towards Italy.'

A century later Joseph Addison estimated the place the 'greatest town on the lake, Cathedral wall opened by earthquake and then shut again by a second quake. Lausanne was once a Republick. One street in the town where every inhabitant has his vote (rare in 1699) and has the privilege of condemming or acquitting any Person in Matters of life and Death.'

Quite soon the visiting English gentry on the Grand Tour found the life there so agreeable and cheap that they settled like migratory birds. John Baker Holroyd (later Lord Sheffield) wrote 'All the world is come to town [Lausanne] and we are eminently brilliant, not an evening scarce without one or two Assemblies. We are not troubled with Playhouse, Ridottos or such like. There is a sort of Club Coffee House the members of which are chosen by ballot. The number is confined to 80 and is at present full. It is a very good collection.'

The young Edward Gibbon spent five years in Lausanne and Geneva 'with pleasure and profit'. So much so that after he made his name with *Decline and Fall of the Roman Empire* he retired to live in Lausanne. 'I have had round my chair a succession of agreeable men and women who came with a smile and vanished at a nod . . .' English travellers came to Lausanne towards the end of the eighteenth century to pay court to Gibbon, just as he and others had previously done to Voltaire. 'Such as I am in Genius or in learning in manners I owe my creation to Lausanne' he wrote.

France had declared war on Prussia and Sardinia and William Beckford found Lausanne '. . . in a violent hurry, all Savoy is bedevilled and bejacobinized and plundered, ravaging is going on swimmingly'. The Lausanne Government he found in sad confusion, half crazy with alarms and suspicions.

William Wordsworth visited Switzerland in 1790 and wrote from Lake Constance, 'My partiality to Switzerland excited by its natural charms, induces me to hope that the manners of the inhabitants are amiable'. But he preferred the French!

Lady Frances Shelley thought that Lausanne in 1816 'with its castle and cathedral look very picturesque, its antiquity is only too apparent from the condition of its dwellings, which look wretched. The castle and the tower of the cathedral built on one of the three hills upon which the city stands rise proudly above the surrounding buildings. The streets are narrow steep and dirty. The outside of the inn, the Lion d'Or looks most forbidding. Our rooms looked towards the lake, opened on to a small terrace overhanging a garden of roses and orange trees. The rocks of Meillerie and the clear lake peeped at us through the trees. Next morning we awoke to find the weather bright and warm while the lake and the mountains shimmered in all the glory of an Italian aria.'

The Charles Dickens family – 'Boz' then aged 34 – with two ladies, six children, four servants and a dog, arrived in Lausanne via Ostend, Mainz and the Rhine steamer, Strasbourg and Basle. They lodged at the Hôtel Gibbon until they found a villa, Rosemount, to suit them, at ten pounds a month. Boz was following in the footsteps of Voltaire, Gibbon, Rousseau, Shelley and Byron. The Dickens family were experienced travellers, having completed the Grand Tour of France and Italy in 1844. Boz frequently visited nearby Geneva and was 'taken aback' at meeting two American ladies smoking cigars, cigarettes and hookahs. All English travellers on their way to Italy for education or 'travelling to economise' now called to pay their respects to Boz at Rosemount. His expeditions to Chamonix, Great St Bernard and Chillon were incorporated into *Little Dorrit*.

The painters came to sketch the incomparable mountains and lakes, J.M.W. Turner between 1840 and 1844 painted a dozen landscapes including 'Lausanne – Sunset', now to be seen at the British Museum. Samuel Prout made the Grand Tour in 1824 and visited and painted Lausanne. William Henry Bartlett's book *Switzerland* was published in 1836 and contains many sketches of the town. Henry Terr's parents lived in Geneva and in 1858 he painted a magnificent *Album of Haute Savoie* of fifty watercolours including several of Lausanne, in which town he married Adèle Pellis. After many Grand Tours (he lived in Venice with Francis Bacon in 1874), he returned to Lausanne and died there in 1880.

The English adopted the town. If the Hôtel Gibbons, Lion d'Or, Grand Pont, Angleterre, Richemond and Beau Rivage were full or considered inadequate, then villas were rented or purchased. An English church was built in 1818 (much used still, on Avenue d'Ouchy). An English library was commenced in 1821 by Isaac Hignou at 7 rue de Bourg. No. 2 became a Club for resident and travelling milords who needed to purchase an English book over a nice cup of tea (as the literature of the time put it). An English cricket and football club followed, as well as various religious movements. The Quakers came to Lausanne in 1839. The Bible Society and the Salvation Army (Armée du Salut) appeared in 1883, and Darbysme, a version of the Plymouth Brethren's doctrine, appeared in 1840. John Wesley's Methodist church arrived in 1840 but was banned in 1846.

VISITING LAUSANNE TODAY

Lausanne has always been a bit of an enigma. Built on quite a steep slope, the Old Town clustered round the cathedral, château, évêché and university, has now accumulated a busy small commercial quarter around it. A mile down the slope is the lakeside port of Ouchy, much as it was when Lord Byron stayed at the Hôtel de l'Ancre with Shelley in 1816. True, the hotels are now grander and more modern (the l'Ancre is now the Angleterre), the Lake Geneva/Lac Léman steamers are slightly more modern, and there are many more yachts, and a modern Métro will take you up to the Old Town rather quicker than a *britchka*. The beauty is self-evident, the lake a brilliant blue, the Alps are snow-topped, the birds sing, and the climate is excellent.

WHERE TO STAY AND WHAT TO EAT

In Lausanne the four-star **HÔTEL VICTORIA**, 46 avenue de la Gare (Tel. 20 57 71), has 100 rooms; the three-star **DES VOYAGEURS**, 19 Grand-St-Jean (Tel. 23 19 02) has 50 rooms; and the two-star **HÔTEL D'ANGLETERRE**, founded in 1780 as L'Ancre, in Ouchy overlooking the lake (Tel. 26 41 45) has 55 rooms. They were all visited by the travellers and are now modernized, with restaurants. Try the '*filets de perche*' in the latter. The Victoria has a discothèque called Le Paddock.

Best of all is the **BEAU RIVAGE** (Tel. 27 78 78), a magnificent hotel founded in 1858. There the modern traveller will find an excellent cuisine, particularly salmon and trout from the lake, washed down with the local Vaudois wines of La Côte, Lavaux, Chablais and Côtes de l'Orbe. Bonvillars Vully produce white wines from the Gamay grape, fruity and full of flavour, such as their Fendant. The red is made from the Pinot grape and tastes earthy ('*du terroir*') and rich.

On your tour of Lausanne call in at the **CAFÉ PINTE BESSON**, rue de l'Ale in the St Laurent quarter. Founded in 1780 it has a good range of local wines. Restaurants serving regional specialities include the **LAPIN VERT**, **BELLERIVE**, **BELLEVUE**, **LE CEP DE VIGNE**, **CHALET SUISSE**, **CHÂTEAU D'OUCHY** and the **AU VIEUX STAND**. Typical Swiss dishes are cheese-based, such as '*raclette*' and '*fondue*', but also '*queniu*', '*gâteau aux raisins*', '*saucisson en croûte*', '*feuilletés du Lac*', and '*filets de bondelle aux petits oignons*'. The **CAFÉ DU JORAT** in Place de l'Ours has delicious fondue.

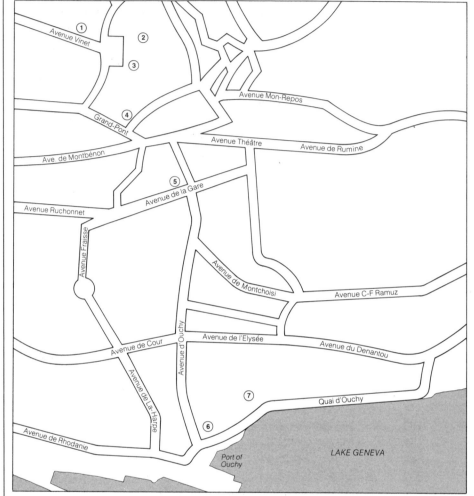

1 University 2 Cathedral 3 Château 4 Hôtel des Voyageurs, 19 Grand-Saint-Jean 5 Hôtel Victoria, 46 Avenue de la Gare

6 Hôtel d'Angleterre, Ouchy 7 Beau Rivage Palace, Ouchy

WHAT TO SEE AND DO

Lausanne has a most efficient **TOURIST OFFICE** at 2 avenue de Rhodanie in Ouchy on the lakeside (Tel. 27 14 27). Every morning except Sundays they have a guided tour of the city, Old Town, cathedral, most of the historic buildings and the Lavaux wine district. The current cost is 20 francs – and well worth it. There are many possible boat excursions on Lac Léman to Evian or Geneva or there are walking tours. Ask for the official guide, *Stadtfuhrer*. The Tourist Office recommends eight different balades, or strolls, round the town starting from the central St Francis Square, five minutes' walk from the railway station. For the determined traveller there is the 'Cultural Circuit' with 35 points of call, which includes besides the cathedral, Ancien Evêché (with its excellent museum) and university, no less than sixteen museums (including the Beaux Arts, the Pipe and the Art Brut which has works by convicts and inmates of lunatic asylums).

Lausanne merits a stay of one or two days, even longer if you wish to explore the wine region, paint, or climb some of the hills and make lake excursions.

AUSTRIA

en route from Venice or Prague

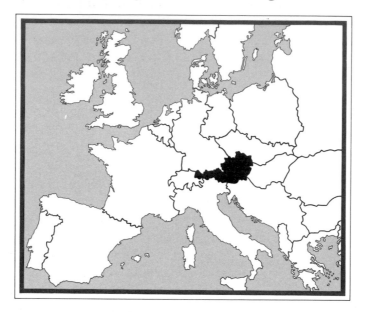

VIENNA

the eternal waltz

Sir Philip Sidney wrote in 1575 that Vienna was the best city in Europe to teach the young traveller the manners of the great world. For three centuries every visitor agreed that the Viennese Court of the Hapsburg Holy Roman Emperors was the most exclusive in Europe, that the best riding and fencing schools were there, and, for the studious, very good libraries.

Three years before Fynes Moryson visited Vienna in 1595 there had been an earthquake. He arrived at vintage time and had bunches of grapes with each meal. He stayed three days to ease his weary horse, paid 24 creitzers for each meal, and for the horses' 'oates and hay' a further 24. It was dangerous to walk the streets in the night as there were 'great numbers

212

of disordered people'. Moryson went on to report, 'Wien a famous Fort against the Turkes. Citie is of a round forme, streets arc narrow but the building is stately of free stone.' The usual route to Vienna was from Venice, Munich or Prague and not down the river Danube from Regensburg.

Lady Mary Wortley Montagu was the first of five distinguished ladies who have written accounts of their visits to the Austrian capital. During 1716 she spent several months there. 'The banks of the Danube [are] charmingly diversified with woods, rocks, mountains covered with vines, fields of corn, large cities and ruins of ancient castles. This town of Vienna has the honour of the Emperor's residence . . . the streets are very close and so narrow one cannot observe the fine fronts of the palaces . . . most of the houses five-six stories high, no house has so few as five/six families in it. The apartments of the great ladies, even the ministers of state, are divided by a partition from that of the taylor or shoemaker. Nobody owns more than two floors, one for their own use and one higher for their servants, the great stone stairs are as common and as dirty as the street . . . the apartments all inlaid, the doors and windows richly carved and gilt and the furniture such as is seldom seen in the palaces of sovercign princes in other countries, fine japan tables, beds, chairs, canopies and window curtains of the richest Genoa damask or velvet, almost covered with gold, lace or embroidery.'

Thomas Nugent's guide of 1750 marvelled at the opulent Viennese society. 'I have seen more splendid equipages and horses here than there are in all Paris. Especially on Court days one sees the greatest profusion and extravagance in this kind of pageantry, the servants being ready to sink under the weight of their liveries, bedawbed all over with gold and silver. There is no place in the world where people live more luxuriously than at Vienna. Their chief diversion is feasting and carousing on which occasions they are extremely well served with wine and eatables. People of fortune will have 18–20 different sorts of wine at their tables. In the winter the Danube is frozen over, ground covered with snow, ladies take their recreation in sledges of different shapes, such as griffins, tygers, swans, scallop shells. Here the ladies sit dressed in velvet lined with rich furs, adorned with laces and jewels with velvet caps on their heads. Sledges drawn by single horses with plumes and feather, ribbon and bells.' Mariana Starke, writing 50 years later, describes the best Viennese wines as 'Weidling, Grinzing, Nussdorf, Pisamberg and Brunn with excellent flavour but not salutory till they become old'.

Lady Elizabeth Craven, on her way to Istanbul, wrote 'there are so many Englishmen here that when I am at Sir Robert Keith's I am tempted to fancy myself in England'. She was delighted by the affability of the

Viennese women, and the range of food – large crayfish, delicious pheasants, artichokes and asparagus. Several visitors complained that society in Vienna was dull, inanimate, that Austrian manners were stiff and that many of the English visitors 'are of a bad sort'. Most visitors appreciated the fashionable Prater, the gardens and parks, the Hofgarten island on the Danube, the Belvedere palaces, the Schönbrunn palace and the Kohlmarkt ice-creams.

The daring waltz was introduced in 1794, and in the next 50 years the Strauss family and Joseph Lanner produced between them over 400 waltzes including *The Blue Danube* and *Tales from the Vienna Woods*. Franz Joseph Haydn, Wolfgang Amadeus Mozart and Franz Peter Schubert had already made Vienna the European capital of music, to be followed by Anton Bruckner and Johannes Brahms early in the nineteenth century.

Catherine Wilmot and her Irish friends stayed at the Hotel Villiers in 1803. She was overjoyed at the paintings displayed in the Belvedere royal gallery of pictures; there were Holbeins, Vandykes, Poussins and Teniers. They went to a Grand Gala at the Prater, 'the most magnificent public walk and drive in Europe. Groups of people eating ices under the trees, drinking coffee, playing on different musical instruments. The Imperial troops drawn up in array each with breastplate, feathered helmet, chivalrous appearance. The Grandees of Vienna, the company numerous and gay, even the peasantry singular in dress, gold wire, solid-looking caps blazing like suns, dark dresses and white slippers. In the L'ace Garden near the Prater one may dance, dine, hear music or breakfast or amuse there as one likes. The Viennese postillions were insolent beyond measure, their appointment exceeding gay, scarlet jackets, gold lace, cocked hat and feather and horn to announce their arrival and departure.'

When Lady Frances Shelley spent a month in Vienna the year after Waterloo, she was armed with letters of introduction from the Duke of Wellington to Prince Metternich and Count Stackelberg. She described the rich musical vivacity of Vienna, the waltzes, charades, theatre, soirées, 'society very rapproché and pleasant'. She found the town small, surrounded by a rampart, and the fashionable promenade took three quarters of an hour in a carriage over unpaved streets. The Faubourgs were comparable to those in Paris, and the palaces she noted were inhabited only in late spring and late autumn. She was met with a 'kindness, attention and bonhomie peculiar to Vienna'. Her husband, she wrote, 'plays at whist, [and] I play a little the queen!' Amongst the quick waltzes she met with a German quadrille and a funny romping Viennese dance called 'Mon Grandpère'.

By 1829 Mariana Starke admitted that there were a dozen good hotels, including La Ville de Londres, the Lamb and Le Cygne. The first coffee houses appeared in Vienna in 1683, and a century and a half later she considered the best to be Schweigger, Neuner, Curty and La Couronne d'Or. Amongst the restaurants Widtmanns, Mehlgrube and the Fisch-Hof were amongst the best. The *traiteur* supplied fried sliced chicken pieces in fricassées to hotel guests.

Of the city's other entertainments she thought the two best theatres were the Burg and the Kärntnertor, and wrote that the opera at the Theatre Royal 'is not striking but the instrumental and vocal performances may be called the best in Europe'. She went on, 'The Prater had six firework displays each year, with over 30 minutes representing temples, grottoes, fountains, parterres of flowers, even fortresses. Shopkeepers and mechanics flock to the Prater to amuse themselves with ninepins, conjurors, see-saws, roundabouts and [to] dine under the trees.' She was impressed by the street traffic – *voitures de remises, fiacres*, sedan chairs and a local carriage called a *bâtarde*. Now with a population five times greater (1.6 million) Vienna has a complex transit system of Metro, trams, buses and taxis.

John Murray's nineteenth-century guides were even more enthusiastic. 'The Viennese cuisine the best in Europe, the beer unequalled.' He commended four white and four red wines and said the best vineyards were at Veslauer and Klosterneuberger. Of the local food, he commended 'Styrian capons, Danube carp and Fogasch perch, Mehlspeisen (puddings), Trout (Forellen) stews, salmon, grayling, chamois venison, blackcock and cock of the woods.'

By 1879 the era of the Grand Tour was over. Vienna's population had risen to one million and it was served by six railway stations. Wildermann was the name of the oldest inn, on 17 Kärntnerstrasse, and the Metropole on Franz Joseph Quai had 400 rooms. English travellers went to the Stadt London or the Victoria in Favoritenstrasse. The best restaurants were E. Sachers (then as now), Fabers, Phillipskys, and Clement's French restaurant in the Liechtenstein Palace. Murray recounted the story of Kulcycki's café, opened in 1863 by a Pole employed by the Duke of Lorraine as a spy. Mr. K. knew that a vast amount of coffee had been left behind by the Turks after the siege of Vienna, and was granted permission with those spoils to open the first coffee house as a reward for his service. Murray commended the ices (*gefrorenes*), Demel's confections (now at 1 Kohlmarkt 14, the most famous bakery in Austria), the silk shawls made by Unden and Hellauer, Viennese gloves by Jacquemar, silk embroidery by Durr and Weiss, porcelain and 'Vienna' china by Lobmeyer, jewellery, Bohemian lace, glassware and fancy leather articles. Tobacco pipe-makers were everywhere, and the best shops were in the Graben, Kohlmarkt, Kärntnerstrasse and St

Stephansplatz: some of the beer halls could hold 1,000 people, among them Drehers, Bischoffs and Likey. There were ten theatres and the new Opera House built in 1869 could take 3,000 people. Concerts could be heard at Musikfreunde, Kursalon in the Stadtpark and the Volksgarten where the Strauss band played to the 'whole beau monde of Vienna'. Military music was played at noon in the Burg: there were many dancing saloons and ballrooms, and the Casino of the Nobles (founded in 1831) was similar to a good London club.

VISITING VIENNA TODAY

Vienna is served by many airlines to Schwechat airport twelve miles to the southeast of the city. There are four main railway stations with lines from the Westbahnhof to France, West Germany and Switzerland, and from the Südbahnhof to Italy, Yugoslavia and Greece. Three large and attractive Austrian towns, Linz, Salzburg and Innsbruck, all lie to the west of Vienna, easily reached by plane, train or autobahn.

The main information centre is at the **TOURIST OFFICE**, 1 Opernpassage (Tel. 43 16 080); **CITYRAMA SIGHTSEEING TOURS** are located at Börsegasse 1 (Tel. 53 41 30).

The best weather in Vienna is generally in May, June and September, but hotel prices are lower from 1 November to March. 'Fasching in Wien' is the carnival week before Lent starts. Specialist travel agencies such as **AUSTRIA TRAVEL**, 46 Queen Anne's Gate, London SW1H 9AU (Tel. 01 222 3660) offer economic winter holidays and a Carnival Special Holiday in Vienna. Several other tourist agencies offer twin city holidays at Vienna and Budapest (visa needed for the latter). The Tourist Office offers discount multiple tickets for museums, advice on public transport discount passes and a range of 31 guided tours in the city and to Grinzing and the famed Vienna Woods. **AUSTRO TOURS** (Tel. 0727–38191) also specialize in tours to Vienna.

WHERE TO STAY

The Grand Tour visitor to Vienna in the twentieth century should consider staying at the **KÖNIG VON UNGARN**, 1 Schülerstrasse 10 (Tel. 52 515 84). This five-star hotel near the cathedral was once the

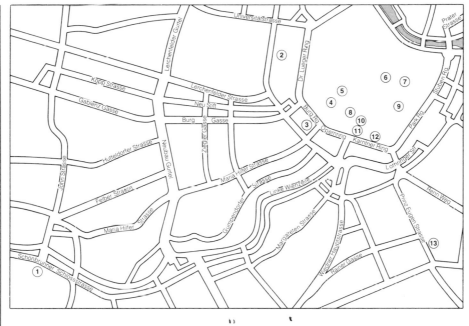

1 Schloss Schonbrunn Palace 2 Rathaus 3 The Kunsthistorisches Museum 4 Hofburg Imperial Palace

5 Spanish Riding School 6 Saint Stephen's Cathedral 7 König Von ungarn, 1 Schulerstrasse

8 Albertina Museum, 1 Augustinerstrasse 9 The Kaiserin Elisabeth, Weihburgasse 3 10 Sachers, Philharmonikerstrasse

11 State Opera 12 Bristol, Karntner Ring 1 13 Belvedere Palace

fifteenth/sixteenth century inn Zur Weissen Rose. **PEDRO'S BUSINESS** is the name of its restaurant, known for its Viennese speciality '*Tafelspitz*', a beef dish. The **KAISERIN ELISABETH**, Weihburgasse 3 (Tel. 52 26 26) nearby, was founded in 1802, and is also a five-star hotel. Wagner and Liszt stayed at the **1892 BRISTOL**, Kärntner Ring 1 (Tel. 52 92 22), and Mark Twain at the **AMBASSADOR**, Neuer Markt 5 (tel. 52 75 11). The famous **SACHERS** dates from 1876, the **DE FRANCE** from 1872, the modest **POST**, where Mozart and Haydn stayed, from 1860. All these hotels are steeped in Vienna's romantic history, most date from the mid or early nineteenth century, all are modernized, comfortable, expensive and have good restaurants.

WHERE AND WHAT TO EAT AND DRINK

Travellers on the Grand Tour would have visited **GRIECHENBEIS**, Fleischmarkt 11, dating from 1500, and the **WILLIAM MARHOLD** restaurant next door, which dates from 1566. A few minutes' walk away is the modest **ZUR LINDE**, Rotenturmstrasse 12, which was an inn dating from 1435. The up-market **GROSSER BIERKLINIK**, Steindlgasse 4, was known in 1566 as Haus zum gulden Drachen (Golden Dragon), and is smart and discreet. Try their '*Tafelspitz*' or '*Esterhazyrindsbraten*' with Sylvaner Riesling from Weinbrau Muldner Durnleis. The **ZUM SCHWARTZEN KAMEEL** (Black Camel), Bognergasse 5, doubles as a wine and spirit importer, and dates from 1618. A speciality here is marinated goose liver in Calvados cream sauce. The baroque-style **DIE SAVOYEN GEMACHER**, 15 Plunkergasse 3, dates from 1720.

Café society has long been a feature of the city. It is essential to visit **SACHERS** and try their '*Sachertorte*', or go to another '*Kaffeehaus*' such as Sigmund Freud's local, **CAFÉ LANDTMANN**, near the Burgtheater. The **CAFÉ MOZART** on the Albertinaplatz, the **CAFÉ TYROLER HOFIN** on the Furichgasse, the **CAFÉ STALLBURG** and the bohemian **CAFÉ HAWELKA** are also worth visiting. **WEIDINGER**, near the Rathaus, claims to be the oldest café in Vienna, and **DEMERS** in the Kohlmarkt dates from 1830. The modern chain Aida have excellent quality coffee at a modest price.

Empress Maria Theresa allowed 700 Viennese families to grow 'Heurigen' wines. Open-air wine gardens and taverns with a pine bough or sprig outside offer jolly evenings sipping young white wine (varietals Grüner Veltliner, Weissburgunder or Riesling) in the communities of Grinzing, Sievering and Nussdorf five kilometres north of Vienna, reached by Metro U4 or Tram No. 38. November 11, Martinmass, is *the* vintage wine date of the year. The best wine '*kellers*' in the centre of town are **ESTERHAZY** and **ZWÖLF APOSTEL**. (Note that '*trocken*' means dry, '*süss*' means sweet.) The **URBANIKELLER**, Am Hof 12, and **MELKERSTIFTSKELLER**, Schottengasse 3, are the oldest wine cellars in the centre of Vienna. The oldest in Grinzing are the sixteenth-century **ALTES PRESSHAUS GRINZING**, 19 Cobenzigasse 15, and **DAS ALTE HAUS RAUSCH RODE**, 19 Himmelstrasse 35.

THE SIGHTS AND SOUNDS OF VIENNA

Old Vienna is contained within a rectangle of connecting boulevards known as the Ring, five kilometres in circumference. All the main sights are within the Ring except for the Schloss Schönbrunn Palace and gardens four kilometres southwest, easily reached by tram or the U4 Metro line, the Belvedere Palace one kilometre southeast, and the

Prater three kilometres east, reached by U3 Metro. The mighty Danube is three kilometres northeast, also reached by U1 Metro, and boat cruises by the D.D.S.G. run daily, May to September, from 265 Handelskai, by the Reichsbrücke bridge.

The **KUNSTHISTORISCHES MUSEUM** on Maria-Theresien-Platz is simply one of the best art collections in the world. A huge room full of Rembrandts, another large room of Breughels, another of Velazquez, many Vermeers. Over four centuries the Hapsburg Emperors brought together an immense collection of early Dutch, Flemish, German, Spanish and Italian paintings. (Like most museums, the Kunsthistorisches is closed on Mondays.) Nearby is the smaller **ALBERTINA**, Augustinerstrasse 1, with 200 superb original etchings and prints, and 20,000 drawings and watercolours by Dürer, Michelangelo, Rembrandt and Rubens. It is closed on Sundays. The **AKADEMIE DER BILDENDEN KÜNSTE** (Fine Arts), 1 Schillerplatz 3, has a terrifying Bosch 'Last Judgement', plus Rubens, Vandykes, Cranachs and much more.

The Belvedere Palace, Prinz-Eugen-Strasse, is surrounded by botanical gardens, and is two kilometres southeast of the town centre, reached by tram or Metro U1. Inside is the **AUSTRIAN GALLERY** with three separate collections: the best is the 'art nouveau' on the third floor. Works by Kokoschka, Klimt and Schiele should be seen in the Upper Palace. (Closed Monday.)

The **SCHÖNBRUNN PALACE**, 13 Schönbrunner Schloss Strasse, has 46 apartments open to the public out of 1,440, and the gardens are fine and extensive. The large **HOFBURG IMPERIAL PALACE** is a complex group of buildings bisecting the Ring, five of which are of great interest. These are the Imperial Apartments, the Schatzkammer (royal treasury), Nationalbibliothek (library/archives), the Stallburg, which houses the famous Spanish Riding School (reserve tickets six months ahead), the Rathaus (town hall) and two major museums.

Famous homes in the city include those of Sigmund Freud, Mozart, Hadyn, Brahms, Strauss, Schubert, Beethoven, Wagner and Léhar.

Among Vienna's many churches, **ST STEPHEN'S CATHEDRAL**, 1 Stephansplatz, has Gothic splendour, catacombs with the remains of the Hapsburgs, and a lift to the North Tower to survey the city and the Danube. The Church of St Charles, the Am Steinhof, Holy Trinity and St Virgil's chapel are all of interest.

The **STATE OPERA**, 1 Opernring 2, is superb. Winter is the best season, and the opera is closed in July and August. Some seats are available on the day of performance but it is best to book ahead. The Vienna Boys' Choir (Wiener Sängerknaben) can be heard at 9.15am Mass each Sunday at the Royal Chapel (Burgkapelle) of the Hofburg, except during July and August. Definitely book two months or more in advance.

Among the 28 theatres and concert halls are the Burg Theatre, the Josefstadt, the Schauspielhaus, the Volksoper and Theater an der Wien, and the English Theatre. And, of course, the two famous Vienna Philharmonic Symphony Orchestras. Beethoven to Franz Léhar, Mahler to Schönberg, the world's greatest musicians have lived and worked in Vienna. The major Vienna cultural festival takes place in May and June each year. Tickets are hard to come by and expensive, although promenaders can get gallery tickets.

Apart from the opera, operettas, theatres, musicals, mime theatre, concerts and ballet (including a biennal Dance Festival), there is a casino, the Cercle Wien in the Esterhazy Palace, and English-language cinemas (Burg and Schottenring Kinos). Free musical concerts (Strauss, jazz, and organ recitals) are performed from 5pm near the Rathaus and the Stephansdom. During summer the Belvedere has free Viennese concerts on Mondays at 5pm.

Plan to spend a minimum of three days in Vienna: longer if you can. The 35 museum and art collections would take at least a month to visit.

SUGGESTED FURTHER READING

The accounts of many travellers, from the early sixteenth century to the late nineteenth century, have provided the historical setting for this book. For readers wishing to know more of these intrepid travellers' adventures, the following are particularly recommended:

Addison, Joseph	*Remarks on several parts of Italy 1701–3* (Published in 1705)
Beckford, William	*Travel Diaries: Italy, Spain and Portugal 1780* (1928)
Birchall, Emily	*Wedding Tour of January–June 1873* (1985)
Bray, William	*Diary of John Evelyn 1640–45* (1818)
Browning, Elizabeth Barrett	*Letters: 1854* (1877)
Boswell, James	*Boswell on the Grand Tour 1765 66* (1955)
Chesterfield, Lord	*Letters: 1753* (1890)
Coryat, Thomas	*Crudities, travells in France, Savoy, Italie 1608–10* (1905)
Crowninshield, Clara	*A European Tour with Longfellow* (1956)
Dickens, Charles	*Letters* (1844)
	Gentleman's Guide in his Tour through France (1770)
Gibbon, Edward	*Memoirs 1764–5* (1966)
Gray, Thomas	*Journals 1740–2* (1890)
Hazlitt, William	*Notes of a Journey through France and Italy 1824* (1904)
Howell, James	*Instructions for Forreine Travell* (1642)
Hillard, G.S.	*Six months in Italy* (1856)
Jameson, Mrs Anna	*Diary of an Ennuyee* (1836)
Lassells, Richard	*The Voyage of Italy* (1670)
Lithgow, William	*Rare Adventures and Painfull Peregrination 1620* (1771)
Massingham, Hugh and Pauline	*The Englishman Abroad* (1962)
Mayne, John	*Journal of Tour of the Continent 1814–15* (1909)
Mead, William Edward	*The Grand Tour in the Eighteenth Century* (1914)
Montagu, Lady Mary Wortley	*Complete Letters 1746–8* (1965)
Miller, Lady Anne	*Letters from Italy* (1776)
Moryson, Fynes	*His Ten Yeares Travell* (1617)
Nugent, Thomas	*Grand Tour of Europe* (1749)
Piozzi, Mrs Hester Lynch	*Journey through France, Italy and Germany* (1789)
Ruskin, John	*Praeterita* (1899)
Shelley, Lady Frances	*Diary 1814–1860* (1912)
Shelley, Mary (Wollenstone)	*Journals* (1840)
Starke, Mariana	*Letters from Italy 1792–1798* (1800)
	Travels in Europe 1800 (1833)
Sterne, Laurence	*Sentimental Journey through France and Italy* (1768)
Smollett, Tobias	*Travels through France and Italy* (1766)
Taylor, Bayard	*Byways of Europe* (1869)
Thicknesse, Philip	*Journey through France* (1777)
Todd, Matthew	*Diary 1814–16* (1962)
Trollope, Mrs Frances	*Travels in Belgium and Germany* (1833)
Twain, Mark	*A Tramp Abroad* (1856)
Walpole, Horace	*The Complete Correspondence* (1737)
Wilmot, Catherine	*An Irish Peer on the Continent 1801–3* (1924)
Young, Arthur	*Travels in France 1787–9* (1889)

INDEX

INDEX